Working with Shakespeare

Howard Mills

HARVESTER WHEATSHEAF

BARNES & NOBLE BOOKS

First published 1993 by
Harvester Wheatsheaf,
Campus 400, Maylands Avenue,
Hemel Hempstead,
Hertfordshire, HP2 7EZ
A division of
Simon & Schuster International Group

First published in the United States of America in 1993 by
Barnes & Noble Books
4720 Boston Way
Lanham, MD 20706

Typeset in 10½/12pt Perpetua and Times
by Keyboard Services, Luton

Printed and bound in Great Britain by
Biddles Ltd, Guildford and King's Lynn

Library of Congress Cataloging-in-Publication Data

Mills, Howard.
 Working with Shakespeare / Howard Mills.
  p. cm.
 Includes bibliographical references and index.
 ISBN 0–389–21009–9
 1. Shakespeare, William. 1564–1616—Criticism and interpretation
History. 2. Shakespeare, William. 1564–1616 —Criticism, Textual.
1. Title
PR2965.M55 1993
822.3′3—dc20   93—13139
                                                         CIP

British Library Cataloguing in Publication Data

A catalogue record for this book is available
from the British Library

ISBN 0–7450–0575–6 (hbk)
ISBN 0–7450–0576–4 (pbk)

1 2 3 4 5 97 96 95 94 93

Contents

I dedicate this book to the memory of my father,
Len Mills (1897–1992)

Preface and Acknowledgements

This book addresses two perceived needs of present-day students, teachers and general readers of Shakespeare: a way of working at first hand with the way he himself worked in putting plays together; and a way of using the wealth of published commentary on Shakespeare.

I rescue from recent attacks the more practical parts of traditional critics, emphasising also their diversity. In referring to their detractors as 'the 1980s critics' I intend no retaliatory indiscrimination. And I am well aware that the latest Shakespearean revolution didn't spring from nowhere on New Year's Day 1980, any more than it dropped dead ten years later – indeed I consider some writings from the early 1990s. But most of the still-influential works I discuss were published in that decade, and very many of them in the middle years 1985 and 1986.

I work with the Riverside Shakespeare, which provides a reliable modern text with adequate textual and explanatory notes, together with a substantial General Introduction and individual Introductions to each play. I have followed its (inevitably in part conjectural) dating of plays. In the interests of smoothness, my quotations liberate conjectural readings from their editorial brackets. But I have retained the sometimes unfamiliar spelling of names (e.g. Bullingbrook, Birnan Wood) even when it is discrepant with spellings in my own text or in my quotations from critics.

Other references are to and quotations from, whenever possible, easily accessible reprints rather than library editions of Complete Works.

A major debt is to my students in England and America with whom I tried out what worked and what didn't. In addition, the comments of Louis Burkhardt, David Ellis, Reg Foakes, Elihu Pearlman and Betsy Wallace led me to throw away what I hope were 'the worser parts' of earlier drafts; they are not implicated in the shortcomings of the final version. More broadly, the give-and-take of Faculty seminars, animated but without animus, gave me a sense of direction and made me sure that any moments of contentiousness in this book will be taken in good part and will get as good as they give in the way of rejoinders. Finally, I am especially grateful to Jackie Jones, my editor at Harvester Wheatsheaf, for her encouragement, patience and perceptive suggestions.

Also gratefully acknowledged are the following publishers: Batsford Ltd, for permission to quote from their 1972 edition of Harley Granville-Barker's *Prefaces to Shakespeare*; Longman Ltd, for permission to quote from their 1989 edition of A. P. Rossiter's *Angel with Horns*; Oxford University Press, for permission to quote from the Oxford Shakespeare, eds S. Wells and G. Taylor, Compact Edition, 1988; and Penguin Books Ltd, for permission to quote from their 1954 edition (repr. 1978) of *Anna Karenin* (1878) by Leo Tolstoy, translated by Rosemary Edmonds.

Introduction

Critics need problems as slugs need cabbages.[1]

I

Heads they win, tails you lose. So might the ghost of Dr Johnson complain, two and a half centuries after his Preface to Shakespeare. In it, he said of Shakespeare 'that, if much of his praise is paid by perception and judgment, much is likewise given by custom and veneration' (Johnson, 1969: 81). In his own day, Johnson got much flak for the second half of that comment, which he reinforces by adding that Shakespeare 'has scenes of undoubted and perpetual excellence; but perhaps not one play which, if it were now exhibited as the work of a contemporary writer, would be heard to conclusion' (*ibid.*). In our day, the first half of Johnson's balanced comment draws fire. For it licenses his claim that Shakespeare is 'the poet of nature, the poet that holds up to his readers a faithful mirror of manners and of life', whose characters 'are the genuine progeny of common humanity . . . his persons act and speak by the influence of those general passions and principles by which all minds are agitated and the whole system of life is continued in motion' (*ibid.*, 59). Such talk is jumped on as the very stuff of 'custom and veneration', of Shakespeare-worship or 'bardolatry'. It depends, we're told, on misguided 'essentialist' notions of unchanging human nature, and it invokes the concept of the genius who is 'not of an age but for all time'.[2] Under attack nowadays is the whole notion of 'trans-historical truths . . . perceived by the unique individual' – unique, and outstanding. Our contemporary 'demystificatory' criticism, it

1

is claimed, 'dismantles the myth of genius' (Dollimore, 1990: 422, 423).

The trouble is that, with the eyewash or bathwater of bardolatry, the demystifiers of the 1980s have thrown out its best antidote, a sense of the individual author not as genius but as craftsman-writer and as dramatist-with-a-deadline, chewing his pen as I do, having a brainwave as I don't, and building on it, working with it. Or losing focus and interest: so that, as Johnson suggests, 'What he does best, he soon ceases to do', he neglects the later part of many plays, and he now and then gets 'entangled with an unwieldy sentiment . . . struggles with it a while' . . . and leaves it rough-and-readily expressed 'to be disentangled and evolved by those who have more leisure' (Johnson, 1969: 67–8). Nobody knew better than Johnson what it was like to be a working writer; nobody brought this better to bear on an understanding of Shakespeare's work.

On the other hand 'working *with* Shakespeare' was what Johnson did mainly as an editor, trying to follow the writer's train of thought through conflicting texts and dated allusions. He lived before the academic takeover of criticism as well as of editing, and indeed long before 'Eng. lit.' was an institution-alised subject of study. He'd have hated the whole idea of students 'working' on Shakespeare, for whom he felt the opposite of his dutiful respect for *Paradise Lost*, which Johnson (as ex-schoolteacher as well as ex-pupil) says makes us 'desert our master and seek for companions' (Johnson, 1968, I: 108).[3] Of Shakespeare he urges anyone 'who desires to feel the highest pleasure that the drama can give, read every play, from the first scene to the last, with utter negligence of all his commentators . . . let him read on through brightness and obscurity'. Otherwise, he 'throws away the book which he has too diligently studied' (Johnson, 1969: 97). My own book has the challenging job of helping study in a way that cultivates rather than kills off the pleasure. 'The want of human interest is always felt,' said Johnson of *Paradise Lost* (Johnson, 1968, I: 108). I want part of the pleasure in working with Shakespeare to be a realistic human interest in Shakespeare himself at work.[4]

Strictly speaking, a genius doesn't have to work, except to record the inspiration that Heaven drops into his/her head. What about the more modest business of planning?

'When we mean to build', says the cautious Bardolph in *Henry IV, Part Two*,

> We first survey the plot, then draw the model,
> And when we see the figure of the house,
> Then must we rate the cost of the erection,
> Which if we find outweighs ability,
> What do we then but draw anew the model
> In fewer offices, or at least desist
> To build at all?
>
> (I, iii, 41–8)

Was Shakespeare this prudent, or more like Hotspur (who got killed off in Part One for his incaution)? 'Model', or design in the sense of a Platonic blueprint, is what I'm sure he never had. Indeed 'a palpable design on us' (Keats's phrase), usually in fourth and fifth acts, sometimes arises from his attempts to pull a play together, to tug the drawstrings around a 'loose baggy monster':[5] most often he appears interested in general themes in so far as they could be exploited for particular dramatic moments rather than using moments to build up a general truth or a well-proportioned whole.

I beg to differ with Johnson, therefore, when he immediately backs up his passage on uninterrupted, 'unrefrigerated' pleasure by maintaining that 'Parts are not to be examined till the whole has been surveyed . . . in its full design and its true proportions; a close approach shows the smaller niceties, but the beauty of the whole is discerned no longer' (Johnson, 1969: 97). It's high time to reverse that order of priorities which has long encouraged students in jumping to premature conclusions and facile overviews. The degenerate issue of Johnson's axiom reassures us that even with the most dauntingly complicated scene or play 'we can again apply our order/disorder formula' 'a simple idea, but one that should help you make sense of any detail or aspect of the plot' (Peck and Coyle's *How to Study a Shakespeare Play*, 1985, repr. 1992: 58, 59). Barely less abject is the survival into the 1980s of the sort of 'Approach through Imagery and Theme' which advises us that, for example, 'Shakespeare has a larger purpose than simply retelling an old story. Lear is spiritually blind, and his lack of vision leads him into chaos and suffering' (this from a 1986 Modern Language Association book on *Approaches to Teaching 'King Lear'*: 82). By way of antidote, my book takes a nuts-and-bolts approach to language and structure. I'm concerned with basic components of plays, and with relative beginners in student work with Shakespeare. This doesn't mean that I start by defining iambic pentameter or the difference between simile and metaphor. That's available in many dictionaries of critical terms and the general and individual-play introductions to Signet, Riverside or other editions. But I work with those and other components, showing the changing ways Shakespeare worked with them, put phrases, lines, speeches and scenes together. This is why detailed analyses form my book's main substance; and – bearing in mind Johnson's contrast of 'parts' and the 'full design' – why a subtitle might be 'Detail into Design'.

Talk of this kind has been so often drowned out by recent polemic that I'm glad to gather allies where I may; and it's encouraging to find them in unexpected quarters. Ann Thompson is one of our subtlest feminist critics and as such has no truck with bardolatry. I draw here, however, on her comments about focal length in her book on *King Lear* (Thompson, 1988a: 52). She favours ' "microlevel" approaches – ones which concentrate on a small area'. One reason which I find persuasive is that they are 'more within the range of what most of us, as students and teachers of *King Lear*, can actually undertake for ourselves'. Another good reason is that 'it can be very liberating to avoid or at least to postpone the rather awesome obligation to provide "an overall view of the play" '. Sometimes rather awesome but, I'd add, often all too facile. Talk comes cheap about grand generalities like Life versus Death. Equally about Transcendent Love versus Everyday Realities: more difficult is an account of the details of *Antony and Cleopatra* or of Donne's 'The Sun Rising'. Even rarer is a sensitive reading thereof: every teacher knows this kind of moment, when he or she is confronted by a student's deafness to rhythm and tone: 'Next, the plunge into sound's physicalities. Miss A, could you let us hear the first four lines? Miss A *loquitur*: "busy old fool unruly sun why dost thou thus through windows and through curtains call on us must to thy motions lovers seasons run" ' (Hugh Kenner in a recent Harvard English Studies volume on *Teaching Literature: What is needed now*, ed. J. Engell and D. Perkins). Joseph Conrad urged that the novelist's task is 'to make you hear' and 'before all, to make you *see*: that – and no more, and it is everything'.[6] Perhaps poets must stress the hearing, and dramatic poets/poetic dramatists the appeal equally to inner ear and mind's eye. A growing number of writers on the practical side of Shakespeare studies (e.g. that Harvard volume, and a special 1990 issue of the *Shakespeare Quarterly*) rightly worry that polemic and theory is breeding colour-blind and tone-deaf students. My book hopes to counteract that.

'Life versus Death', one of the grand generalities I mentioned just now, is the example of another unlikely ally of mine. Gary Taylor is best known for his Oxford editing of the plays and for his study (*Reinventing Shakespeare*) of their afterlife in adaptations and in the cult of bardolatry. Rarely noticed is his 1985 book, published in England as *Moment by Moment by Shakespeare* and in America as *To Analyze Delight: A hedonist criticism of Shakespeare*. Beside recommending the book heartily (especially its chapter on a scene of *King Lear* which I also analyse), I follow the direction implied by both titles and by these comments in his introductory chapter: 'my subject is the pleasure of moments . . . Criticism too often consists in filtering out pleasure in the pursuit of meaning, in reducing poems to their lowest common denominator ("life vs. death") . . . I am interested in unity only insofar as it contributes to the pleasures of the single moment' (Taylor, 1985: 13, 1). And he turns to pure praise Johnson's famous faint blame that Shakespeare 'was much more careful to please than to instruct' (*ibid.*, 1; cf. Johnson, 1969: 66).

This helpfully links pleasure to moments, rather than to wholes; and my book will end with the similar insistence of Bertolt Brecht on pleasure as indispensable, in his close analysis of 'the pleasures of the single moment' in one Shakespeare scene. But Brecht's self-directed humour is only too aware that disinterested perception, let alone weighing and interpretation, of detail is coloured by knowing how the entire play works out, and that pleasure in moments always coexists with our compulsive 'hunt for the truth that is "behind it all"' (Brecht: 1964, 265) – as Taylor also realises. And my own focus on details and moments moves out to consider how far they are articulated – into articulate human speech, and into larger groupings of speech and scene and sequence. It's simply a question of priorities and of the main direction of attention. If a subtitle of this book might perhaps have been 'Detail into Design', it could certainly not have been 'Design into Detail'.

II

'Read every play from the first scene to the last, with utter negligence of all his commentators,' urged Johnson. The present book, however, seeks to introduce and to appraise commentators of the past decade or so, not least because they have challenged the very idea of such direct or 'innocent' approaches to Shakespeare. Each chapter will try out a variety of recent and mainly theoretical approaches in terms of their practical performance on this or that scene or speech. This Introduction offers a preliminary survey: do these recent critics seem to be working with Shakespeare or against the grain of his work? Are they aligned with that approach of mine which I've just been outlining, or are they the Enemy? So far, my signals have been mixed, castigating most 1980s critics for casting out baby with bathwater but welcoming two of them for commending pleasure in detail. In the ten or so pages that now follow, I will show how far I go along with prevailing critical currents and where I part company. This can best be begun with that very question of 'innocent' reading.

Shakespeare, I noted, sometimes betrays 'a palpable design on us'. Likewise critics – as Brecht again saw – may have ideological designs on us and on the text, the more insidious the more they are unadmitted or unconscious. One valuable contribution of the 1980s has been to show that such traditional critical authorities as Tillyard and Dover Wilson, who offered to describe Shakespeare's adherence to a conservative ideology of his day, had a hidden programme for nationalism and stability in their own time. Far safer the explicit bias of Coleridge, in for instance his patriotic and right-wing comments on *Richard II*. An extension of that exposure has been to develop the point made long ago by George Orwell that all writing is political and that 'the opinion that art should have nothing to do with politics is itself a political attitude'.[7] I therefore quite take the point that in the bad old days 'practical criticism' treated literary texts 'as self-contained organisms, "words on the page" in glorious isolation from any social or historical context' (as Jonathan Bate, 1989: 8, puts it), while being ingloriously unaware of or unstraightforward about its own social assumptions. Recent critics are right to be wary of the would-be pragmatism of the Eliot era which contrasted comparison-and-analysis with 'interpretation' and maintained that 'there is no method except to be very intelligent' (Eliot, 1975: 75, 55). One safeguard is to emphasise that intelligence has to include self-awareness. Another is to adopt what one recent critic has called counter-strategies, anti-procedures, 'as a means of unthinking some of the strategies of appropriation that may be common critical practice' for critics and students (Tennenhouse, 1986: 6). And if, as I think, the most common critical practice is to jump to conclusions, race to overall views, our anti-procedural priority should be what another 1980s critic calls 'having the local reading undo an established symmetry', undermining 'totalizing structures' by Shakespeare's 'subversive motility, moment by moment' (Parker and Hartman, 1985: 39, 43).

Having swum so far with the critical current, I am now anxious to scramble ashore. My reason will emerge if I place in context that stress on 'subversive motility'. It occurs in an essay by Geoffrey Hartman from an influential mid-1980s collection of which he was an editor, entitled *Shakespeare and the Question of Theory*. The volume's Introduction by co-editor Patricia Parker sounds the 1980s theme by noting that larger developments in critical theory have prompted 'a wholesale reconsideration of the Shakespearean corpus' and 'called into question traditional ways of thinking about, classifying, and interpreting texts' (*ibid.*, vii). For Hartman, 'local reading' was one traditional way of attempting 'rigor', practised by a previous generation: by English equivalents (such as F. R. Leavis and William Empson) of the American 'New Critics' – those who taught *me* and many another present-day teacher of a certain age. But their rigour, says Hartman, didn't go far enough. Equally 'another form of rigor, historical scholarship' (he instances Leslie Hotson's once celebrated *The First Night of 'Twelfth Night'*) could be 'outrageously speculative' but put speculation to the service of 'unscrambling perplexing expressions or normalizing daring ones', and delivered us from 'a verbal vertigo it exposes' by making the play a *roman à clef* with a covert but coherent overall meaning (*ibid.*, 40). Whereas in Hartman's Shakespeare verbal vertigo is all:

> there is no mystery, no *Abgrund*, except language itself, whose revelatory revels are being staged, as if character were a function of language, rather than vice versa . . . No wonder modern critics have felt a Dionysian drift in the play, a doubling and effacing of persons as well as a riot of metaphors working against distinctions. (*ibid.*, 43, 46)

Hartman's flamboyant style, emulating the wordplay he celebrates, is bound to make the more lacklustre my claim that our approaches diverge in degree, not kind. Take but degree away, untune that string, and you have Hartman's headlong Hotspur-like pursuit of 'a kinship between Derridean wordplay or Bakhtinian heteroglossia and Shakespeare's own inveterate punning' (*ibid.*, vii).

Hartman's cry of 'out upon all half-measures!' is redoubled in Malcolm Evans's book *Signifying Nothing* (1986), which mocks the compromise or caution of such 'practical critics' as Empson and Leavis and even of M. M. Mahood whose 1957 book on *Shakespeare's Wordplay* Hartman praises as 'still the most sensitive exploration of the subject' (Parker and Hartman, 1985: 42). Mahood, protests Evans (1986: 194–5), lacks the courage of her own implications, pulls back from the 'abyss' of language (cf. Hartman's 'verbal vertigo') which is in limitless play cut off from referential anchorage to 'realities' and from authorial control or design. And the same root-and-branch, abyss-and-dizziness idea recurs in influential 1980s commentaries I'll consider in later chapters: Terence Hawkes on *Hamlet* and Terry Eagleton on *Macbeth*.

All the critics I've just been citing came close in date: Hawkes was reprinted in Parker and Hartman's 1985 volume, Evans and Eagleton appeared a year later in what Evans came to call the *annus mirabilis* of revisionary criticism. But their closeness is more than in timing. Eagleton contributed an admiring Foreword to the second edition of Evans's book, which in turn warmly praised Eagleton and Hawkes (granting them twelve and six index-entries respectively). And Hawkes outlined the theoretical background to their similar stances in a subsequent survey of 1980s criticism.

That survey is one of three 'inside jobs' – written, that is, by people who have themselves contributed substantially to the critical movement they survey – that I recommend strongly to newcomers. They are:

(a) Terence Hawkes, 'Shakespeare and New Critical Approaches', in *The Cambridge Companion to Shakespeare Studies*, ed. S. Wells (Cambridge, 1986);
(b) Jonathan Dollimore, 'Political Criticism of Shakespeare', in *Oxford Bibliographies: Shakespeare, new edition*, ed. S. Wells (Oxford, 1990);
(c) Ann Thompson, 'Shakespeare and Feminist Criticism', in *The Shakespeare Myth*, ed. G. Holderness (Manchester, 1988).

I draw gratefully on all three here.

The structuralist movement, Hawkes notes, had questioned the old notion of language as a clear window to reality: it is not transparent but stained glass which 'imposes its own shapes, colours and formations on the world we see' (Wells, 1986: 288). Accordingly (a big jump, this), a literary work has only its own internally consistent structures, not a system of correspondences to outside reality. But the limitation of structuralism, says Hawkes, lay in 'its commitment to fitting every aspect of a text into the overall pattern or structure it perceives' (*ibid.*, 290) – merely another version of the urge for unity, the design-deciphering into which traditional criticism often fell. The inevitable reaction, suggests Hawkes, was poststructuralism's seizing on 'breaks in the pattern' and 'contradictory features' to indicate 'a world which consists, finally, of no ultimate . . . presence but a multiplicity of competing sign-systems referring endlessly in their "free play" of differences one to another' (*ibid.*, 291–2). By this view, literary texts are 'endlessly, like language itself, in free play' (*ibid.*, 292).

Dollimore, in the second survey I recommend, complements Hawkes's stress on language theory by focusing more on social concerns. But in fact the two areas are intertwined. Deconstruction, says Hawkes, 'ultimately aims to subvert . . . the whole

Western view of the world' (*ibid.*, 291). In the critical collection *Political Shakespeare* (Dollimore and Sinfield, 1985) Dollimore (with co-editor Alan Sinfield) had affirmed in his own work a 'commitment to the transformation of a social order which exploits people on grounds of race, gender and class' (*ibid.*, vii). The link between a belief in unstable language and an interest in destabilising society is signalled by the recurrent word *subversive* (or *subvert* – see Hawkes quoted above). Hartman's reference (Parker and Hartman, 1985: 45) to the 'subversive motility' of Falstaff's language resembles Eagleton on 'the witches' subversiveness' (Eagleton, 1986: 4): 'a stability of signs – each word securely in place, . . . settled meanings, shared definitions' – forms 'an integral part of any social order' (*ibid.*, 1) and the witches' 'riddling, ambiguous speech', signifying 'a world of non-meaning and poetic play', 'promises to subvert this structure' (*ibid.*, 2). So that a would-be revisionist critic's suggestions for 'Questioning the Consensus' ring a touch hollow when they open his chapter entitled 'Shakespearean Tragedy: the Subversive Imagination' (Ryan, 1989)!

A caveat must come here. Not everyone leaps on deconstruction as a bandwaggon heading for a levelling revolution, or sees Shakespeare in his time headed that way. Dollimore's survey – the second of the three I recommend strongly – points out the central divisions of recent criticism: 'partly because of the complexity in the representation of historical and social process *within* Shakespearean drama itself', there is 'a thriving debate as to whether those plays are more conservative than challenging or vice versa; in particular . . . did his plays reinforce the dominant order, or do they interrogate it to the point of subversion' (Wells, 1990: 414)? And Dollimore has identified the three salient critical groups: the mainly British cultural materialists (*ibid.*, 407–8), the mainly American new historicists (*ibid.*, 407, especially end of middle paragraph), and the feminists (*ibid.*, 415 ff.). 'New historicists have inclined to the first view, cultural materialists to the second, while feminism and gender critique have operated in both categories.' I'd add that the first group has above all brought out that a society, and a play, may simultaneously license and 'contain' – let freedom have its exercise but on a firmly held leash; or, to change metaphors, give it enough rope to hang itself.

III

If, therefore, the contributors to *Political Shakespeare* are all steered by a 'commitment' to political change, political approaches have overall been varied. Given his polemical tone in *Political Shakespeare* and elsewhere, Dollimore's survey is itself scrupulously impartial. My own concern is to introduce 1980s criticism in the level tones of his and Hawkes's surveys. But in order further to define my own stance, and to maintain that it makes no naïve claim for detail opposed to design, I need to point out a few paradoxes in these new critics and some resulting hazards they may pose for students.

The first has to do with the new stress on heterogeneity, in Shakespeare and in criticism. 'A diverse variety of alternatives' challenge the previously dominant paradigm, noted the editor of *Alternative Shakespeares* (Drakakis, 1985: 1–2); and in *Political Shakespeare* Kathleen McLuskie advises us that feminist criticism in particular 'can only be defined by the multiplicity of critical practices engaged in by feminists' (Dollimore and Sinfield, 1985: 88). Yet the reader will be more aware of solidarity than pluralism in the united front against the critical past, the enthusiastic mutual citations and the ignoring of distinguished latterday traditionalists. And an agreed vocabulary functions like masons' or oddfellows' nods and winks. This is *foregrounded* or *privileged* or *prioritised*, that is *marginalised*. I've already illustrated the predilection for *subversion* which gives a favourable colouring to the old totalitarian phrase about 'subversive elements' that tended to be *liquidated* or *eliminated* rather than merely *marginalised*. This last term, like *subversive*, is used to connect the linguistic and social realms: Eagleton says that the witches' 'realm of non-meaning' 'hovers at the work's margins' (Eagleton, 1986: 2), and Dollimore develops a list of 'the subordinate, the marginal, and the displaced' that have been receiving belated critical attention (Wells, 1990: 409). There is in many such critics a contradiction between the already-quoted hostility to 'settled meanings, shared definitions' and their standard shared vocabulary that seems to come from some even more drastically revised and even more drastically thinned Dictionary of Critical Terms. One finds in 1980s criticism what Greenblatt saw as the relation between

Elizabethan society and theatre: 'a network of trades and trade-offs, ceaseless borrowings and lendings . . . collective exchanges and mutual enchantments' (Greenblatt, 1988: 7). Thus the newcomer may well have the impression of confronting a large but exclusive striking force with its own interlocking series of passwords. The reason is that the new critical dialect leans on tenets developed off-stage, as it were, or before the curtain went up. In the bad old days, when Shakespeare was praised for having 'looked upon mankind with perspicacity, in the highest degree curious and attentive', his great moments were accessible 'to common apprehension, unassisted by critical officiousness; since, to conceive them, nothing more [was] requisite than acquaintance with the general state of the world, and those faculties which he must always bring who would read Shakespeare' (Johnson, 1969: 78, 56). The position is less encouraging now that Eagleton remarks playfully (well, sort of) that 'it is difficult to read Shakespeare without feeling that he was certainly familiar with the writings of Hegel, Marx, Nietzsche, Freud, Wittgenstein and Derrida' (Eagleton, 1986: ix–x), while Drakakis (1985: 23) officiously puts us on to eleven major European theorists who provide that 'rich and heterogeneous foundation' for the even longer list of 1980s critics whom Evans (1986: 13) warns that 'anyone concerned with Shakespeare . . . must . . . be aware of'. All this awareness calls for an equal dose of wariness, in that those named are more often invoked as authorities than quoted in detail for inspection and questioning. We might be tempted to throw up our hands and recall Eliot's warning that 'When there is so much to be known, when there are so many fields of knowledge . . . when everyone knows a little about a great many things, it becomes increasingly difficult for anyone to know whether he knows what he is talking about or not' (Eliot, 1975: 55). Obviously, any self-respecting teacher will do the homework suggested, but any realistic one will know that it is beyond the time and competence of the average student. Teaching, like politics, is the art of the possible. No wonder the editors of *Shakespeare Reproduced* lament that

> many university-press books do not get widely read. And for the few who do read such books, the practice of reading and/

or writing criticism and the practice of teaching can be discrete activities, even as undertaken by a single individual. It is only too easy to read and/or write as a born-again poststructuralist/ Marxist and still teach like an unregenerate New Critic. (Howard and O'Connor, 1987: 5)

This is why a typical student primer like Andrew Gurr's *Studying Shakespeare* (1988) mentions Evans and others but doesn't tangle with their newfangled ways. No wonder, either, that students have turned to more shamelessly spoonfeeding guides which offer an all-purpose formula or a moralistic cliché (e.g. Peck and Coyle's *How to Study a Shakespeare Play*, or the MLA essay, quoted above, p. 3).

We all wince when, in David Lodge's *Changing Places*, the doggedly earnest student describes his essay on Jane Austen to ultra-trendy Morris Zapp: 'I've done it on her moral awareness.' But the new concern with marginalised groups can lead to pious generalisations as tritely predictable as the worst moments in the old humanist criticism. Homogeneity of attitude here is largely unavoidable, there being (I fully agree) no two ways with sexism, racial prejudice, anti-semitism or persecution of homosexuals. Each year, for example, we're inflicted with yet more essays on *The Tempest* which, after a due display of free-playing linguistic fireworks, come out with the solemn conclusion that Colonizing People is Wrong. More broadly, the voice of what Kiernan Ryan in 1989 attacked as the 'crudely reductive, moralistic type of reading' is simply redirected when he himself rails at 'the iniquitous structure of economic, social and sexual relationships which breed despair and ultimate devastation of exploiters and exploited alike' (Ryan, 1989: 73); a social structure of which marginalised figures are 'a living indictment'; with an 'intolerable price still being paid in needless human suffering to keep our society divided': or when, in a heteroglossia of critical newspeak and moral oldspeak, he tells us that *Romeo and Juliet*, 'subversive and protesting' about 'patriarchal society', 'compels us to face without illusions the appalling cost in possible human happiness', 'foregrounding the conflict between the rebellious lovers and the verbal conventions which encode and enforce those constraints' (Ryan, 1988: 120). We are not only, as Johnson knew, 'perpetually moralists' (Johnson, 1968, I: 63), we are also incorrigible moralisers. Taking stock in 1970 rather as Ryan did in 1989, D. J. Enright complained of 'a curiously trite moralising' in Shakespeare criticism (Enright, 1970: 10), and Ryan and other 1980s writers should have narrowed their attack from moral commentary as a whole to trite, newspaper-cliché indignation and moralistic righteousness. And those who throw stones shouldn't live in glass houses camouflaged as whited sepulchres.[8]

A further passage from Johnson will remove from my reservations any merely negative aspect, any hint of a weary 'there's nothing new under the sun'. I've already quoted the paragraph from his preface that draws most fire nowadays, about Shakespeare portraying 'those general passions and principles by which all minds are agitated, and the whole system of life is continued in motion'. But 'motion' also occurs in a lesser-known passage which speaks of the uncertain 'advances of truth' whereby 'the opinions prevalent in one age, as truths beyond the reach of controversy, are confuted and rejected in another, and rise again to reception in remoter times. Thus the human mind is kept in motion without progress' (Johnson, 1969: 87).[9] The positive present-day application of this could be to defuse a good deal of confrontationist polemic, to remind us that dividing-lines are not purely aligned with chronology or schools/traditions, and so to encourage more eclecticism in the way that students and teachers draw on published criticism. In particular, it prompts me to work for the qualified rehabilitation of those critics of the remoter past, especially Johnson and Coleridge, who are nowadays not so much read as paraphrased and caricatured at third hand. More broadly, I aim to show how recent critical developments stretch and sophisticate rather than supplant or discredit traditional procedures.

Certainly I've no wish simply to suggest that the poor critical habits are always with us; it's rather that many critical opportunities, preoccupations and pitfalls alike are perennial. For example, I regard it as an advantage in Ryan that his description of stylistic diversity contains an echo of T. S. Eliot. The progress of the Elizabethan dramatists, wrote Eliot, 'is a process of splitting up the primitive rhetoric, developing out of it subtler poetry and subtler tones of conversation, eventually mingling, as no other school of dramatists has done, the oratorical, the conversational, the elaborate and the simple' (Eliot, 1932: 91).

In Shakespeare, Ryan similarly notes, 'the kaleidoscopic composition of the text cross-cuts the varieties of verse with the varieties of prose, braiding together the demotic and the educated, stylised high-flown rhetoric with the more earthbound manoeuvres of everyday usage, and not only within the play as a whole or through dialogue, but often within the discourse of the same character' (Ryan, 1989: 38). These passages differ in emphasis and scope. Ryan, unlike Eliot, has his eye on sociopolitical causes and consequences. And while both are left as generalisations, Ryan's is about 'any Shakespeare play' (*ibid.*, 38), Eliot's even more broadly about all Elizabethan dramatists but with a compensating eye on development. But both have proved equally suggestive, and equally questionable, in my following chapters. The novelty of Ryan's formulation lies only in its vocabulary, and I will be questioning whether it is helpful to describe the plays' stylistic diversity as (in Ryan's jawbreaking phrase) 'the constitutive heteroglossia of Shakespearean drama' (*ibid.*, 39).

I hope, therefore, to avoid the polemical shrillness, special pleading and either-or confrontationism endemic to 1980s critics which even Ryan's retrospective suggestions found infectious. They had good reason for waving wildly to catch attention. Those critics have only recently been picked up by critical anthologies (e.g. the new Casebooks): they do not appear in the back section of the Signets, nor have they influenced introductions to recent volumes of the New Cambridge and other would-be 'modern' editions – or coloured the scandalously scanty revision (after some twenty years!) of the *Oxford Bibliography* and the *Cambridge Companion*, in which those surveys by Hawkes and Dollimore are indeed marginalised. And Ann Thompson notes wryly, in the third survey I recommended, that she is the token feminist in the volume. This is one reason why I give them space. But the overall 1980s argument for drastic change is not helped by wilful ignorance of the past and a correspondingly deluded exultation that 'the improving, sensibility-refining fish of humanist literary studies are now mostly belly-up in the academic backwaters, and not before time' (Evans, 1986: 283).[10]

IV

But in its wish to sort out promptly a question of method, and clarify my own stance in relation to recent developments, this Introduction has given somewhat undue prominence to my intended presentation of published critics in the chapters that follow. To recycle my earlier theatre metaphor, they will enter left and right as called for, with my own direct commentaries holding centre-stage.

Those commentaries link a cross-section of major plays from diverse genres and periods and, through that, of aspects of poetic and dramatic craft. This lets students develop their knowledge of plays in chronological order side by side with analytic skills in steadily broadening focus (from how a line hangs together to gender issues and genre distinctions). By restricting the number of plays I can give them detailed if selective attention, and can reach back to earlier ones for further illustration while discussing a specific technique in relation to a later play. Thus, for example, a sort of compound interest is built up when *Henry IV, Part One*, first considered in Chapter One in terms of formal and colloquial verse, is again drawn on in Chapter Three, which describes varieties of speech structures. The latter topic is also illustrated in part by *King Lear*, which returns in Chapter Four to help show what I mean by the 'mercuriality' of Shakespeare's scene structures and in Chapter Five to help show what feminists mean by 'the patriarchal bard'. The other recurring plays are *Richard II*, *Romeo and Juliet*, *Hamlet*, *Antony and Cleopatra* and *The Winter's Tale*, with *Henry IV, Part Two*, *Measure for Measure*, *Macbeth* and *Coriolanus* making single appearances.

Prominent in my commentaries are comparisons – with alternative texts, later adaptations or excerpts on the same subjects from literary genres other than drama. I also provide in chapter appendices raw materials for other comparative exercises that have worked well in my own teaching.

A final comment on any eyebrow-raising at this traditional habit of taking Shakespeare chronologically and (apart from some of those comparisons) Shakespeare alone. This reflects the teaching situation which, like or lament it, almost everywhere still prevails. It remains true that 'Shakespeare nearly always stands alone, the pre-eminent "major figure". Typically, his plays are arranged to display a developmental teleology' (Howard and O'Connor, 1987: 5). And most critics, the major American new historicists Greenblatt and Tennenhouse as much as the Englishmen Eagleton and Ryan, continue to follow chronology and also to leave other dramatists to other commentators. More hybrid courses are becoming established, although typically in Britain if less so in North America at graduate school or under a programme of cultural studies rather than in English Departments. My own book is based on a practical recognition that the dominant context of study in Britain, America and elsewhere, continues to be courses on Early Shakespeare and Later Shakespeare, or simply Shakespeare, His Art and Development.[11]

Chapter One

Voices

In *Troilus and Cressida*, a play from the middle of Shakespeare's career, the Prologue speaks of his lines' relation to 'author's pen or actor's voice'. This first chapter shows the earlier Shakespeare starting to use his pen and exploit actors' voices, so as to make us think we hear the voices of distinct, individual characters. The start is uneven: often we get toneless, anonymous speeches all too obviously penned by an author. And this unevenness, frequently smoothed over by old and new critics alike, must therefore be a recurring larger concern of this chapter on voices.

I

Where to start? Teachers dither, writers of guides to Shakespeare study differ. The critics mentioned in my Introduction may all observe chronology but don't start where Shakespeare himself started work, around 1590 with the three *Henry VI* plays or *Titus Andronicus* and *The Comedy of Errors* in the early 1590s. Greenblatt gets down to business with the *Henry IV* plays (late 1590s); Eagleton with *Richard II* (1595) after his proleptic account of *Macbeth* from ten years later; Ryan with *The Merchant of Venice* (1596–7). The last, which suits Ryan's interest in marginalised characters and hypocritical hegemonies, gets increasing prominence nowadays and is rescued from its status as a harmless text for school productions, being rivalled only by *The Taming of the Shrew* (1593–4) with its freshly explored feminist relevances.

Lecturing on Shakespeare nearly two centuries ago, Coleridge turned to *Romeo and Juliet* of 1595–6 as a first illustration of general principles and as evidence of Shakespeare finding his feet. He 'now proceeded to *Romeo and Juliet,* not because it was the earliest or among the earliest of Shakespeare's works, but because in it were to be found all his excellencies, such as they afterwards appeared, in his more perfect dramas, but differing from them in being less happily combined' (Coleridge, 1989: 135). My own reason for starting with the probably just earlier *Richard II* (1595) is that it contains, unhappily combined, the best and worst of Shakespeare.

With me as with Coleridge there will be a constructive purpose in dwelling – later in this opening section of my present chapter – on the weaker parts. But nobody will get hooked on Shakespeare for diagnostic purposes, and that's why I'll start not with Act I scene i line 1 (usually a good habit) but with one of the play's high 'moments'. The first such moment, many would say: while some find the play a harmonious whole, others feel that only here did Shakespeare find his true subject and find Richard's authentic voice.

It comes from the central, the pivotal, scene (III, ii), and furthermore forms the centre of that scene: the King returns from his Irish campaign to find his followers have deserted him for his challenger, Bolingbroke, and he reflects on his 'hollow crown'. Nobody, it appears, would quarrel with Harold Bloom's calling the speech 'an astonishing outburst' – on Shakespeare's part as much as Richard's – after he has quoted it in full in the Introduction to his critical anthology on the play (Bloom, 1988: 3). So that in trying to describe its 'astonishing' 'intensity' and variety of 'linguistic registers' (to weave together phrases about this speech from Bloom, Greenblatt and Ryan) I risk labouring the obvious. But as many commentators – including Greenblatt – take it as read, and as many students don't read it, register or take it in, here goes:

AUMERLE
Where is the Duke my father with his power?
RICHARD
No matter where – of comfort no man speak:
Let's talk of graves, of worms, and epitaphs,
Make dust our paper, and with rainy eyes
Write sorrow on the bosom of the earth.
Let's choose executors and talk of wills;

And yet not so, for what can we bequeath
Save our deposed bodies to the ground?
Our lands, our lives, and all are Bullingbrook's,
And nothing can we call our own but death,
And that small model of the barren earth
Which serves as paste and cover to our bones.
For God's sake let us sit upon the ground
And tell sad stories of the death of kings:
How some have been depos'd, some slain in war,
Some haunted by the ghosts they have deposed,
Some poisoned by their wives, some sleeping kill'd,
All murthered – for within the hollow crown
That rounds the mortal temples of a king
Keeps Death his court, and there the antic sits,
Scoffing his state and grinning at his pomp,
Allowing him a breath, a little scene,
To monarchize, be fear'd, and kill with looks,
Infusing him with self and vain conceit,
As if this flesh which walls about our life
Were brass impregnable; and humor'd thus,
Comes at the last and with a little pin
Bores thorough his castle wall, and farewell king!
Cover your heads, and mock not flesh and blood
With solemn reverence, throw away respect,
Tradition, form, and ceremonious duty,
For you have but mistook me all this while.
I live with bread like you, feel want,
Taste grief, need friends: subjected thus,
How can you say to me I am a King?

                                        (III, ii, 143–77)

'But what is there to take in?' students often ask. 'It's just talk; or rather, a set speech – and a longwinded one too!' One rejoinder is that Drama is Conflict, including inner conflict; that as the Brussels doctor observes in Conrad's *Heart of Darkness*, the real changes take place inside, and that as Bloom says, 'Richard is crucially changed' by this 'outburst' (*ibid.*). As for audiences, one might try appealing to the evidence that Elizabethans attended as much to verbal colour as to the colourful robes and the carnivalesque spectacle stressed of late by New Historicist critics like Greenblatt and Tennenhouse. But in our day this is the time for students to skim and audiences to clear their throats or rustle their chocolate papers until something *happens*.[1]

But for God's sake . . . 'arresting' would be as apt a description as Bloom's 'astonishing' for Richard's 'For God's sake let us sit upon the ground'. He intentionally arrests the action, stops the clock, explicitly bans hope and good news ('of comfort no man speak') and, by the pre-emptive strike of his own listing of picturesque catastrophes, implicitly arrests the procession of messengers who have been bringing bad news. The tactic therefore resembles that of the lover in Donne's poem 'The Canonization' who breaks in with 'For God's sake hold your tongue, and let me love'; and Richard's 'For God's sake let us sit upon the ground' . . . reminds me of the way that F. R. Leavis was arrested by another Donne opening (of 'The Good-Morrow'): we stop reading the dusty literary past, and 'read on as we read the living'.[2] In Richard's case, however, the impression Shakespeare contrives (my book will hold on to the fact that even directness in drama is an achievement of artifice) is of our not reading a living poet but hearing a living person.

Richard's line follows the exclamation 'For God's sake' with the added force of a histrionic gesture and an injunction ('. . . let us sit upon the ground': see my comment on *Deixis* in Chapter Five, p. 212). Thereafter, all there is to see will require the mind's eye and not the opera glasses. To wrench apart and reduce to wretched diagrams these overlapping mental pictures: (1) Mr Death besieges not only the King's castle but his person, his body, his eggshell of a skull. Death is a fifth column, a traitor within the gates; while the King keeps court in his palace, Death sets up his camp or court within the King. (2) Death is the 'allowed fool' or licensed jester who dogs the King's heels to mock him; the 'antic . . . scoffing his state and grinning at his pomp'. Back in *Henry VI, Part One* (IV, vii, 18), a character calls out to 'Thou antic Death, which laugh'st us here to scorn': the Riverside footnote takes 'antic' there as an adjective, 'grinning like a clown, as in the pictorial representations of the *danse macabre*' (or Dance of Death). Skulls, like clowns, are said to grin. (3) At the same time the sinister Mr D. has a powerful job in the theatre – director, rival star or stage manager, who watches from the wings with tolerant amusement while the King struts and frets and 'monarchises' (hams up the role of monarch).

But what animates these pictures and lets them coalesce is a form of wordplay. The 'crown' is what a King wears on his head and also what lies beneath it – the crown of his skull. His 'temples' are the front of his skull as well as period idiom for what we'd call the protection or security zone of several miles around his sacrosanct presence (to Death, however, nothing is sacred). The third key word, 'court', has a hint of secondary meaning, as a court of law; with perhaps a glance at the Day of Judgment. A further means of fusion is to use the palace building or battlements as a source of metaphor in talking about the human body: thus 'this flesh which walls about our mortal life'.[3]

But again, none of this would arrest us if it weren't for the flamboyant and mercurial play of voice tones. 'Farewell, king!' sounds a bit like 'Bye – bye, Mr Punch!':[4] Richard here mimics Death's mockery as his little pin despatches the monarchiser with ludicrous ease. But immediately after that, Richard with the utmost gravity prohibits another form of hollow mockery, courtly flattery: 'cover your heads, and mock not flesh and blood/With solemn reverence . . .'. That ceremonious last phrase is elaborated (and mocked?) in 'throw away respect,/ Tradition, form, and ceremonious duty' before the preceding bare phrase 'flesh and blood' is picked up in the blunt mono-syllables and hammerblows of 'I live with bread like you, feel want,/Taste grief, need friends'.

It is precisely this impression of modulated human speech, rather than of reading a speech set down for the actor, that has often aroused speculation about 'the fundamental nature' of the speaker. I've two important reasons for wanting to direct students away from that road. Here's the first.

My comments so far are the sort for which I've found students grateful, opening up the passage and showing how it works. I've said nothing controversial, let alone original, which is hardly surprising with such a celebrated and central passage. I'm roughly in the position of Gary Taylor, whose 'analysis of delight' 'cannot consist of brilliant and subtle new interpret-ations, since its purpose is not to offer new insights, but to explain how everyone arrived at the old ones' (Taylor, 1985: 13) – though I'll be a little less modest as my book goes on. My main

cry to students is, don't rush to interpret but for God's sake first
enjoy, enjoy! I'm glad, therefore, that Harold Bloom, before he
goes on to psychologise and moralise, records that:

> I know of many readers and students who agree with Dr.
> Samuel Johnson [later called 'best of critics'] in his judgment
> that *Richard II* 'is not finished at last with the happy force of
> some of his other tragedies . . .', yet even these recalcitrants
> thrill to the justly famous cadences of 'For God's sake let us sit
> upon the ground/ And tell sad stories of the death of kings'.
> (Bloom, 1988: 4)

Others, however, enforce the point I made in the Introduction,
that 'crudely moralistic' and 'reductive' commentary is alive and
kicking in the very people who in recent years have professed to
decry it. Thus Eagleton wades straight in, fists flailing: 'As a
"poet king", Richard trusts to the sway of the signifier; only by
translating unpleasant political realities into decorative verbal
fictions can he engage with them. While Bolingbroke's enemies
are invading, Richard wants to sit down and concoct narcissistic
narratives about the death of Kings' (Eagleton, 1986: 10).
(Apart from 'signifier' this could have been written a hundred
years or more ago.) Far more favourable to Richard but equally
moralistic in manner is Holderness: 'this speech is a penetrating,
tragic insight into the hollowness of "Power" without power'
(Holderness, 1992: 69). All such comments bypass the pleasures
of the passage as a performance, its colour and texture, in a haste
to reach its moral point. They illustrate Taylor's complaint that
'criticism too often consists in filtering out pleasure in the pursuit
of meaning' (Taylor, 1985: 1). They are themselves the best
antidote for veneration of the Bard by making him sound
pompous and platitudinous.
  We can get back to the passage itself by asking how they could
possibly anchor such pronouncements to its style. Here's an
elaboration of Holderness's favourable view: Richard expresses
'a wisdom that power and prosperity could not teach him – the
vulnerability of Kings . . . like Lear, he is obliged to recognise –
and willingly accepts – his common humanity with his subjects'.[5]
It can't be so straightforward, when that plainest language about
bread, need and grief is followed by the flicker of play in

'subjected thus': 'cast down' and 'a subject, not a ruler' –
here's one word that's sophisticated, a flourish, if not betoken-
ing residual facetiousness. And in the passage's imitation of
Death's mockery isn't there residual facetious hyperbole, near-
irresponsibility? It reminds me of the short but revealing scene
that ends Act I, when Richard delights in doing all the voices as
he describes to his cronies the future usurper's 'courtship to the
common people'. *That* speech ends with two lines that wipe the
smirk off his face: Bolingbroke behaved 'as were our England in
reversion his/And he our subjects' next degree in hope' – this
climactic exaggeration of Richard's, it dawns on him, could turn
into sober truth. When, by the middle of Act III, Richard sits on
the ground faced with the plain imminent fact of deposition, I'm
tempted to say that he relishes his performance more than
realises the point – even while it is a performance that purports
to be against performances (against 'monarchising').

More monarchising than moralising, then? To press for an
either/or answer would be to squeeze the life out of the passage
whose fascination is precisely in being somewhere on the
borderline between insight and indulgence; Coleridge (1989:
130) speaks of a 'parade of resignation'. Just where, we can't tell
– the advantage of it being in poetic and dramatic form, rather
than part of a prose biography or a Court Statement, is that we
can't ever tell. To anticipate some comments on *Hamlet* I draw
on later, Richard is set 'gingerly' on a knife-edge and the
question whether he inclines more this way or that is 'best left to
the individual reader, actor, or producer' (Knight, 1989: 300).
Not only best but necessarily left, for poetic drama by its nature
won't tell us what prose fiction can. Compare Richard's speech
with George Eliot on a possibly similar case of qualified
humility. In *The Mill on the Floss* Maggie Tulliver, when her
family's fortunes collapse, seeks consolation in

> something that will present motives in an entire absence of
> high prizes, something that will give patience and feed human
> love when the limbs ache with weariness and human looks are
> hard upon us – something, clearly, that lies outside personal
> desires, that includes resignation for ourselves and active love
> for what is not ourselves. Now and then that sort of
> enthusiasm finds a far-echoing voice that comes from an

experience springing out of the deepest need . . . From what you know of her, you will not be surprised that she threw some exaggeration and wilfulness, some pride and impetuosity, even into her self-renunciation; her own life was still a drama for her in which she demanded of herself that her part should be played with intensity. And so it came to pass that she often lost the spirit of humility by being excessive in the outward act; she often strove after too high a flight and came down with her poor little half-fledged wings dabbled in the mud. (Book IV, Chapter Three)

The difference is that in the dramatic excerpt 'you seem to be *told* nothing, but to see and hear everything' (Coleridge again).[6] The point-hunting critics I quoted just now might be referring to a prose paraphrase or a narrative version of Richard's speech.

My other quarrel with many commentaries on the 'hollow crown' has to do with moments and wholes, actual details and alleged unifying designs. This runs parallel with the question I've just been nagging about, which concerned texture versus moral design, or pleasure versus point. In both respects, what goes on too often – despite much modern talk about heterogeneity and heteroglossia – is a process of homogenising. I can best get at this by a return to the old practical criticism with which I was busy in the opening pages of this chapter and by picking up Ann Thompson's terms cited in the Introduction. Here is both how I would discuss Richard's speech in terms of microcosms and macrocosms – and why such an approach eventually runs aground.

How then might this speech be seen as a 'miniature' of Shakespeare at large and used to alert students to aspects of his inheritance and emerging habits? First, it could exemplify his period's own concept of micro- and macrocosms. Elsewhere in Shakespeare this invoked the relation of human to heavenly worlds. Man embodies in little space the infinite riches of the Universe, as in Hamlet's 'What a piece of work is man . . .' (II, ii). Or the larger cosmos reacts to the smaller; as when, in *Macbeth* (II, iv), 'the heavens, as troubled with man's act,/ Threatens his bloody stage' (the idea combines here with a grimmer version of the theatre image Richard also uses), or when Salisbury and a Captain give an early sketch for that *Macbeth* scene (*Richard II*, II, iv). But in our hollow-crown speech the general concept has to do rather with the relation of inner and outer realms: Richard imagines his enemies as both human and metaphysical – besieging armies, and Death – and the latter is both external and internal; a few pages back I touched on the way that Death is at once drilling through from the outside but is also 'within the hollow crown'. In working with Shakespeare chronologically I would build on this with similar images in *Julius Caesar* ('the state of a man, Like to a little kingdom, suffers then/The nature of insurrection' – II, i) and *Macbeth* ('My thought . . . Shakes so my single state of man' – I, iii). At this early stage I would look back on what Shakespeare was drawing on from earlier figures of Death in the plays *Mankind*, *Everyman* and *The Castle of Perseverance*, seeking also to link Richard's vision of 'grinning' Death with that strand of sadistic mocking recurrent in medieval drama and visual art, even in Crucifixion scenes (see Appendix 1A). Finally, to remove any remote period air of Ye Quainte Olde Middle Ages, I would adduce later poetic portrayals of enemies that are partly outside a victim and partly the traitor within the gates. Thus Blake's tree of evil:

> The Gods of the earth and sea,
> Sought thro' Nature to find this Tree,
> But their search was all in vain:
> There grows one in the human brain

('The Human Abstract'); or his rose that is sick in itself as well as destroyed by 'the invisible worm/That flies in the night' ('The Sick Rose').

It would also be possible to consider Richard's speech as a microcosm of this particular play: it gives a vigorous twist and onward push to several terms and images that have already been bobbing along in the text. For a start, its series of references to the earth and ground reverse the optimism of Richard's fond evocation of his Kingdom's 'dear earth' in the same scene's opening lines. I'd be tentative about some wider links: for instance, of Death's terse 'Farewell king!' (terminal not only in the sense of ending the line and a long sentence) with the single-word line of the exiled Bolingbroke's equally brief 'Farewell' in I, iv – and perhaps with the King's and Queen's farewells in V, i (see below). Other long-distance echoes are more resounding: in II, i Gaunt has warned Richard that 'A thousand flatterers sit within thy crown/Whose compass is no bigger than thy head', while Northumberland (in a choric passage near the end of that scene) reassured Ross that 'even through the hollow eyes of death/I spy life peering'. That scene is in turn itself a microcosm of the play's method, the closing choric part picking up the key terms 'heart', 'tongue', 'deeds', 'thoughts', 'speech' used by Gaunt at its opening and already sounded in Act I.

But of course this kind of thread-tracing cuts across considerations of quality. And it would be equally important to show how a scene of this play is a microcosm of Shakespeare's developing style – how, for example, obvious and/or elaborated similes bow out as metaphors to enter by the back door in the guise of personification. The vision of life peering through death's eye-sockets (like a living person behind a death-mask, or light at end of a tunnel) is a surprise and relief after some predictable and protracted tossing to and fro of the storm image – fearful tempest, no shelter, our fault for not keeping open a weather-eye, and so on. Since R. D. Altick's famous article on 'Symphonic Imagery in *Richard II*' (1947; reprinted in the Signet edition, the *Casebook*, and several other anthologies) it has been common to claim unity for the play by virtue of its 'iterative symbolism and imagery' (PMLA, 1947: 339). But a valuable point of Altick's is that in this earlyish play iterative images may be 'conventional' and 'marred by diffuseness', lacking the mature 'condensation, the compression of a universe of meaning into a single bold metaphor' (*ibid.*, 365).

We should keep this qualitative caveat in mind when coming back to our central scene, III, ii. The way in which its hollow-crown speech picks up images and terms which run through that scene as much as through others tempts us to integrate it effortlessly into its context, seeing unity even through Richard's wildly oscillating moods. This is the Coleridgean approach, the perilously convenient paradox of unity-in-diversity perceiving 'the utmost consistency of character in Richard' through 'the most rapid transitions – from hope to despair, from the extravagance of love to the agonies of resentment, and from pretended resignation to the bitterest reproaches' (Coleridge, 1989: 120). Mercuriality ('the most rapid transitions') is after all what I will be going on (in Chapter Four) to describe in later plays from *King Lear* to *The Winter's Tale*. But the point I have to stress for the main purpose of the present chapter is that I can call III, ii mercurial only as long as I can hear Richard's 'very self and voice'. And I hear no voice at all when we lurch immediately on to this:

RICHARD
. . . How can you say to me I am a king?
CARLISLE
My lord, wise men ne'er sit and wail their woes,
But presently prevent the ways to wail;
To fear the foe, since fear oppresseth strength,
Gives in your weakness strength unto your foe,
And so your follies fight against yourself.
Fear and be slain – no worse can come to fight,
And fight and die is death destroying death,
Where fearing dying pays death servile breath.
AUMERLE
My father hath a power, inquire of him,
And learn to make a body of a limb.
RICHARD
Thou chid'st me well. Proud Bullingbrook, I come
To change blows with thee for our day of doom.
This ague fit of fear is overblown,
An easy task it is to win our own.
Say, Scroop, where lies our uncle with his power?
Speak sweetly, man, although thy looks be sour.
(III, ii 177–93)

I certainly hear no differentiation between voices – the division between speakers is purely a structural device in a passage of ingenious patterned verse. The arbitrarily assigned speakers work together, as do the insistent onomatopoeia, assonance, paradox, antithesis and symmetry inside lines and/or couplets, at times approaching the knottiness of tongue-twisters ('Where fearing dying pays death servile breath': around the rugged rocks the ragged rascals ran).

It would be as inappropriate *there* to think in terms of voice or character as it would *here*:

QUEEN
I cannot but be sad; so heavy sad,
As, though in thinking on no thought I think,
Makes me with heavy nothing faint and shrink.
BUSHY
'Tis nothing but conceit, my gracious lady.
QUEEN
'Tis nothing less: conceit is still deriv'd
From some forefather grief; mine is not so,
For nothing hath begot my something grief,
Or something hath the nothing that I grieve –
'Tis in reversion that I do possess –
But what it is that is not yet known what
I cannot name; 'tis nameless woe, I wot.
                                          (II, ii, 30–40)

(Compare the end with 'Peter Piper picked a peck of pickled pepper' or 'the Leith police dismisseth us'.) And in V, i the opening dialogue between Richard, Queen and Northumberland is abruptly switched off for this chilly cleverness on the most hackneyed of Petrarchan conceits:

QUEEN
And must we be divided? must we part?
RICHARD
Ay, hand from hand, my love, and heart from heart.
QUEEN
Banish us both, and send the King with me.
NORTHUMBERLAND
That were some love, but little policy.
QUEEN
Then whither he goes, thither let me go.
RICHARD
So two together weeping make one woe.
Weep thou for me in France, I for thee here;
Better far off than, near, be ne'er the near.
Go count thy way with sighs, I mine with groans.
QUEEN
So longest way shall have the longest moans,

RICHARD

Twice for one step I'll groan, the way being short,
And piece the way out with a heavy heart.
Come, come, in wooing sorrow let's be brief,
Since wedding it, there is such length in grief.
One kiss shall stop our mouths, and dumbly part;
Thus give I mine, and thus take I thy heart.

QUEEN

Give me mine own again, 'twere no good part
To take on me to keep and kill thy heart.
So now I have mine own again, be gone,
That I may strive to kill it with a groan.

RICHARD

We make woe wanton with this fond delay,
Once more, adieu, the rest let sorrow say.

(V, i, 81–102)

Individual voices (especially if line 84 really is supposed to be spoken by Northumberland) are overridden by composite pattern which again nears to tongue-twisters – especially in 'Better far off than, near, be ne'er the near'.

II

Richard II is not the first or last play which abandons presence, gesture and voice for anonymous ingenuity – anonymous in that lines are arbitrarily distributed between speakers. What matter to my ongoing argument about the study of Shakespeare are the various options open to us in dealing with such changes from one style to another. Before illustrating those options, it is worth stressing that my intention is not to do a New Criticism praise/blame, or Neoclassical beauties/blemishes job, let alone assume that the more colloquial kind of blank verse is automatically superior to patterned couplets. What concerns me is the abrupt alternations of styles; and an aptly neutral description is provided by the term *unconformities*.

That is a term used by a critic who adopts the first of the options I wish to illustrate. A. P. Rossiter (1989: 23) says that 'whether you approach *Richard II* from the angle of the texture of the verse, the verse-styles, character, plot or theme, you encounter what geologists call "unconformities" ' – broken surface layers with outcrops of earlier, lower strata. What thus breaks through may be a rhymed source-play or an earlier version by Shakespeare; plot problems may result from the dramatist taking for granted a knowledge of another old play (*Woodstock*): but the net result is that parts of our play are 'unconformable' with others. (See extended quotation in Appendix 1B.) Rossiter's word and view is taken up by Kristian Smidt in his *Unconformities in Shakespeare's History Plays* (1982).

Both Rossiter and Smidt are loud in their preferences: an alternative reaction has been to view unconformities quite neutrally as analogous to geological faults but not as artistic blemishes. But many critics go further, vindicating the play's couplets, even at their most patterned and pat, as psychologically appropriate. Thus, after the hollow-crown speech, 'Carlyle's quibbling and sententious platitudes characterize the well-meaning but ineffectual Bishop' (Hill, 1961: 108). A variant is to detect difference-in-similarity, as when Hill continues that 'Carlyle's bishoply manner is neatly offset by the incisive speeches of Aumerle' (nothing is said about Richard's ensuing couplets); or similarity-in-difference, as when A. R. Humphreys (1967: 58) says of V, i that 'the deposed King and Queen make a stylistic ceremony of their grief, lyrical-sentimental at the beginning, formal-artificial at the end, but ceremonious in both cases'. And on the Queen and Bushy in II, ii Humphreys (*ibid.*, 44) again combines an aspiring and a drooping evaluative eye: here 'are first suggested those qualities, responsive and moving, though impractical, which are to gain for Richard the sympathies' of audiences; Coleridge, less sympathetic but equally smoothing over cracks, speaks of 'the characters all talking high, but performing nothing' (Coleridge, 1989: 128) and thus mirroring Richard himself. To extend the chronological range of these critics, here is Andrew Gurr's 1984 editorial introduction, on Act I: 'Gaunt is an honest man who uses couplets to express conventional wisdom. Blank verse is for him an intense and personal form of expression' (Gurr, 1984: 33). If that sounds too kindly, then Gurr's next paragraph begins: 'The honesty of Gaunt's blank verse and its contrast with the trivialising character of his rhymes is one aspect of what is probably the play's most fundamental concern, the distance between words and what they represent' (*ibid.*, 33). A more extreme mid-1980s example is Harry Berger Jr. On II, i he suggests that

> the opposed selves are bound to their proper ritual represen-
> tatives in l. 17, with their proper ritualized representation in
> ll. 18–19, an event *celebrated* [my italics] with the play's first
> rhymed couplet . . . The shift in these lines from enjambed,
> internally stopped blank verse to end-stressed rhymed verse
> reinforces the shift from uncertain syntax and rapidly
> changing impressions to the too predictable formulas of
> chivalric rhetoric, which in this case produces an oxymoronic
> relation between what is said and how it is said . . . the shifts
> described above combine to mark the most fundamental
> process that structures this drama: the passage and transfor-
> mation of conflict from the tongueless caverns of some
> 'hidden imposthume'; to the safety of the sanctioned artifice
> and 'fair designs' of ritualized combat and behavior . . . in
> *Richard II* the conspicuous trifles, the stiff and stilted
> formulas, of ritual are the palisades that impose quarantine
> against the miasma. (Parker and Hartman, 1985: 226–7)

Berger also speaks of Richard's 'jingling rhymes whose flippancy sharpens the calculated tone of affront' (*ibid.*, 217) and of Gaunt 'smoothing faults all round – and the smoothness penetrates the syrupy rhymes and rhythms' (*ibid.*, 225). (Berger's *Imaginary Audition*, 1989, analyses in detail the entire play.)

That phrase 'smoothing faults all round' would fit the critical procedure Berger himself exemplifies, whereby the faults are attributed not to the play or the author but to the characters. A third group of critics also smooth over the unconformable places in the interests of some higher thematic or doctrinal interest. Let us take a fresh example from the play, the scenes of Aumerle's plot in Act V, the tone of which often causes problems for actors or readers. Humphreys thinks these 'should be retained and the lure of farce resisted' because 'they are about serious things, treachery, loyalty, anger, love, forgiveness', although he concedes that they are 'immaturely handled' (Humphreys, 1967: 58). No such qualitative qualification in Tennenhouse:

Another occasion for Henry to display his authority occurs when Aumerle, his conspiracy discovered, begs forgiveness, and Henry grants it. With this, Shakespeare completes the contrast between Richard and Henry. Richard lacks the power of generosity as well as the capacity for ruthlessness. Henry possesses both and can manifest either power in extreme as he so chooses. No less important than granting his cousin Aumerle forgiveness is Henry's condemnation and pursuit of all those who plotted against him. He vows, 'Destruction straight shall dog them at their heels . . ./They shall not live within this world, I swear' (V, iii, 139, 142) . . . It is significant that by staging this scene of forgiveness for Aumerle's parents, the Duke and Duchess of York, Henry recasts his authority in a comedic form. 'Our scene is alt'red from a serious thing' (V, iii, 79), he observes, when the Duchess begs an audience to plead for her son. Having just examined the comedies, one should find this scene a familiar one. By this stroke, we might say, Shakespeare acknowledges the conceptual link between his two major Elizabethan genres. (Tennenhouse, 1986: 81)

In practice it is difficult to separate such thematic justifications of unconformities from those made on psychological grounds. It is easier, and more important, to draw a line between those who face apparent problems even if they end by vindicating Shakespeare, and others (notably Berger) who never mention Shakespeare or think of the words coming 'from author's pen' rather than welling up from a character's deeper recesses.

I dwell on this for two reasons. First, I think one can readily extend to students Smidt's observation that 'the general reader would be better served by an assurance that a tangle is a tangle' (Smidt, 1982: 9); and the student will readily feel the scepticism or discouragement that Alfred Harbage wrote about: 'Evidence of blindness to defects or inconsistencies casts suspicion upon testimony about merits or consistencies. The most subtle and convincing verbal analysis of a fine passage loses authority when the critic finds identical virtues in a passage far from fine' (Harbage, 1966: 35). The 1980s have marginalised any awareness that these plays were written by a human being, because of a commendable modern wariness of bardolatry. But the two things need not be inseparable bedfellows. Smidt's final pages verge on a roundabout route to the notion of Shakespeare as Superman, but a saner note prevails in M. M. Mahood's 'Unblotted Lines: Shakespeare at work', which talks of his 'habit of plunging into a play before he has fully conceived its direction or outcome' in the spirit of 'how do I know what I think till I see what I say', confident that 'the important thing is to press on in search of the right track, knowing that once this is found the audience will forget any aberrations': 'the plays abound in loose ends, false starts, confusions and anomalies of every kind' not least because 'it is not his habit to go back and tidy up, to sweep up the clippings' (Mahood, 1972: 10–12). And Mahood reminds us that there was something far more bardolatrous about the old, turn-of-the-century school of Textual Disintegrationists which excised all unconformities as textual corruption or revisers' interference unworthy of Shakespeare. We should all be grateful, she rightly says, for Sir Edmund Chambers's 'cool declaration' in 1924 that Shakespeare was 'often careless and perfunctory' (*ibid.*, 3).

If my main purpose were to write a critical history of Shakespeare criticism, I would show how the notion of Shakespeare the impulsive artist and the erratic learner-as-he-went along is absolutely not time-specific. It governs Johnson's edition, and strongly influences Coleridge's notes if not so frankly his lectures. It recurs in Bradley, whose 'astonishment at the powers that created' *Antony and Cleopatra* gains credence from his acknowledgement that Shakespeare 'took little interest in the character of Octavius' and little care to make it clear (Signet, 1963: 226, 241). With Aufidius in *Coriolanus* Bradley says that 'in reading some passages in his talk we seem to see Shakespeare yawning as he wrote' (Signet, 1988: 266). Equally, what strikes me most powerfully in Tillyard when I reread him in response to the repetitive contempt of the 1980s, is not the right-wing colour of his politics but the colourfulness of his evaluative response. He is forthright that *Richard II* 'is imperfectly executed': the imperfections 'are undoubted and must be faced', they include 'a good deal of verse which is indifferent', with couplets that may have a function but 'as poetry are indifferent stuff' (Tillyard, 1944: 245–6). 'Ceremonial' is Tillyard's word for that function – this must be Humphreys's source in the passage I quoted earlier – but it is not an excuse-all in Tillyard. Again, the critic's yawns makes us sit up the more at his enthusiasms. When he goes on to *Henry IV* there is the paradox that, like Johnson, Tillyard the right-winger has far more relish for Falstaff than any of our present-day theorists of the spirit of Carnival. He warms equally to the 'infectious vitality' of Hotspur, whose 'eye [is] sharp with the zest of a man who adores the solid and reassuring traffic of the world' (*ibid.*, 280, 284).

'Even Homer nods': it ought to release students from attitudes of unquestioning veneration (bound to be hypocritical) if they are allowed to think that authorial nods and yawns, rubs and botches, lags and spurts, may exist.

Conversely, in their refusal to think about the possibility of unconformities – whether textual faults, incompleteness of revision, or authorial unevenness of attention and changes of direction – many critics new and old imply despite themselves a position indistinguishable from the excesses of bardolatry (at worst the faults or limitations they notice are ideological ones). In the introduction to his *Shakespearean Negotiations*, Greenblatt has in mind the legacy of New Criticism when he says that 'the textual analyses I was trained to do had as their goal the identification and celebration of a numinous literary authority, whether that authority was ultimately located in the mysterious genius of an artist or in the mysterious perfection of a text' (Greenblatt, 1988: 3). But it is to newer-than-New critics like Tennenhouse and Berger, no less than to Wilson Knight or Coleridge in their unrestrained moments, that we can apply Greenblatt's complaint about 'the impression conveyed by powerful critics that had they but world enough and time, they could illuminate every comma of the text and knit together into unified interpretive vision all of their discrete perceptions' (*ibid.*, 4). Fissures, such as that between the hollow-crown speech and the hollow fill that follows it, are thereby ignored.

The matter is central to my dissenting dialogue with Kiernan Ryan. He, too, attacks the New Critics, laughs at Wilson Knight and rejects Coleridge. But he endorses, in effect, the most extreme of Coleridge's ideas: that the characteristically Shakespearean power is found in 'any Shakespeare play' (Ryan's phrase, not Coleridge's) and in any and every part of it. This idealistic view is made plausible by identifying the common, uniting element as diversity. But Ryan is thereby offering only a latter-day protean variant on the Romantic view, much derided by recent critics, that Shakespeare is *par excellence* what Keats termed 'the chameleon poet'. And Ryan actually adopts the corresponding Coleridgean term, writing of 'Shakespeare's protean imagination', his 'protean compulsion to displace the dramatic perspective across a spectrum of disparate identities and irreconcilable attitudes' (Ryan, 1989: 3, 38).

III

That protean compulsion, Ryan goes on, 'is what makes possible the structural identification of Shakespeare's greatest plays with the common interests of humanity as a whole rather than with the interests of one section of society at the expense of the rest' (*ibid.*, 38). This would be a neo-Johnsonian stance (cf. Johnson's view of the plays as 'the genuine progeny of common humanity') were it not that in Ryan's vision of 'the work's vision' one section of society becomes greatly prioritised.

Ryan is a left-wing optimist. Not so the American New Historicists who think 'the plays that meditate on the consolidation of state power' let out populist underdogs on a very firm leash: 'Shakespeare's plays are centrally, repeatedly concerned with the production and containment of subversion and disorder' (Greenblatt, 1988: 40). I will outline for your consideration Tennenhouse's application of this idea to *Richard II* (Tennenhouse, 1986: 79–80).

The play shows 'a split in the body politic' being mended by making the state 'contain' the 'heterogeneous elements of carnival'.

> This makes the hierarchy of state seem less at odds with nature, at once more inclusionary and less arbitrary in its laws. Although we do not usually think of Henry Bullingbroke in such terms, Shakespeare does give him the features of inversion which necessarily challenge the law. In preparing for battle against Mowbray, Bullingbroke is 'lusty, young, and cheerly drawing breath' (I, iii, 66). As Henry

leaves England, Richard accordingly describes his rival as one who enjoys the popular support of the 'craftsmen', 'an oyster-wench', and a 'brace of draymen'. These elements, Richard notes, regard Henry as if 'England [were] in reversion his,/ And he our subjects' next degree of hope' (I, iv, 35–6). Even the support enabling Henry to challenge the king – in its mixing of ages, sexes and social ranks – sounds more like a carnivalesque troop than a disciplined military force.

Tennenhouse finds the carnival idea of 'inversion' in this description:

> White-beards have arm'd their thin and hairless scalps
> Against thy majesty; boys, with women's voices,
> Strive to speak big, and clap their female joints
> In stiff unwieldy arms against thy crown;
> Thy very beadsmen learn to bend their bows
> Of double-fatal yew against thy state;
> Yea, distaff-women manage rusty bills
> Against thy seat: both young and old rebel . . .
>
> (III, ii, 112–19)

And he notes that the King describes his challenger 'in language more appropriate for a Falstaff than an English king; Bullingbrook is "a thief", as well as a "traitor", one "Who all this while hath revell'd in the night"' (III, ii, 47–8). So that when he comes to power, 'Henry restores the body politic to wholeness. His England incorporates the robust features of festival.'

I present Tennenhouse's case at some length because it could stimulate discussion of the play from a viewpoint that will still be fresh to many students, even though its concern with Carnival has become a new critical orthodoxy. My own reaction to the passage is that it is disabled by tone-deafness. On the revealing scene iv of Act I, for example, it doesn't hear the different tones of voice in which speakers talk of Bolingbroke's departure into exile – while Scroop is edgily contemptuous, Richard revels in dramatising the anecdote and mimicking both exile and citizens until the sobering double-take of his two closing lines. In this respect and others, throughout the entire first act and with Gaunt in the opening of the second, Richard himself can well be seen as combined lord of misrule and court jester. And in the third act he serves as his own licensed fool.

The position taken by Tennenhouse is fairly orthodox in the New Historicism. But Greenblatt directs his guiding formula of 'production and containment' at the *Henry IV* plays, and his brief recall of *Richard II* appears to accept the hollow-crown speech as 'clean':

> There are moments in *Richard II* when the collapse of kingship seems to be confirmed in the discovery of the physical body of the ruler, the pathos of his creatural existence: [he quotes the last five and a half lines of the hollow crown speech]. By the close of *2 Henry IV* such physical limitations have been absorbed into the ideological structure, and hence justification, of kingship. It is precisely because Prince Hal lives with bread that we can understand the sacrifice that he and, for that matter, his father have made.

Greenblatt quotes the father in his role as insomniac monarch:

> Why rather, sleep, liest thou in smoky cribs,
> Upon uneasy pallets stretching thee,
> And hush'd with buzzing night-flies to thy slumber,
> Than in the perfum'd chambers of the great,
> Under the canopies of costly state,
> And lull'd with sound of sweetest melody?
>   (III, i, 9–14)

and comments:

> Who knows? Perhaps it is even true . . . . But . . . this sleeplessness was not a well-kept secret: the sufferings of the great are one of the familiar themes in the literature of the governing classes in the sixteenth century. Henry IV speaks in soliloquy, but . . . his isolation only intensifies the sense that he is addressing a large audience: the audience of the theatre. We are invited to take measure of his suffering, to understand – here and elsewhere in the play – the costs of power. And we are invited to understand these costs in order to ratify the power, to accept the grotesque and cruelly unequal

distribution of possessions: everything to the few, nothing to the many. The rulers earn, or at least pay for, their exalted position through suffering, and this suffering ennobles, if it does not exactly cleanse, the lies and betrayals upon which this position depends. (Greenblatt, 1988: 53–4)

Ryan spiritedly attacks this kind of diagnostic approach as defeatist and reactionary. 'It seems ironic that the new breed of historicists confirms rather than refutes the fundamental supposition of traditional critics like Tillyard that Shakespeare was an entirely conventional thinker, whose plays necessarily express the political, moral and philosophical outlook of those who ruled his world [except that they] explain the drama's ideological conformity far more complexly'; and 'it leaves merely negative or cynical reasons for bothering to study such a contaminated Shakespeare at all' (Ryan, 1989: 7, 8). My own objections are more strongly towards the 'curiously trite moralising'[7] this New Historicism licenses – for instance, about 'the grotesque and cruelly inequal distribution' of possessions: 'everything to the few, nothing to the many' (Greenblatt, 1988: 54) – a plangent note amplified by Ryan himself, especially on the tragedies. We've long been familiar, from Christian critics before Marxists, with this comfortable indignation, this moralising no less trite for being vehement, prompted by remarks like Lear's 'I have taken too little thought of this' or Gloucester's wish that 'distribution should undo excess'. More worrying is that Greenblatt's commentary betrays not even a flicker of amusement. He stubbornly resists any tendency to laughter, as Johnson said of Swift (Johnson, 1968, II: 169). It seems an odd resistance in the face of the *Henry IV* plays, especially paradoxical in writers who, like Greenblatt, Ryan and Tennenhouse, are much concerned with the spirit of Carnival! The notion of containment is all very well, but these critics are only too able to contain their laughter when it comes to describing the thing contained.

IV

In the past few pages, I have been presenting the routes two New Historicists take from *Richard II* to *Henry IV*. I will myself now propose an alternative way to link those plays. This cuts across considerations of ideology (whether that of the plays or of the critics); and it works unhagiographically with the notion of an author. Of 'author's pen' finding and exploiting 'actor's voice'. Not, emphatically, an infallible author, nor one who has anything much to say (or betray), but very much the opportunistic 'apprentice hand'. I take this up with the part of York.

Note that I don't speak of 'the character of York'. Like the chameleon poet in Keats's and Coleridge's idea, he has no character; or at best it's made up as Shakespeare goes along – and remade quite without scruple to fit the dramatic needs of the moment. I want to take up one of those moments and consider, not who York is, but how he sounds.

> . . . God for his mercy, what a tide of woes
> Comes rushing on this woeful land at once!
> I know not what to do. I would to God
> (So my untruth had not provok'd him to it)
> The King had cut off my head with my brother's.
> What, are there no posts dispatch'd for Ireland?
> How shall we do for money for these wars?
> Come, sister – cousin, I would say – pray pardon me.
> Go, fellow, get thee home, provide some carts,
> And bring away the armor that is there. [*Exit Servingman.*]
> Gentlemen, will you go muster men? If I
> Know how or which way to order these affairs
> Thus disorderly thrust into my hands,
> Never believe me.
>
> (II, ii, 98–111)

(Contrast later revisers' versions: Appendix 1C.) Disorderly is indeed the word for it. This is the voice of the old buffer, blustering and flustered, distractedly and disjointedly addressing half a dozen people while forgetting who is who and wheeling about with appropriate gestures.

This (despite half-attempts in the *Henry VI* plays) is Shakespeare hitting off something new. But I want to stress equally my twin point, the unconformity of this with much else – both with other speakers in this scene and with York himself in other scenes.

Now the Harmony School of critics has no trouble smoothing this in. We've already seen them smoothing in the minor-Metaphysical lines assigned to the Queen and Bushy at the start of this scene. And they go on, plausibly enough, to see careful design in the abrupt entry of York and of the 'practical' world of pressing events. Certainly, a broad contrast (and a powerful one) may be drawn between the Queen's leisurely introspection and York's urgent distraction. But that depends on jumping over York's first speech immediately on entry, which I see no way of harmonising with the 'disorderly' one I've already quoted.

QUEEN
. . . O, full of careful business are his looks!
Uncle, for God's sake speak some comfortable words.
YORK
Should I do so, I should belie my thoughts.
Comfort's in heaven, and we are on the earth,
Where nothing lives but crosses, cares, and grief.
Your husband, he is gone to save far off,
Whilst others come to make him lose at home.
Here am I left to underprop his land,
Who, weak with age, cannot support myself.
Now comes the sick hour that his surfeit made,
Now shall he try his friends that flatter'd him.
(II, ii, 75–85)

This is a competent bit of patterned writing from Shakespeare's pen, unrhymed but constructed largely in couplet units, with the familiar pleasures of symmetry and antithesis. It is therein less extreme than the Queen's speeches which I quoted back in Section I. But it is closer to her style than to that of York's own following speeches, and also submits happily to being entwined with hers with the help of three of the play's recurring terms that end her feedline and his opening lines: 'looks', 'words', and 'thoughts'.

In this scene, and in the play as a whole, the impression conveyed by unconformable verse styles assigned to York's actor is that there are at least two Yorks: the dignified if indignant spokesman of tradition and rectitude – dignified, like

Gaunt, by age if also made unformidable by it; and the
flustered, vacillating old fart. True, Shakespeare tries to pull
those together in the next scene, at Berkeley Castle (II, iii),
but in the present one the solemn element is ludicrously
miscalculated. He starts 'Tut, tut! Grace me no grace, nor
uncle me no uncle . . .' but then come the lines Rossiter
rightly quotes to support the view that some of the play's
blank verse is worse than its couplets: 'Why have those
banish'd and forbidden legs/Dar'd once to touch the dust of
England's ground?' The speech recovers its dignity, but with
York Shakespeare can't or won't harmonise opposite strands
in the portrayal of age as he does with Polonius – 'dotage
encroaching on wisdom', is how Johnson (1969: 139) puts it –
or with Lear and Gloucester. At the very least, Coleridge
(1989: 117) goes too far in promoting York to one of 'the
three principal persons in this play' and in claiming that 'the
keeping [consistency] was most admirable', constructing a
coherent character portrait and elaborating a psychological
comparison with Richard.

How do these comments on York lead me out to adjacent
plays? I am countering the New Historicists', and Ryan's, stress
on 'heteroglossia' and 'multivocality' with something more
modest, but I think more realistic: Shakespeare hitting on or
learning how to do one particular kind of voice, and how to bend
blank verse to the individual speech rhythm, then carrying *that*
over to *Henry IV* – and beyond.

But one adjacent play relevant to my theme may have been
written just before *Richard II* and may deserve the credit for that
stylistic discovery.

V

Romeo and Juliet is almost entirely ignored by 1980s critics, even
the feminists. Nevertheless, it has always been popular both in
itself and in the many distinguished musical adaptations (e.g. by
Berlioz, Tchaikovsky, Gounod, Milhaud, Prokofiev) which
confirm that it is not vacuous to talk about the play's musical
structure of contrasting voices, tempos and moods. And a recent
issue of the *Shakespeare Quarterly* (Summer 1990) which

concentrated on *teaching* Shakespeare returned to this play again and again.

If it has appealed to old and young, this is partly because the play constantly contrasts youth and age. Such a contrast emerges intermittently in *Richard II*: Gurr notes that an indistinct feature 'of the shifting balance in the play is the generation gap' (Cambridge, 1984: 17); and its first line has young Richard addressing 'Old John of Gaunt' and 'time honored Lancaster'. This is equally true of *Henry IV, Part One*: the King figures as 'The Old Man' (parental as well as national authority, and sounding about four score years and ten under the cares of office) who is contrasted with Falstaff as a carefree 'old boy', and who himself contrasts 'my young Harry' with 'this young Percy' (I, i, 86, 92). This Percy, Hotspur by nickname and nature, is in turn contrasted with the caution, even coldness and calculation, of his father, uncle and other allies. But this youth–age contrast is pressed most insistently in the start of *Romeo and Juliet*. After the opening brawl, the Prince castigates 'old Capulet, and Montague' for having 'made Verona's ancient citizens . . . to wield old partisans, in hands as old'; and (as Montague puts it) 'set this ancient quarrel new abroad'. In the second scene Capulet tells Paris that ' 'tis not hard, I think, for men so old as we to keep the peace'. He then turns to the very young, to his daughter as 'hopeful lady of my earth', in lines which also look back on his own long life and which thus parallel the nurse's talk about her life and Juliet's in the third scene.

But Shakespeare's twist is to combine in old Capulet the comic stereotype of tyrannical father with 'the hot blood of youth' we heard racing in Hotspur (and which is also transfused into Capulet's nephew Tybalt): let me jump ahead for a first illustration to the scene (III, v) after Tybalt's death and Romeo's banishment, when father is thwarted in plans for his daughter's wedding. 'It made me mad,' exclaims Hotspur of the 'popingay'. 'God's bread, it makes me mad!' cries Capulet of the 'mammet' Juliet; and he mimics her as Hotspur mimics the messenger.

> . . . A whining mammet, in her fortune's tender,
> To answer, 'I'll not wed, I cannot love;
> I am too young, I pray you pardon me'.
>
> (III, v, 184–6)

In his anger, he lashes out in turn at daughter, wife and nurse. But – to recall my earlier talk about unconformities – I leave a question-mark over the start of this encounter which either resorts to or parodies an expansive style of analogy. The first lines are perhaps deliberately made appropriate to a (so far!) genial as well as prolix old-timer like Capulet:

> When the sun sets, the earth doth drizzle dew,
> But for the sunset of my brother's son
> It rains downright.
> How now, a conduit, girl? What, still in tears?
> Evermore show'ring?
>
> (126–30)

But the continuation, stretching out to eight and a half lines the tedious conceit that 'In one little body/Thou counterfeits a bark, a sea, a wind', though roughly apt as playful paternal mockery, has more of very early Shakespeare than of a particular speaker. This reservation of mine will be matched by one about the ball scene in Act I, to which I now turn.

Old Capulet welcomes his young guests with nostalgia for his own salad days:

> I have seen the day
> That I have worn a visor and could tell
> A whispering tale in a fair lady's ear,
> Such as would please; 'tis gone, 'tis gone, 'tis gone.
>
> (I, v, 21–4)

As the dancing gets under way he reminisces with his equally elderly cousin:

> Nay, sit, nay, sit, good cousin Capulet,
> For you and I are past our dancing days.
> How long is't now since last yourself and I
> Were in a mask?
> COUSIN
> By'r lady, thirty years.
> CAPULET
> What, man? 'tis not so much, 'tis not so much:

'Tis since the nuptial of Lucentio,
Come Pentecost as quickly as it will,
Some five and twenty years, and then we mask'd.
COUSIN
'Tis more, 'tis more. His son is elder, sir;
His son is thirty.
CAPULET
                    Will you tell me that?
His son was but a ward two years ago.
                                        (30–40)

Note the elderly habit of repetition – ' 'Tis gone, 'tis gone, 'tis
gone', ' 'tis not so much, 'tis not so much', ' 'tis more, 'tis more' –
and the amazement at how time flies. As Mahood (1957: 62)
says, this is a sketch for the old codgers Shallow and Silence in
Henry IV, Part Two. Next, young Romeo admires young Juliet
('Did my heart love til now?'), and is recognised as an enemy by
young Tybalt, who then quarrels with old Capulet over his wish
to challenge Romeo. This is the climax of that quarrel:

I'll not endure him.
CAPULET
                    He shall be endured.
What, goodman boy? I say he shall, go to!
Am I the master here, or you? go to!
You'll not endure him! God shall mend my soul,
You'll make a mutiny among my guests!
You will set cock-a-hoop! you'll be the man! . . .
You must contrary me! Marry, 'tis time. –
Well said, my hearts! – You are a princox, go,
Be quiet, or – More light, more light! – For shame,
I'll make you quiet, what! – Cheerly, my hearts!
                                        (76–88)

If I may spell out what links this with York and with Hotspur: an
old man, who has talked of having bowed out of both family
feuds and masked flirtation, getting angry at a young man's
anger; fleeting half-mimicry of Tybalt ('You'll not endure
him! . . . You will set cock-a-hoop! you'll be the man!');
all this muttered, and alternating distractedly with shouts of

encouragement to the guests ('Well said, my hearts!' and 'Cheerly, my hearts!') and orders to the servants ('More light, more light!'). Similarly, his first speech in this scene was addressed in quick succession to all groups present: 'Welcome, gentlemen! . . . Ladies. . . . Ah, my mistresses . . . Welcome, gentlemen! . . . You are welcome, Gentlemen! . . .' Then:

> Come, musicians, play.
> A hall, a hall! give room! and foot it, girls.
> More light, you knaves, and turn the tables up;
> And quench the fire, the room is grown too hot

before he turns to his cousin ('Ah, sirrah . . .'). In both speeches the words signal aptly varied gestures and tones of voice as he wheels round to address different people – servers, musicians, guests and relatives, dancers and wallflowers.

Of course, old Capulet here contributes to a larger pattern of contrast in the scene. He and Tybalt help convey the bustle and noise of the party that began with the servants' run-off-their-feet distracted preparation ('You are looked for and called for, asked for and sought for in the great chamber – we cannot be here and there at once': this continues the 'tail' of the earlier scene – iii – when they set off to deliver invitations). This turbulence is the turning world in which Romeo and Juliet form a still centre.

Every student knows that, in their exchange which forms the centre of as well as occupies the middle of this scene, Romeo and Juliet jointly create a sonnet; and the sense of interweaving and of stasis which that conveys is heightened by contrast with the servants' distracted prose and Capulet's disjointed blank verse. None the less – and I now make my parallel with the case of York – that contrast is imperfect, for in this same scene Capulet and Tybalt sometimes break into rhymed verse, measured and well ordered if not over-patterned. As if taking his cue from Romeo's rhymed reaction to Juliet (in his speech beginning 'O, she doth teach the torches to burn bright . . .') Tybalt ends his angry recognition of Romeo with a rhyming couplet and, when Capulet questions him, rhymes with Capulet (as he does again a little later), and adds another rhyming couplet. And after Capulet's distracted reproof ('Go to . . . Cheerly, my hearts' –

quoted in full above), Tybalt withdraws muttering, angrily but rhymingly and antithetically:

> Patience perforce with willful choler meeting
> Makes my flesh tremble in their different greeting.
> I will withdraw, but this intrusion shall,
> Now seeming sweet, convert to bitt'rest gall.
>
> (89–92)

This kind of verse is much more like the lovers' sonnet that immediately follows than like Capulet's preceding bluster. Making due allowance for Shakespeare's enduring predilection for rhymed 'get-off lines', he is still (as with York) infirm of purpose or proficiency in creating a voice in anger or distraction; although this unsteadiness shows more with Tybalt than with Capulet. With this play it is not realistic to posit (as one can with *Richard II*) the outcropping of a previous, patchily revised play in verse, although the source-poem may be poking through.[8] A strong impression is of stylistic seepage within Shakespeare's own text: one character starts (for example) rhyming and this overruns some later speeches, overruling character – or voice distinctions. A pejorative analogy might be the non-congruence of forms and colours in the early days of colour printing; a favourable one would be the deliberate overwash of several forms in some modern painting. Whether the equivalent in Shakespeare is intentional or hapless, it warns us of the limits to his mimesis of voices, even when he has hit upon a voice which is at once so distinctive and – as we'll soon see with Hotspur – adaptable to characters young as well as old.

To end this section on *Romeo and Juliet* I reproduce Coleridge (1989: 135–7) on Capulet, and on the play as exemplifying an early stage in Shakespeare's development. A memorable image of Coleridge's envisages a 'war embrace' and eventual alliance between the poet and the philosopher in Shakespeare (*ibid.*, 29): here he writes of the poet or sheer lover of language and the dramatist, and he sees them in *Romeo and Juliet* as still wrestling with each other. Coleridge elsewhere idealises the young lovers and, as Hazlitt saw, sentimentalises by spiritualising them. But towards Shakespeare himself he is not here uncritically idolising: I began this chapter with his view that in *Romeo and Juliet*

Shakespeare's 'excellences' were 'less happily combined' than in later plays. He does trace a consistent thread in the representation of Capulet,

> worthy noble-minded old man of high rank with all the impatience of character which is likely to accompany it. It is delightful to see the sensibilities of nature always so exquisitely called forth, as if the poet had the hundred arms of the polypus, thrown out in all directions to catch the predominant feeling. We might see in Capulet the way in which anger seized hold of everything that comes in its way, as in the lines where Capulet is reproving Tybalt for his fierceness of behaviour which led him to insult a Montague and disturb the merriment [he quotes lines 82–8]. The line 'This trick may chance to scathe you – I know what –' was an allusion to the legacy Tybalt might expect; and then, seeing the lights burn dimly, Capulet turns his anger against the servants, so that no one passion is so predominant but that it always includes all the parts of the character, – so that the reader never had a mere abstract of a passion, as of anger or ambition, but the whole man was presented, the one predominant passion acting as the leader of the band to the rest.

None the less the play as a whole lacks coherence and proportion:

> to borrow a phrase from the painter, the whole work was less in keeping: there was the production of grand portions: there were the limbs of what was excellent; but the production of a whole, in which each part gave delight for itself, and where the whole gave more intellectual delight, was the effect of judgement and taste not to be obtained but by painful study, and in which we gave up the stronger pleasures, derived from the dazzling light which a man of genius throws over every circumstance, and where we were chiefly struck by vivid and strong images. Taste was a subsequent attainment, after the poet had been disciplined by experience . . .

And Coleridge adds a comment that should give encouragement

to students: 'it would be a hopeless symptom . . . if he found a young man with perfect taste'.

Elsewhere (*ibid.*, 153) Coleridge quotes Benvolio and old Montague on Romeo's love for Rosaline (I, i) as proving that Shakespeare meant the play 'to approach to a poem – which, and its early date, are proved likewise by the multitude of rhyming couplets.' And he warned that, because in *Romeo and Juliet* 'the poet is not entirely blended with the dramatist . . . Capulet and Montague frequently talked language only belonging to the poet, and not so much characteristic of passion' or of the particular characters in whose mouth it is placed (*ibid.*, 140). That caveat, which present-day enthusiasts for heteroglossia appear to ignore, should also be kept in mind with the portrayal of York and of Hotspur.

VI

Richard II, as Rossiter says, has 'no real beginning', certainly not one that carries us clearly on to the 'coherent middle'. But *Romeo and Juliet* so immediately pushes forward with a vigorous play of contrasts that my reservations may be brushed aside as quibbles about little local difficulties. Even more so with the comments I now make about *Henry IV, Part One*, where I'll focus on the last scene in the opening act's confident tripartite structure.

We've heard Henry lament, in the first scene, that no sooner has he defeated one set of enemies than others rise up, including those who had been his friends and accomplices. What is worse, with a son like Hal, who needs enemies? – if only it could turn out that there had been a switch of babies and his real son was Hotspur! Shakespeare satisfies our curiosity by introducing Hal (and Falstaff, his surrogate father) in scene two, which partly confirms and then challenges Henry's charge of 'riot and dishonor'; and by introducing in scene three that other 'son who is the theme of honor's tongue'. The parallel is reinforced by the two sons' contrasting speeches on honour: Hal's calculating soliloquy 'I know you all . . .' and Hotspur's impulsive fantasy about plucking 'bright honor from the pale-faced moon'. Isn't the speaker of that icy first speech not perhaps a chip off the old block after all; and is Hotspur really the kind of son Henry would be glad to have, any more than the monarchising 'vile politician' Henry is the kind of father Hotspur would appreciate?

In Marlowe's *Edward II*, still in Shakespeare's eyes and ears while writing the mid-1590s plays I'm discussing, the effete and irresponsible nature of the court is brought home by adapting a stock motif (one common in verse satire up to and including Donne, who elaborated the vital added ingredient of mimicry). King Edward's favourite Gaveston doesn't waste time before telling us that he 'must have wanton poets, pleasant wits' and pretty-boy pages clad 'like sylvan nymphs' (I, i). Hence young Mortimer's impatience in this set piece:

> Uncle, his wanton humour grieves not me:
> But this I scorn, that one so basely born
> Should by his sovereign's favour grow so pert,
> And riot it with the treasure of the realm,
> While soldiers mutiny for want of pay.
> He wears a lord's revenue on his back,
> And, Midas-like, he jets it in the court,
> With base outlandish cullions at his heels,
> Whose proud fantastic liveries make such show
> As if that Proteus, god of shapes, appear'd.
> I have not seen a dapper Jack so brisk.
> He wears a short Italian hooded cloak,
> Larded with pearl, and in his Tuscan cap
> A jewel of more value than the crown.
> Whiles other walk below, the king and he
> From out a window laugh at such as we,
> And flout our train, and jest at our attire.
> Uncle, 'tis this that makes me impatient.
>
> (I, iv)

'Impatient' is also a recurrent word for Hotspur, not least in his debut scene. He is one of those who, the King complains, 'tread upon my patience', and his father sees that 'imagination of some great exploit/Drives him beyond the bounds of patience'. Hotspur himself speaks of 'my grief and my impatience' in a speech which could well be Shakespeare's emulation of Marlowe's which I've just quoted; Henry demands that Hotspur hand over prisoners taken in a recent battle, and Hotspur fences:

. . . My liege, I did deny no prisoners,
But I remember, when the fight was done,
When I was dry with rage and extreme toil,
Breathless and faint, leaning upon my sword,
Came there a certain lord, neat, and trimly dress'd,
Fresh as a bridegroom, and his chin new reap'd,
Show'd like a stubble-land at harvest-home.
He was perfumed like a milliner,
And 'twixt his finger and his thumb he held
A pouncet-box, which ever and anon
He gave his nose and took't away again,
Who therewith angry, when it next came there,
Took it in snuff – and still he smil'd and talk'd:
And as the soldiers bore dead bodies by,
He call'd them untaught knaves, unmannerly,
To bring a slovenly unhandsome corse
Betwixt the wind and his nobility.
With many holiday and lady terms
He questioned me, among the rest demanded
My prisoners in your Majesty's behalf.
I then, all smarting with my wounds being cold,
To be so pester'd with a popingay,
Out of my grief and my impatience
Answer'd neglectingly, I know not what –
He should, or he should not – for he made me mad
To see him shine so brisk and smell so sweet,
And talk so like a waiting-gentlewoman
Of guns, and drums, and wounds, God save the mark!
And telling me the sovereignest thing on earth
Was parmaciti for an inward bruise,
And that it was great pity, so it was,
This villainous saltpetre should be digg'd
Out of the bowels of the harmless earth,
Which many a good tall fellow had destroyed
So cowardly, and but for these vile guns
He would himself have been a soldier.
This bald unjointed chat of his, my lord,
I answered indirectly, as I said,

And I beseech you, let not his report
Come current for an accusation
Betwixt my love and your high Majesty.
                              (I, iii, 29–69)

This, however, gets the substance of his impatience, its
provocation, but not entirely its pace or temperature. These
come, briefly, as the King sweeps out with the order for 'Send us
your prisoners, or you will hear of it' and Hotspur, 'drunk with
choler' as his father says, bursts out

And if the devil come and roar for them,
I will not send them. I will after straight
And tell him so, for I will ease my heart,
Albeit I make a hazard of my head.
                              (125–9)

The choler is in full flood by the time Worcester concedes that
while the King refuses to ransom Mortimer from the Welsh,
'those prisoners you shall keep':

                              Nay, I will; that's flat.
He said he would not ransom Mortimer,
Forbade my tongue to speak of Mortimer,
But I will find him when he lies asleep,
And in his ear I'll hollow 'Mortimer!'
Nay,
I'll have a starling shall be taught to speak
Nothing but 'Mortimer', and give it him,
To keep his anger still in motion . . .
Why, look you, I am whipt and scourg'd with rods,
Nettled, and stung with pismires, when I hear
Of this vile politician, Bullingbrook.
In Richard's time – what do you call the place? –
A plague upon it, it is in Gloucestershire –
'Twas where the madcap duke his uncle kept,
His uncle York – where I first bow'd my knee
Unto this king of smiles, this Bullingbroke,
'Sblood!
When you and he came back from Ravenspurgh –

NORTHUMBERLAND
At Berkeley Castle.
HOTSPUR
                    You say true.
Why, what a candy deal of courtesy
This fawning greyhound then did proffer me!
'Look, when his infant fortune came to age',
And 'gentle Harry Percy' and 'kind cousin' –
O, the devil take such cozeners! God forgive me!
Good uncle, tell your tale – I have done.
                                        (218–56)

What I am suggesting is that Shakespeare is indeed protean but
only up to a point and in a purely practical way: having hit (even
though it's a bit hit-and-miss) on a tone and a rhythm for
flustered old York and old Capulet, he adopts it – appropriates
it, if you like – for blustering young Hotspur.

I'll draw out some aspects of that last quotation, before setting
the passage in context:

(1) Snapping dovetailing of speeches: Hotspur interrupts others,
jumps down their throats: Worcester's concession and Hotspur's
opening phrases are two halves of one line. A little earlier:

HOTSPUR
I cry you mercy.
WORCESTER
                    Those same noble Scots
That are your prisoners –
HOTSPUR
                    I'll keep them all! . . .

(2) Rhythmic versatility, starting with '*Nay* I *will*; *that's flat*'. (My
stresses, as in the following quotations.) This perhaps takes off
from an early exchange in *Edward II*:

WARWICK
Bridle thy anger, gentle Mortimer.
YOUNG MORTIMER
I *cannot*, nor I *will not*; I *must speak*

and points towards an exchange in *Antony and Cleopatra* (II, ii):

MAECENAS

　　　　　　　　　　　　　　　　　　　　　　　　Now Antony
Must leave her utterly.

ENOBARBUS

　　　　　　　　　　　　Never, he *will not* . . .

(Compare Antony, III, iv: '*Nay, nay* Octavia, not only *that –/ That* were excusable, *that* . . .' and Enobarbus, III, vii: 'But *why, why, why?*' and 'Well, *is* it, *is* it?')

(3) Individuality of voice through dialect: if 'nay' isn't regional, 'flat' is surely north country. There's a touch of regional humour (the blunt northerner type) carried over into regional speech rhythms (as elsewhere in the *Henry IV/V* plays, especially the Glendower–Hotspur confrontation).

(4) Hotspur's verbal clowning. An early touch of that, rather than of authorially imposed patterning, comes in the sequence 'heart'–'head'–'hazard' of his first lines after the King leaves (quoted above). When Worcester begins to speak of the Scottish prisoners and Hospur interrupts ('I'll keep them all') he goes on: 'By God, he shall not have one Scot of them,/No, if a scot would save his soul, he shall not.' (A scot is a fee – usually a small one, as in 'scot and lot'; cf. the still surviving expression 'scot-free'.) This leads on to the scene with Glendower, and with his wife: '"What is it carries you away?" "Why, my horse, my love, my horse."' She calls him a 'mad-headed ape', and then a 'paraquito' because in mocking timorousness he mimics her: 'So far afoot I shall be weary, love.' In our Act I scene he mimics the courtier-messenger, then Bolingbroke, and then the starling he'll train in turn to mimic human speech and squawk 'Mortimer!' at the King. Shakespeare is in his stride in this play, able to reproduce voices but also have them in turn mimic other voices. Other instances are Hotspur on Glendower's 'tales of the moldwarp and the ant,/Of the dreamer Merlin' etc.; Hal mimicking Hotspur who kills twenty Scots before breakfast and then complains 'Fie on this quiet life: give me work'; and Kate telling Hotspur he's been talking in his sleep. The great scene of mimicry in this play has Hal and Falstaff 'doing' each other and each doing the King.

　　But, to go back to I, iii, it is equally important to my suggestions about the unsteady growth of Shakespeare's growing skill that Hotspur's voice, like York's and Capulet's, comes and goes. His anecdote of the messenger, while free of the toneless regularity of the Marlowe passage, is leisurely rather than impatient. His next speech, a response to one from the King about 'revolted Mortimer', is equally expansive and even prettily poetical with its personification of 'gentle Severn', which 'affrighted with their bloody looks/Ran fearfully among the trembling reeds'. He here gets into the rut of an epithet–noun/epithet–noun pattern: 'gentle Severn's sedgy bank', 'changing hardiment with great Glendower', 'hid his crisp head in the hollow bank'. (The compressed metaphor of the lines that follow is more trenchant: 'Never did bare and rotten policy/Colour her working with such deadly wounds' – cf. the King in V, i on facing 'the garment of rebellion/With some fine colour that may please the eye . . . never yet did insurrection want/Such water-colours to impaint his cause.') A final example of patterning in Hotspur's account of the Severnside combat is: 'Three times they breath'd and three times did they drink', which strikes a note more like that of 'the great Glendower' whom Hotspur has mentioned immediately before. (Cf. Glendower in III, i: 'Three times hath Henry Bullingbrook made head/Against my power; thrice from the banks of Wye/And sandy-bottom'd Severn have I sent him/Bootless home and weather-beaten back' – at which Hotspur sounds a very different note: 'Home without boots, and in foul weather too!/How scapes he agues, in the devil's name?) Hotspur's next big speech, sparked off by Northumberland and Worcester confirming that Richard had proclaimed Mortimer his heir, begins: 'Nay, then I cannot blame his cousin King,/That wish'd him on the barren mountains starve'; he goes on to contrast Henry with Richard. This is a long stretch of fossil speechifying that has nothing idiosyncratic to him and a good deal common to all Shakespearean politicians, including those whose measured discourse the scene elsewhere contrasts with his hotheaded spurring-on. It is full of the doublets and triplet phrases to which generations of platform windbags have resorted: thus 'the line and the predicament', 'nobility and power', 'jeering and disdained contempt', 'fool'd, discarded and shook off', 'ruminated, plotted and set down'. When Hamlet thus combines words they often both strengthen and diversify each other; not so with Hotspur, who verges on redundancy.

The habit in fact surfaced in the vignette of the messenger – 'rage and extreme toil', 'breathless and faint', 'neat and trimly dressed', 'my grief and my impatience'. (More inventively diverse are 'slovenly unhandsome corpse', 'betwixt the wind and his nobility', and 'holiday and lady terms'.) And the habit pervades not just Hotspur's lines but the whole scene, irrespective of speaker: Worcester, for instance, tells Hotspur that 'I'll read you matter deep and dangerous,/As full of peril and adventurous spirit . . .', while the King contributes 'cold and temperate', 'danger and disobedience', 'bold and peremptory', 'promise and exception', and 'lost and forfeited'.

I've just collected examples of a Shakespearean habit particularly prominent in this whole play – it verges on a tic. But my present concern is purely with a double point about I, iii, where I have sought to show unconformities within the lines assigned to one speaker, Hotspur, and also inappropriate conformities between the speeches of diverse characters. A prevailing style irrespective of speaker; a habit of phrasing common to all (whether we call it Shakespeare's tic-of-the-moment or hear in it all those politicians who are still shocked and saddened at a barbaric and repellent act which is illegal, unacceptable and wrong); a tempo dictated not by temperament but by leisurely similes, elaborated personifications and picturesque detail – through all this we hear, intermittently, a voice that the play goes on to build up as idiosyncratically Hotspur's. And that voice is adapted from, has a close family relationship to, York's in *Richard II* and Capulet's in *Romeo and Juliet*.

Let me end these comments on *Henry IV, Part One* by relating them to the focuses of recent critics whom I discussed earlier when talking of *Richard II*. Ryan writes of Shakespeare's habitual *diversities* of style which embody conflicting viewpoints; and these Shakespeare indeed achieves with especial ease in the Hal–Falstaff scenes. The *unconformities* I have just been illustrating in Hotspur's first scene, however, impede such diversity. But this is perhaps nitpicking, for the scene is explosively funny as well as politically explosive (the 'rebels' have a strong case). And by far the most disturbing aspect of Greenblatt's chapter on the *Henry IV/V* plays is that in all its forty-five pages he makes only the briefest passing reference to Hotspur. Tennenhouse is equally neglectful. And this in writers who profess a concern with the carnivalesque faces of rebellion. But then they don't laugh at or with Falstaff either. It's not that they think common humanity is misguided in finding much of the play funny; they write as if they haven't even noticed. This is one – to me funny-haha as well as funny-peculiar – example of the way that recent critics of Shakespeare, preoccupied with how the plays identify 'with the common interests of humanity as a whole', don't pause to listen to the common interest that humanity as a whole has had in Shakespeare.

* * *

Appendices to Chapter One

1A

Several of the late-medieval Morality Plays culminate in a confrontation between the personified figures of Death and Mankind (or Everyman, or Humanum Genus). In *The Castle of Perseverance* (early fifteenth century) Death announces that 'with this point I will pierce him' and that 'I strike you a blow, Mankind, to your heart's core'. In vain 'Humanum Genus' cries out to 'Good Sir World' for help. He has already left the protection of the castle, into which he had been led by Confession and Penitence and which was then protected by various Virtues and besieged by Vices. The staging plan in the manuscript of the play shows the castle in the middle of a sort of circus ring, with God, the Devil, World, Flesh and Covetousness at various compass points on the circumference.

Also behind Shakespeare is the Dance of Death in which skeletons or tattered, rotting corpses or Death himself drag people into a jig around the gravestones. (Holbein made many depictions of this.) Such ghastly grinning jollity had a family relationship to the ambivalent stance of medieval passion plays and paintings – which resurfaces in such Shakespearean scenes as the blinding of Gloucester in *King Lear* (e.g. the jocularity of 'let him smell his way to Dover' and Regan's helpful suggestion that if one eyeball is left in, 'one side will mock another'). Richard's achievement (or masochism?) is to see himself from Death's own viewpoint as he grins from the wings.

On all this and other aspects of Shakespeare's inheritance from the Middle Ages, the best books are still A. P. Rossiter's *English Drama from Early Times to the Elizabethans* and J. Huizinga's *The Waning of the Middle Ages*.

1B

This passage opens Rossiter's chapter on *Richard II* (1989: 23–9):

> The ancients had a thrifty habit of scrubbing parchments and using them again: these written-over documents are called palimpsests. It is a pity that frugal Elizabethan dramatists did not use parchments for play-books: we should not then need to rely on the hazardous ultra-violet of interpretative criticism or the infra-red of critical bibliography, to decide whether to treat a play as a palimpsest or some other kind of problem, such as lack of coherence in its author's mind, divided aims, and the like . . .

A diagram then introduces Rossiter's geological metaphor:

> There is a kind of fold (or "fault") in the play; Acts I and II are on one side of it, III and IV on the other; and in Act V something comes up to the surface which one is very strongly tempted to call "half-revised Old Play" . . .
>
> If ours is the character-approach, we find a lack of continuity between the Richard of Acts I and II and the melancholy introvert reimported from Ireland. Those who praise the play as character piece most highly, seem to *begin* their reading with Act III; and to 'explain' the autocratic, capricious Richard of the first two acts as an imperious adolescent playacting. This does not cover up *the lack of inside* in the early Richard . . .
>
> To generalize, most commentators direct attention to a play which they *can* manage, and tacitly divert it from 'misfits' they cannot; and in this there is no great critical difference between 'character' and 'thematic' approaches. Both do vaguely agree in taking measures to smooth over a kind of 'fold' between Acts II and III . . .
>
> If we look at the verse, it is a crude discrimination to say there are three styles: rhyme (mainly couplets) and two sorts of blank verse – that of the Deposition, say, and an 'earlier' kind. The 'early' type in fact ranges from a flattish competence (Act I, or Bolingbroke at V, iii, 1–12, 'Can no man tell me of my unthrifty son? . . .') to a jumbled incompetence, aptly described by York's comment on the state of England at II, ii, 121–2:
>
>> All is uneven,
>> And everything is left at six and seven.
>
> The couplets vary as much, although this is less striking, as Shakespeare wrote within a convention that did not *hear* bad couplets as we hear

them; and in Acts I and II especially they pop in and out most disconcertingly. The worst in both kinds, rhyme and blank verse, is distressingly or comically bad. As a *formal* type of play in what Dover Wilson calls 'deliberately patterned speech', it contrasts strikingly with the operatic consistency of *Richard III*.

Examine the texture of the verse, and Eliot's 'patterned speech' *is* there; mainly in the 'early' type of verse, but also in some of the other. It is easiest seen where not very good: where it represents the heavily over-written Elizabethan High-Renaissance manner, over-ingenious with a mainly *verbal* wit, and obtrusive. It is obtrusive, I mean, in Keats's sense: 'Poetry should be great and *unobtrusive*, a thing which enters into one's soul and does not startle or amaze it with itself, but with its subject.'
e.g.

> The setting sun, and music at the close,
> As the last taste of sweets, is sweetest last,
> Writ in remembrance more than things long past
> (II, i, 12–14).

There is a marked degree of what Keats would call 'obtrusiveness' in such writing. Frigid ingenuities accompany it, such as this from Northumberland:

> And hope to joy, is little less in joy
> Than hope enjoy'd
> (II, iii, 15)

or the Queen's tortuous lines where she has conceived a grief and wrenches her imagination to find out what has caused it . . .

Rossiter summarises his criticism bluntly: '*Richard II* . . . seems to me to have no real beginning; a coherent middle; and a ragged, muddled end.'

(From *Angel with Horns: Fifteen lectures on Shakespeare* (1961) by A. P. Rossiter (1989), Longman. Reproduced with permission.)

1C

In Nahum Tate's 1681 version York says:

> Death, what a tide of woes break upon us at once. Perverse woman to take this time to die in, and the varlet her son to take this time to play the villain in: would to Heaven the King had cut off my head as he did my brothers. Come, sister – cousin, I would say; pray pardon me. If I know how to order these perplexed affairs, I am a sturgeon. Gentlemen, go

muster up your men, and meet at Berkeley Castle. I should to Plashy too, but time will not suffer [allow]; the wind's cross too, and will let us hear nothing from Ireland, nor boots it much, if they have no better news for us, than we have of them. All's wrong: oh! fie, hot! hot!

(Cornmarket Press facsimile, London 1969, p.19; I have slightly modernised spelling and punctuation.) Lewis Theobald's 1720 version, which combines the original's II, ii and II, iii in its opening scene, regularises the verse:

Heaven of his mercy! What a tide of woes
Comes rushing on this ruined land at once!
My lords of Salisbury, Ross and Willoughby,
What would your wisdom counsel me to do?
I would old York had dropped into his grave
E'er taken this unwieldy task of power;
Here am I left to underprop the land,
Who, weak with age, can scarce support myself:
I fear me, Bolingbroke comes on too fast.

(Cornmarket Press facsimile, London, 1969, p. 1 – again slightly modernised.)

Chapter Two

Words

I

'How long a time lies in a little word,' reflects Bolingbroke when Richard airily slices four years off his banishment; 'such is the breath of kings.' This chapter shows how the breath of editors and interpreters can make a world of difference by the words they choose to reproduce or to probe.

It would of course be unrealistic to hold the line of a whole chapter quite so narrowly on individual words, or even their combination in phrases. And fairness demands that my textual comparison must be flexible enough to pick up questions of voice from the previous chapter as well as anticipate briefly the following chapter on speech structures. But the aim throughout will be to test Blake's famous declaration that to generalise is to be an idiot and that the truth lies in minute particulars.

For illustration we'll stay with one play, *Hamlet*. Or with *Hamlet*s. Present-day preferences are against any quest for one definitive text or interpretation, and in favour of what a mid-1980s volume called *Alternative Shakespeare(s)*. This affects criticism (e.g. Hawkes's *Telmah*, or *Hamlet* backwards); study of stage interpretation (e.g. J. C. Trewin's *Five and Eighty Hamlets*); and editing (e.g. the Oxford *Hamlet* which gives students two for the price of one by providing alternatives from the second, 'good' Quarto to its own Folio-following text: see Appendix 2A on this and the two Oxford *Lear*s). I'll end this chapter with a look at Hawkes's case and another comparable, contemporaneous one (by Margaret Ferguson) which is especially searching in its attention to the play's 'little words'. As a transition, the middle part of my chapter expands on the subject of wordplay as one kind of detail with powerful design-building potential that is crucial to those two critical readings.

That subject of wordplay starts to be salient in the first half of this chapter (Sections I–IV). But what this first half mainly proposes is a textual comparison – of sorts. It will doubtless appear, in scholarly terms, far more irresponsible than the Oxford (or other) editors' work but has often proved equally engrossing and illuminating to students. I compare the Riverside version with the *first* Quarto. No scholarship at all goes into the devising or the pursuit of this comparison, although it's fine by me if some comes out of it. Students may become fascinated by detective investigations of the provenance and (non-)authority of the first Quarto and, more importantly, of their modern hybrid text. I merely place the texts parallel, as below, and ask them to look upon this version, and on this. I hope the emergent preference won't be as clear-cut as Hamlet meant Gertrude's to be when he thrust the pictures of Gertrude's two husbands under her nose. The first Quarto is often dismissed out of hand as 'the bad Quarto', quoted in Riverside's notes only 'to help the reader in appreciating its debased nature' (Riverside, 1974: 1186). All power, therefore, to the editors of a 1992 reprint, which I gratefully use as my source, whose introduction 'attempts to view the play as a work of art in its own right rather than as an analogue to the received text' (FQ, 1992: 10). My own priority is simply to sharpen students' eyes by noticing differences of detail; detail that is invisible in their frequently preferred aerial photos taken from some stratospheric height above the play. I choose the prayer and closet scenes (III, iii and III, iv) because they are in the centre of the play and have always been pivotal in critical disputes. (Later in this chapter I turn by contrast to a scene from Act IV too often 'marginalised' by critics although 'foregrounded' by those to whom I give space.)

II

In the sequence that first concerns us, Hamlet, having (he thinks) made Claudius reveal his guilt in the mousetrap scene, comes across him defenceless and at prayer: but he talks himself out of killing Claudius there and then, and goes off to his mother's 'closet' to attack her – verbally. Here is the start, Claudius's soliloquy:

FIRST QUARTO

Kin O that this wet that falles upon my face
Would wash the crime cleere from my conscience!
When I looke up to heaven, I see my trespasse,
The earth doth still crie out upon my fact,
Pay me the murder of a brother and a king,
And the adulterous fault I have committed:
O these are sinnes that are unpardonable:
Why say thy sinnes were blacker then is jeat,
Yet may contrition make them as white as snowe:
I but still to persever in a sinne,
It is an act gainst the universall power,
Most wretched man, stoope, bend thee to thy prayer,
Aske grace of heaven to keepe thee from despaire.

hee kneeles.

RIVERSIDE

O, my offense is rank, it smells to heaven,
It hath the primal eldest curse upon't,
A brother's murther. Pray can I not,
Though inclination be as sharp as will.
My stronger guilt defeats my strong intent,   40
And, like a man to double business bound,
I stand in pause where I shall first begin,
And both neglect. What if this cursed hand
Were thicker than itself with brother's blood,
Is there not rain enough in the sweet heavens   45
To wash it white as snow? Whereto serves mercy
But to confront the visage of offense?
And what's in prayer but this twofold force,
To be forestalled ere we come to fall,
Or [pardon'd] being down? then I'll look up.   50
My fault is past, but, O, what form of prayer
Can serve my turn? 'Forgive me my foul murther':
That cannot be, since I am still possess'd
Of those effects for which I did the murther:
My crown, mine own ambition, and my queen.   55
May one be pardon'd and retain th' offense?
In the corrupted currents of this world
Offense's gilded hand may [shove] by justice,
And oft 'tis seen the wicked prize itself
Buys out the law, but 'tis not so above: 60
There is no shuffling, there the action lies
In his true nature, and we ourselves compell'd,
Even to the teeth and forehead of our faults,
To give in evidence. What then? What rests?

> Try what repentance can. What can it not?   65
> Yet what can it, when one can not repent?
> O wretched state! O bosom black as death!
> O limed soul, that struggling to be free
> Art more engag'd! Help, angels! Make assay,
> Bow, stubborn knees, and heart, with strings of steel,
> Be soft as sinews of the new-born babe!   71
> All may be well.   [*He kneels.*]

Those hunting for faults might point out that Claudius's first line in Riverside (hereafter R) ends in a dead metaphor, 'smells to heaven' (although it is still dead-and-alive in colloquial use today). But the phrase makes concrete and sensory the abstract 'offense'. So, more swiftly, does the epithet 'rank'. The latter is one of the play's simple but recurring and reverberating words (like 'breath' or 'earth' in *Richard II*, or 'stick' in *Macbeth*). It smacks particularly of Hamlet himself, who is its most frequent user (thrice in the closet scene). And it seeds itself into related phrases, suggesting 'rank weeds' which are both indecently 'fat and pursy' (lush and 'broad-blown, flush as May') and offensively smelly and festering (like 'rank sweat' or any corrupt habit, like any 'fat weed', that roots and 'rots itself in ease').[1] By omitting 'rank', the first Quarto (hereafter FQ) misses one way of weaving this speech into the rest of the text (particularly of this scene and the next).[2]

Although its very first phrase is swiftly distinctive, R is not above using traditional formulae. If FQ contrasts 'blacker than jet' with 'white as snow', R's Claudius has a 'bosom black as death' which 'rain' (instead of FQ's 'tears') would wash 'white as snow'. But it is a matter of washing, not his face as in FQ, but his hand, and washing it whiter than new even if that hand were 'thicker than itself with brother's blood'. 'Thicker' rescues this phrase from being an unthinking trope: it evokes the fraternal blood-bond (. . . thicker than water) as well as sticky congealed blood (as in *Macbeth*).

There again, you see an abstraction turned offensively physical: and R plugs away at this kind of conversion throughout the speech. The main method is one I described in the previous chapter as metaphor dressed as personification. 'Offense', when summoned again (l. 47), has a human face which it is Mercy's job to confront (the personification brings out the physical face-to-face in 'confront'). Looking him squarely in the face and facing him with it, Mercy may say 'You'll be forgiven, but only if you say you're really sorry – and if you also act as if you're really sorry by handing over the booty, for how "may one be pardon'd and retain th' offense?"' (l. 56). That last word nags away at Claudius: two lines later 'Offense', too, has a hand, this one 'gilded' (ready to palm off the Law with a golden backhander; perhaps the word also suggests deceit, guilt gilded over – 'all that glitters', etc.) which can shove by Justice in 'the corrupted currents of this world' or the dirty carryings-on of the corridors of power. Likewise, 'the wicked prize itself buys out the law', while 'faults' have teeth and forehead, and 'inclination' is as 'sharp as will'. We sometimes talk of poets bringing dead metaphors to life; this speech in R revivifies abstractions through personification, wherever possible by bluntly stressed Anglo-Saxon one-syllable verbs like 'buy out' and 'shove'. (One of many similar personifications in the next scene is 'reason panders will'.) By contrast FQ rests content with a string of pious abstractions: 'crime', 'trespass', 'fault', 'sins', 'contrition'. No imagined physical confrontations here. Is this in the interests of brevity (the soul of wit, Polonius tells us)? But FQ still has space for the vacuous line 7: 'O these are sinnes that are unpardonable'.

As the comparison of words, phrases and images runs poor FQ into the ground, let us broaden our focus to include questions of voice and structure. In a comment which I quoted in the Introduction, and which could sum up the aspect of Shakespeare's early development that I traced in Chapter One, Eliot spoke of the dramatist splitting up the 'primitive rhetoric' and mingling 'the oratorical, the conversational, the elaborate and the simple'. In those terms, FQ doesn't look especially early or 'primitive': it is not inflated or bombastic even if it flinches from colloquial words like 'rank', 'shove', 'shuffle', 'buys out'. But in verse structure it looks like a throwback to the more patterned parts of *Richard II*. The speech is built of end-stopped line units that frequently combine into couplets which, although unrhymed, are held together by the old over-insistence on symmetry and antithesis: e.g., 'heaven-earth' (ll. 3–4); 'sins black' – 'contrition white' (ll. 7–8). And alliteration is laid on with a trowel, binding one half-line to the other and that line to its twin: thus the opening 'couplet' has 'wet', 'world', 'wash'; 'falls', 'face'; 'crime', 'clear', 'conscience'.

More important, this version has no change of tempo or direction, no air of sudden discovery. By contrast R is remarkable for the degree to which it follows the wayward movement of a mind 'to double business bound', self-searching and self-divided, 'standing in pause' and then racing ahead only to be brought up dead in its tracks, finally trailing off in a lame half-line, 'All may be well'. The prevailing pace, however, is swift, partly to convey Claudius's urgent hammering at an intractable problem, partly because he has much more to say on that problem here than in FQ: his position looks grim; he can't pray, because he can't repent, because he won't give up what he murdered for; criminals often get away with it in this world, but not up there. What little of this FQ shares comes as a smooth sequence of statements, whereas R repeatedly runs its head against a wall and takes the form of, not simply question and answer but demand and retort. An extreme instance of this, rearranged between the two voices in Claudius, will also bring out the economy of phrasing which heightens the tight turns of thought, the savagely swift return of the ball: it will show also the insistent stressing (cf. Chapter One, pp. 53–4) which plays fast and loose with iambic patterns and which, when one voice echoes the other, devastatingly slams the retort home by moving the stress to another word. (The final serve-and-return retort and counter-retort are both questions.)

1ST CLAUDIUS	. . . To give in evidence.
2ND CLAUDIUS	What *then*? What *rests*?
1ST CLAUDIUS	Try what *Repentance* can.
2ND CLAUDIUS	What can it *not*?
1ST CLAUDIUS	Yet what *can* it, when one cannot *repent*?
	(64–6)

I spoke just now of 'the degree to which' R moves waywardly: as the following chapter on speech structures will illustrate further, even the most apparently spontaneous or 'disorderly' speech of Shakespeare has an underlying rhetorical structure. In this instance, the structural discipline that in Shakespeare's time was part of spiritual discipline – of systematic self-interrogation –

combines with theatrical practicalities, with providing footholds or path-markers for the actor. New sentences and directions of thought nearly always begin in R at a caesura rather than at the start of a line or 'couplet' as in FQ; but they none the less recur regularly as structural devices (see ll. 38, 43, 46, 50, 64, 65, 67, 69). (Similarly, even Hamlet's most apparently uncontrolled attacks on his mother in the next scene are built upon these half-line footholds: one speech has 'such an act . . .' and 'O, such a deed . . .'; the next, 'Have you eyes? . . . Ha, have you eyes? . . . , Sense sure you have . . . , What devil was't . . . , O shame, where is thy blush? . . .' and 'proclaim no shame . . .'.) And alliteration continues to unite lines across the caesura (see especially ll. 46 and 51), unbroken lines conversely being divided by alliteration (*s-s/b-b* in l. 71). Chain-links are further forged by 'knees' – 'heart' in l. 70 and 'sinews' – 'new' in l. 71.

These points might be laboured by comparing the versions of Hamlet's ensuing speech (texts in Appendix 2B), where FQ this time has much more of R's concreteness and most of the telling lines or phrases ('incestuous pleasures', 'relish of salvation', 'trip him that his heels may kick at heaven'). And FQ's 'his sins brim full' is quite good – although R's 'grossly, full of bread' is sadly missed ('gross' recurs in this play as much as 'rank') and R's 'broad blown, as flush as May' links back to Claudius's 'rank' offence. But the big difference is between FQ's on-the-one-hand/on-the-other structure ('I [= aye] so . . . no, not so . . .') and in R the unplanned, unpredictable veering of Hamlet's mind as his native hue of resolution is sicklied over with the pale cast of thought ('Now might I do it' – 'And now I'll do it' – 'and so 'a goes to heaven' – 'And so I am revenged . . .'). A structure is sketched in R (it goes on: 'That would be scanned' – 'Why, this is . . . not revenge . . .'. 'And am I then revenged? – 'No!') but the main impression is of impulse losing impetus. The monosyllabic opening 'Now might I do it pat', corresponding to instantaneous motor-reactions as arm jerks to sword, trickles away as his brain chews over 'now' and 'might'. By contrast, FQ presents an equable rehearsing of pros and cons; a rehearsal that seems rehearsed.

But what is the *point* of all these detailed points of difference, students may ask: is it all just a way of passing the time and exercising the eye, like those twin pictures in comics where you're invited to spot the fifteen or fifty trivial differences? The start of an answer is that the differences with Hamlet's speech bear – like a steamhammer – on a longstanding argument about this scene. Johnson (1969: 140) was jolted by Hamlet's professed, vindictive reasons for delay here as 'too horrible [ie. horrifying] to be read or to be uttered'. The Romantic rejoinder (see Coleridge and Bradley) was that these are self-deceiving pretexts for further delay on the part of a pathological procrastinator. The Freudian interpretation, that Hamlet won't murder Claudius even when it's handed to him on a plate because he unconsciously identifies with the man who replaced Hamlet's father in Gertrude's bed – this is a minor variant on the Romantic view. And I can entertain that view only if the reasoning, or rather the rationalisation, unwinds itself as in R and does not form a neat premeditated pro-and-con debate as in FQ.

The choice of an interpretation on that matter still leaves open our reaction to Hamlet. If Johnson, taking the speech at face value, thinks the sentiments 'horrible', Jenkins (the New Arden editor) argues from within and outside the play that they are Christian and orthodox. If Coleridge and Bradley sought to let Hamlet off the Johnsonian hook, they thereby convict him of radical self-ignorance. And that conviction will be confirmed, in this scene at least, by the contrast with Claudius. Such a contrast is set up by the unique structure of this scene: immediately after the play-within-a-play we have a soliloquy-within-a-soliloquy. And it's clear that the question, Which text? goes beyond stylistic niceties when we see that the impression of Claudius's painful, unflinching self-probing is strong in R and virtually absent from FQ. The latter has him admit guilt, acknowledge that forgiveness is a lot to ask of heaven, but end in kneeling for prayer which he may well think will be successful. The Claudius of R can't even pray, can only go through the motions of lip-service: the closing 'all may be well' can't but sound feeble after the rigour of his own reasoning that all must be ill and after the early four stressed monosyllables 'pray can I not'.

An instance of the vital importance of verbal 'minute particulars' is the scene's closing couplet. R has

My words fly up, my thoughts remain below:
Words without thoughts never to heaven go

which can also be taken as a comment on Hamlet's soliloquy that
– in R – 'unpacks his heart with words'. And this is lost in FQ
which, by small change in words, destroys the irony and changes
the couplet into another, more banal point relevant only to
Claudius himself as he is conceived in FQ:

My words fly up, my sinnes remain below,
No King on earth is safe, if God's his foe.

I would want to stress the sheer amoral textual pleasures of the
prayer scene in R: the irony that, if only Hamlet paused in
talking to himself and listened to Claudius, he would know that
his professed reason for postponing vengeance was invalid; and
the further irony that, while Hamlet thinks he has cornered
Claudius and exposed his guilt in the mousetrap scene, Claudius
has got Hamlet surrounded here in his soliloquy that surrounds
Hamlet's. Who is spying on whom; who runs rings around
whom? – these are pleasures enjoyed by everyone in the play,
not least Hamlet himself, and everyone in the audience: and this
scene gives the questions an ingenious new twist. *Hamlet*, says
Barbara Everett, 'could even be called the first ever detective
story or civilized thriller' (Everett, 1989: 11; cf. Mahood, 1957:
111–12). But we can't stay morally neutral for long, even if we
don't push matters to an absolute choice of black, white/right,
wrong in the manner of Wilson Knight's demand: 'Which then,
at this moment in the play, is nearer the Kingdom of Heaven?'
(see Appendix 2C).

III

Wilson Knight and others understandably tie that scene to the
next, and here again FQ and R have drastic differences. I reprint
FQ for you to align with the modern text.

Enter Queene and Corambis.

Cor. Madame, I heare yong Hamlet comming,
I'le shrowde my selfe behinde the Arras.   *Exit Cor.*
    Queene Do so my Lord.
    Ham. Mother, mother, O are you here?
How is't with you mother?
    Queene How is't with you?
    Ham. I'le tell you, but first weele make all safe.
    Queene Hamlet, thou hast thy father much offended.
    Ham. Mother, you have my father much offended.
    Queene How now boy?
    Ham. How now mother! come here, sit downe, for you shall heare me
speake.
    Queene What wilt thou doe? thou wilt not murder me:
Helpe hoe.
    Cor. Helpe for the Queene.
    Ham. I a Rat, dead for a Duckat.
Rash intruding foole, farewell,
I tooke thee for thy better.
    Queene Hamlet, what has thou done?
    Ham. Not so much harme, good mother,
As to kill a king, and marry with his brother.
    Queene How! kill a king!
    Ham. I a King: nay sit you downe, and ere you part,
If you be made of penitrable stuffe,
I'le make your eyes looke downe into your heart,
And see how horride there and blacke it shews.
    Queene Hamlet, what mean'st thou by these killing words?
    Ham. Why this I meane, see here, behold this picture,
It is the portraiture, of your deceased husband,
See here a face, to outface *Mars* himselfe,
An eye, at which foes did tremble at,
A front wherein all vertues are set downe
For to adorne a king, and guild his crowne,
Whose heart went hand in hand even with that vow,
He made to you in marriage, and he is dead.
Murdred, damnably murdred, this was your husband,
Looke you now, here is your husband,
With a face like *Vulcan*.
A looke fit for a murder and a rape,
A dull dead hanging looke, and a hell-bred eie,
To affright children and amaze the world:
And this same have you left to change with this.
What Divell thus hath cosoned you at hob-man blinde?
A! have you eyes and can you looke on him
That slew my father, and your deere husband,
To live in the incestuous pleasure of his bed?

Queene O Hamlet, speake no more.

Ham. To leave him that bare a Monarkes minde,
For a king of clowts, of very shreads.

Queene Sweete Hamlet cease.

Ham. Nay but still to persist and dwell in sinne,
To sweate under the yoke of infamie,
To make increase of shame, to seale damnation.

Queene Hamlet, no more.

Ham. Why appetite with you is in the waine,
Your blood runnes backeward now from whence it came,
Who'le chide hote blood within a Virgins heart,
When lust shall dwell within a matrons breast?

Queene Hamlet, thou cleaves my heart in twaine.

Ham. O throw away the worser part of it, and keepe the better.

Enter the ghost in his night gowne.

Save me, save me, you gratious
Powers above, and hover over mee,
With your celestiall wings.
Doe you not come your tardy sonne to chide,
That I thus long have let revenge slippe by?
O do not glare with lookes so pittiful!
Lest that my heart of stone yeelde to compassion,
And euery part that should assist revenge,
Forgoe their proper powers, and fall to pitty.

Ghost Hamlet, I once againe appeare to thee,
To put thee in remembrance of my death:
Doe not neglect, nor long time put it off.
But I perceive by thy distracted lookes,
Thy mother's fearefull, and she stands amazde:
Speake to her Hamlet, for her sex is weake,
Comfort thy mother, Hamlet, thinke on me.

Ham. How is't with you Lady?

Queene Nay, how is't with you
That thus you bend your eyes on vacancie,
And holde discourse with nothing but with ayre?

Ham. Why doe you nothing heare?

Queene Not I.

Ham. Nor doe you nothing see?

Queene No neither.

Ham. No, why see the king my father, my father, in the habite
As he lived, looke you how pale he lookes,
See how he steales away out of the Portall,
Looke, there he goes.   *exit ghost.*

Queene Alas, it is the weakenesse of thy braine,
Which makes thy tongue to blazon thy hearts griefe:
But as I have a soule, I sweare by heaven,

I never knew of this most horride murder:
But Hamlet, this is onely fantasie,
And for my love forget these idle fits.
   Ham. Idle, no mother, my pulse doth beate like yours,
It is not madnesse that possesseth Hamlet.
O mother, if ever you did my deare father love,
Forbeare the adulterous bed to night,
And win your selfe by little as you may,
In time it may be you will lothe him quite:
And mother, but assist mee in revenge,
And in his death your infamy shall die.
   Queene Hamlet, I vow by that majesty
That knowes our thoughts, and lookes into our hearts,
I will conceale, consent, and doe my best,
What stratagem soe're thou shalt devise.
   Ham. It is enough, mother good night:
Come sir, I'le provide for you a grave,
Who was in life a foolish prating knave.

                      Exit Hamlet with the dead body.

The high tension and grim humour of the closet scene depends
on the mother, who has summoned Hamlet for a good ticking
off, being herself pinned by the ears, if not by the arms, in a
parental scolding from her son – while the old man meant to
overhear and in emergency to intervene soon sprawls at her feet,
having survived only twenty lines. (More tonal variation to
enjoy: loquacious Polonius promises – in R – that 'I'll silence me
even here'.) Swiftness is all; this time the jerk of Hamlet's arm to
his sword and sword to his victim outspeeds the movement of
words to his mind. FQ is even briefer than R, but at cost of the
whole point in R:

CORAMBIS
Helpe for the Queene.
HAMLET
I a Rat, dead for a Duckat.
Rash intruding foole, farewell,
I tooke thee for thy better.

Hamlet *says* he mistook Corambis (= Polonius) for Claudius,
but there's scant room for that before his recognition of the 'rash
intruding fool' in the preceding line.
   Only R then has the word 'rash' thrown back at Hamlet in

Gertrude's horror at his 'rash and bloody deed'. But in both texts, Hamlet counters by a comparison with regicide and incest; and in both she reacts ambiguously with 'kill a King?!' For the detective in us, eager to know who knew who dunnit, this is as grippingly opaque as Lady Macbeth's responses are to the *dramatis personae* who – as in all the best murder stories – gather in shock in the drawing room in the small hours. (To the news that King Duncan is dead in her guest room she offers the 'off' phrase 'What, in our house?' and, as suspicious questions close in, faints – or feints.) But FQ soon tidies up any ambiguity about Gertrude by having her assure us that 'as I have a soule, I sweare by heaven/I never knew of this most horride murder' (ll. 98–9). A more drastic difference in plot is implied by the closing passage of the scene. In FQ she 'will conceale, consent, and doe my best,/What stratagem soe'r thou shalt devise'. In R this is pre-empted by her complicity in the stratagem already devised against him: mum's the word, she promises, but

> HAMLET
> I must to England, you know that?
> GERTRUDE
>   Alack,
> I had forgot. 'Tis so concluded on.

Accordingly, whereas FQ's Hamlet abruptly draws towards an end with just two lines of telescoped scorn for Polonius, the sixteen lines he speaks in R include a counter-stratagem.

But that closing speech in R does more than keep the detective thriller primed for Act IV: it serves as an epitome of the whole scene, and of much more in the play, by cramming together clashing tones and provoking in us conflicting elements of sympathy and recoil. We hear a volatile mixture of moral gravity, grave- or gallows-humour and jocular callousness ('I'll lug the guts'), self-righteousness, and a smack of Iago or Richard Crookback in the way that pleasure and action (killing two lame ducks – his old college buddies – with their own stone) make the hours seem short: 'O, 'tis most sweet/When in one line two crafts directly meet.'

If you follow up the comparisons proposed in Appendix A, you'll know that the gleeful plan to blow up Rosencrantz and

Guildenstern with their own bomb comes in the first nine lines of Hamlet's last speech, lines which R takes from the *second* Quarto but which were cut in the Folio. (Shakespeare's second thoughts??) None the less the volatile mixture found there in concentrated form is writ large through the entire closet scene in R. And FQ by contrast damps down each extreme and all but irons out the transitions. No 'have you eyes . . .' (R, ll. 65ff.) in FQ, and little of Hamlet's rank imagination about Claudius 'like a mildewed ear, Blasting his wholesome brother' (instead we have 'a face like Vulcan' and 'a hell-bred eye', routine Elizabethan stage-Gothick attempts to put the frighteners on us). No 'rank sweat', 'enseamed [= greasy] bed', 'stewed in corruption', 'honeying' or 'nasty sty': whereas R's Hamlet thus rubs Gertrude's nose in it, that which arises from R's sheets in steam evaporates innocuously in FQ's vapid theological abstraction which (as in the prayer scene) converts the offensively physical into pious metaphor: 'to sweat' not in an actual 'enseamed bed' but 'under a yoke of infamy'. But as striking as such differences in vocabulary and imagery are the differing speech structures and voice rhythms. In R, Hamlet unpacks his heart with self-proliferating sequences of phrases. Thus he dwells on 'such an act that blurs', 'calls', 'takes off', 'sets', 'makes' and 'plucks' – that furthermore blurs the grace *and* blush of modesty. To live stewed *and* honeying *and* making love – in rank sweat *and* enseamed bed *and* a nasty sty. With a murderer *and* a villain *and* a slave *and* a vice *and* a cutpurse *and* a King; one of shreds *and* patches.

Those speeches of potentially endless proliferation career out of control past Gertrude's three pleas for pause and mercy. Those pleas are themselves far more elaborated and strong in R; a parallel is thereby set up between Gertrude's startling arousal from her usual bovine state[3] and Claudius's self-knowledge in the previous scene. An explicit link is made with Hamlet's previous intention to 'speak daggers, though use none'; her cry that 'these words like daggers enter in mine ears' confirms that Hamlet has struck home and that the rest of his ranting is redundant or gratuitous. This adds point to the ghost's intervention – in R, but not in FQ, he actually interrupts Hamlet in mid-flight as Gerturde's three pleas have failed to do – and his reiteration (blurred in FQ) of his Act I injunction to go easy on Gertrude.

FQ also skimps the purely dramatic impact of the ghost's intervention and the ingenious deictics of this triangle of stage-presences in which one (the ghost) is visible and audible to only one of the others. Thus in swiftest succession in R (all three crammed into two lines) the ghost orders 'Speak to her, Hamlet', Hamlet obediently asks her 'How is it with you, lady?' and the lady rejoins 'Alas, how is't with *you*?' (my stress). Soon her question 'Whereon do you look?' produces Hamlet's 'on *him*, on *him*! Look *you* how pale *he* glares . . . Do not look upon *me* – Why, look you *there* . . . Look where *he* goes, *even now*.' Equally absent from FQ are two elements in this sequence of questions and pointings: Gertrude's description of Hamlet's hair standing on end and his eyes popping out on stalks; and her sublimely straightforward reply to Hamlet's demand, 'Do you see nothing there?' – 'Nothing at all, yet all that is I see.' The latter ties in with a constant preoccupation of the play, what Coleridge (1989: 72) called a due balance between the internal and external world or the perceived and the created. It also contributes to the play's recurrent contrasts between hypersensitive imaginative susceptibility and ludicrous literal-mindedness. In this respect, it picks up other moments in the play when people think they can play on Hamlet like a pipe or a penny whistle; it pre-echoes Lady Macbeth's 'When all's done, you look but on a stool' when her husband gibbers at the ghost of Banquo.

Gertrude's innocent literal-mindedness in her flat line of simple monosyllables ('Nothing at all, yet all that is I see') varies the scene's tone, verging on humour at her expense and stemming any rush of sympathy at her heartfelt words before the ghost intervenes. It also leads her to write off Hamlet as crazy, and this in turn prompts him to prove her wrong and to obey the ghost ('step between her and her fighting soul') by slowing his tempo and altering his tone to measured and kindly if stern admonition (R, ll. 139–79). But her return to bovine helplessness in 'What shall I do?' – immediately after he has patiently and expansively *told* her what to do – sparks off a return to sarcasm ('Not this, by no means, that I bid you do') and nasty physical detail in the same kind of proliferating sequence that I indicated in earlier speeches ('Let the King tempt *and* pinch *and* call – [*and again*] let him . . .'). Little of all this is present in FQ, even though students who work speech by speech through the comparison will perhaps complicate the impression, intensified by my own attempt at brevity, that FQ is a distorting abbreviation or pale imperceptive imitation of R.

If I thus raced ahead in evaluative championing of R, I have tried not to jump prematurely to moral evaluation of the characters. Johnson's observation, cited in my Introduction, that we are perpetually moralists, and his reminder that we inevitably and 'necessarily distinguish, reject and prefer' (Johnson, 1968, II: 148), will explain why words like 'obsessed', 'hypersensitive' and 'bovine' cropped up in my analysis. But my main focus was on dramatic excitement, and the way that this is heightened in R by the linguistic assault on our mind's eyes and nose, the changing voice rhythms, and the surprise changes of direction. And all of that in fact confounds attempts at moral conclusions. The scene might settle the argument about Eliot's famous essay 'Hamlet and His Problems' and about much Freudian criticism, by leading us to conclude that Shakespeare knew what he was writing about even though Hamlet didn't know what deep down really directed his words.[4] But we can't build a moral judgement on any such psychological interpretation of Hamlet if we can't form any steady judgement of Gertrude (whether about her implicaton in the murder or repentance at remarriage), as I showed we can't in R's closet scene, even if we can, boringly, in FQ's. And I don't offer the suspension of moral judgement as itself a moral virtue on our part or Shakespeare's – it's another facet of amoral dramatic pleasure as we're flung this way and that.

IV

None the less, critics have often pushed moral judgements to the forefront. These judgements have been diverse. Wilson Knight stands with Lawrence and Eliot in the early-modern reaction against the longstanding view of Hamlet as a sweet prince in a corrupt world. What concerns me more here is the diversity of ways critics have arrived at their general judgements from the play's 'particulars'. In this respect, Johnson and Wilson Knight, who broadly share a dislike of Hamlet in the prayer scene, go their different ways. Johnson finds his soliloquy jarringly discrepant in 'Hamlet, represented as a virtuous character': he baulks at it as an unconformity, almost pushes it aside as an excrescence (Johnson, 1969: 140). By contrast Wilson Knight builds on it, links the prayer scene with the closet scene that follows and the mousetrap scene that precedes it, and generalises that 'the question of the relative morality of Hamlet and Claudius reflects the ultimate problem of the play'. (See Appendix 2C.) This doesn't quite resort to the stratagem of which Eliot warned, in a passage from his essay 'The Function of Criticism' (Eliot, 1932: 33) that lies behind the wariness of his Introduction to Wilson Knight's book: whereas 'comparison and analysis need only the cadavers on the table', interpretation is 'always producing parts of the body from its pockets and fixing them into place'. But Wilson Knight projects on to the rest of the play his strong preference for Claudius in Act III, entangling himself in special pleading for him as the 'typical kindly uncle' with 'eminently pleasant traits' apart from the little matter of the murder (Knight, 1989: 34, 36). He deliberately presses over-heavily the other side of the scales to counteract the one-sidedness of Bradley and earlier commentators (a better account of Act III may be that Shakespeare himself is deliberately unsettling a balance established through Acts I and II). Wilson Knight admits as much at the start of his '*Hamlet* Reconsidered' a quarter-century later. But each of these essays equally provides us with the means of disputing its general conclusions by the particular moments in the play that it evokes; evocations as detailed as the disconnected notes on specific moments by Johnson and Coleridge.

Coleridge's writings on *Hamlet* contain extremes of particular and general. He is well known for his diagnoses of the hero, less so for his detailed analysis of the opening scenes' poetic and dramatic technique. Similarly, Eliot's parallel description of those scenes in 'Poetry and Drama' (Eliot, 1975: 132–47) is far less known than the broad, diagnostic 'Hamlet and His Problems'.

Of the recent critics, Eagleton and Ryan belong completely to the generalising tradition. They work by broad contrasts. 'If *Othello* portrays a man in hot pursuit of nothing, *Hamlet* reverses the perspective and tells the story from the standpoint of that nothing itself,' begins Eagleton (1986: 70), who ends (*ibid.*, 73–5) with an equally neat, absolute contrast with another 'kind of nothing', Coriolanus. Ryan caricatures the view of some composite figure 'the moralist critic' and then simply 'proceeds on the opposite assumption' (Ryan, 1989: 48). What both Ryan and Eagleton equally hasten to is not the pleasure but, in Ryan's own phrase, 'the point of Shakespearean tragedy'. Not surprisingly, the point is banal and stale. Eagleton's is a minor variation on the central Bradleyan diagnosis of melancholia: 'the particular form of negativity which Hamlet experiences is melancholia, which, rather like paranoid jealousy [note the fragile transition from the pages on *Othello*], drains the world of value and dissolves it into nauseating nothingness' (Eagleton, 1986: 70–1). Ryan embraces the sentimental old idea of Sweet Prince in Corrupt World: 'Hamlet's tormented reluctance to surrender to the role of revenging prince expresses a legitimate rejection of the constitutionally "rotten" way of life which festers within the "prison" he *perceives* Denmark to be'; and his tragedy is 'having to live and die on the degrading terms of such a world' (Ryan, 1989: 48; my stress: Ryan takes at face value Hamlet's perception of others and of himself). We are told that 'Shakespeare's greatest tragedies compel us to probe beyond moralism, to analyse the premises of the society which could trap such an individual in such a predicament in the first place' (*ibid.*, 47–8), but the analysis offered is rank moralism redirected, from Hamlet to Denmark.

Two other recent critics throw their energies into trying to avoid generalisation. Before introducing them, however, I will dwell on an aspect of verbal detail especially important to their cases.

V

'Wordplay was a game that Elizabethans played seriously': so begins M. M. Mahood's study of *Shakespeare's Wordplay*. While she disclaims the attempt at 'an exhaustive and final discussion of the subject', the book has until recently been regarded as definitive. Derivative might be the right word for my own comments, if not my examples: systematic they certainly aren't, and indeed I'd rather attune students to wordplay by showing how it can't be systematised, let alone circumscribed as a purely literary activity. For I share Mahood's aim, 'to quicken the reader's response to this aspect of his poetic art and so perhaps to add something to his enjoyment of Shakespeare'. I can't write with her wit, but can perhaps do something to make students (who by and large don't play with words in their talk with each other) look less alarmed or earnest about it than they do if one drops names like 'stichomythia' or 'isocolon'. After all, wordplay is everyday and all around you.

Puns pay. Close your Shakespeare and open your *Yellow Pages*. Mine, under 'Hairdressers', give A Cut Above, Hair We Are, Hair Lair, Hair Waves, Hair to Stay, Fresh Hair and About Faces. Read the newspaper while you wait your turn and headlines could include 'LONG-HAIRED PUPIL SUSPENDED BY HEAD' or 'HEADLESS BODY IN TOPLESS BAR' (I won't clutter this section with footnotes but I've not invented any of my examples). And talking, as we were (or Richard was), of 'crowns', one local stylist is the Crown of Glory Salon. (Next door is Little Shop of Flowers. Nearby is the Plumb Center.)

Wordplay surfaces in talk as often as print. 'Only a crown, your Majesty,' replied the Prime Minister when King George III asked how much it would cost to fence in London's royal parks. Freud tells us someone defended a book to a hostile reviewer by saying that it had been thoroughly revised, indeed virtually rewritten: 'That's just made it re-rotten,' snapped back the critic. (Compare Hamlet's opening retort about his uncle being more kin than kind.)

Wordplay can both express and conceal one's meaning. Nursery rhymes like that in which Jack fell down and broke his crown originated as political squibs safe from censorship. Hamlet's 'kin'–'kind' retort is a broad aside, almost a broadside, a little less than overt and more than covert. The Fool tempts Lear into the trap of wordplay with a riddle:

FOOL
Nuncle, give me an egg, and I'll give thee two crowns.
LEAR
What two crowns shall they be?

FOOL

Why, after I have cut the egg i' th' middle and eat up the meat, the two crowns of the egg. When thou clovest thy crown i' th' middle and gav'st both parts, thou bor'st thine ass on thy back o'er the dirt. Thou hadst little wit in thy bald crown when thou gav'st thy golden one away.

Wordplay can be accidental, through mistranslation, for example; as when an oriental bar barring unaccompanied ladies put up a sign: 'WOMEN CAN ONLY BE ENTERED THROUGH THEIR HUSBANDS'. Or accidentally-on-purpose: how deliberate is Hamlet's 'very vile phrase' (as her father calls it), 'the beautified Ophelia'? And was my student's phrase for her, 'painstakingly beautiful', an innocent malapropism for 'breathtakingly' and/or 'painfully' (= awesomely, terribly), or was it influenced by Hamlet's 'beautified' and his recurrent talk about women painting? Did Robert Maxwell's valet think before saying that suicide was implausible as the previous day 'he seemed very buoyant'?

Wordplay overlaps with metaphor; often by jumping a spark between figurative and literal meanings. When we're told that Perdita, in *The Winter's Tale*, 'crowns' each action with her next, we think of 'tops' or 'outshines', but we also look back to reinterpret the word when we find she is a long-lost princess. Or words play with alliteration and assonance. M. M. Mahood (1957: 95–6) finds this, as well as the link between wordplay and metaphor, in Sonnet 60:

Nativity, once in the main of light,
Crawls to maturity, wherewith being crown'd,
Crooked eclipses 'gainst his glory fight.

'"Crooked", in its figurative sense of "malignant" belongs to the astrological figure, while its literal sense evokes the pictorial image of the sliver of an eclipsed sun, curved like a scythe.' The sequence 'crawls'–'crown'd'–'crooked' (stressed by positions at line-start, line-end and line-start) resembles that of 'hunted'–'had'–'hated' in Sonnet 129 about 'The expense of spirit in a waste of shame'. To take another context featuring two of those words Mahood dwelt on: the dying Henry IV recalls with remorse

By what by-paths and indirect crook'd ways
I met this crown . . .

The metaphorical sense of 'crook'd' – which for us is the same as
being metaphorically 'bent' or 'devious' or 'dodgy' – is just held
in check by the original meaning 'curved' which is called for by
the (metaphorical!) context: curvy back roads and roundabout
routes. (Compare the ambiguous word 'craft', as with the 'vile
politician' Bolingbroke 'wooing poor craftsmen with the craft of
smiles'.) A final suggestion about wordplay and alliteration: if
Hamlet's 'more than kin and less than kind' depends on
distinguishing between similar sounds as well as between
semantically related words, can we therefore count as another
instance of wordplay his comment in the closet scene that he
'must be cruel only to be kind'? Henry IV's enemies whose
'griefs are green'? Lady Macbeth fearing about her husband that
'What thou wouldst *highly*,/That thou wouldst *holily*'? Or
Macbeth himself hoping that he'll catch, with Duncan's 'sur-
cease, success'? (quite apart from the wordplay of 'success' in
itself, i.e. succession to the throne and successful outcome).

Wordplay can be, in Mahood's words, 'delicate, ingenious
and profound' – and emotionally intensifying as well as expressive of emotional pressure (the overflow of powerful feelings).
Or it can be facile and trivialising. Tolstoy's genial Oblonsky oils
the social wheels with puns; after advising a friend about his
wife's infidelity he mulls over a conundrum: 'What is the
difference between me and a chemist? A chemist makes
solutions and no one is any the better – but *I* arranged a solution
which made three people happier.'

Such punning, like that of clowns in early Shakespeare
comedies, is crashingly obvious. At the other extreme there's a
blurred or crooked border between the ingenious or far-fetched
and the conjectural or tenuous. In that no-man's-land, I think,
lie these three in *Macbeth*: (a) Mahood's speculation that
Macbeth's complaint, in the banquet scene, that the slain now
rise 'With twenty mortal murders on their crowns/And push us
from our stools', suggests the meaning that 'twenty mortal
wounds cannot prevent Banquo's children succeeding to the
throne'; (b) Mahood's view that those same 'heirs' to the throne
are behind Old Siward's assertion that 'Had I as many sons as I

have *hairs*,/I would not wish them to a fairer death'; (c) A. P.
Rossiter's suggestion (Rossiter, 1989: 225) that the phrase
'troops of friends', in Macbeth's Act V list of all he has lost, is not
a dead metaphor or our modern 'vague collective, but a sharp
figure antithetical to the troops of enemies' who are closing in on
Dunsinane Castle. To turn from *Macbeth* to a conjecture about
Hamlet: it's pleasing that Bradley, rarely credited with such an
interest in language and wit, suggests that just as Hamlet's first
words, to Claudius, play with words, so do his last words to
Claudius. ('Is thy union here?' – union = his uncle's marriage
and the prize pearl in the poisoned cup.) For Bradley this
exemplifies Hamlet's 'nimbleness and flexibility of mind', its
'strange lightning' (Bradley, 1905: 150, 151). (Incidentally,
Mahood acknowledges that observation of Bradley's; Ferguson,
on whom see below, does not.) A final query about borderline
conjectures: should I have looked with an aspiring or a drooping
eye at the student who took my point about the multiple
meanings of 'rank', and found in Claudius's 'O, my offense is
rank' an allusion to the 'advancement' that Hamlet says he
lacks?

VI

'"A little more than kin and less than kind": play on words due
either to 1. exuberant activity of mind . . . 2. imitation of it as a
fashion . . . 3. contemptuous exultation . . . the language of
resentment . . . or lastly, the language of suppressed passion,
especially of hardly smothered dislike.' This comment of
Coleridge's (1989: 82) indicates the broadly traditional view,
covering the main points he shares with Mahood – and with
Freud. To all three, wordplay is either conscious if often covert,
or it wells up unbidden. The assumption is that in a play or novel
either the writer or the speaker will be in control.

But a discrepancy looms. Mahood, for example, sometimes
sees wordplay as an expression of character: 'One quality is
shared by all Shakespeare's punning characters, whether
heroes, villains, lovers, *raisonneurs*, jesters: a vitality, a
supercharged mental energy, that makes them pack as much
meaning into a word as it can be made to carry' (Mahood, 1957:

168). Elsewhere, it expresses the author, and she doubts the whole idea of packing meanings into words: 'No one could play so long and brilliantly with words as Shakespeare did without asking himself: "what is the relationship of words to things – the meaning of meaning?"' (*ibid.*, 169). This 'verbal scepticism' of Shakespeare's (*ibid.*, 177), his 'battling thoughts of language' (*ibid.*, 185), becomes uppermost for Mahood, dictating her last twenty pages. But it also dominates her early chapter on *Richard II* which ends its first paragraph thus: 'to doubt the real relationship between name and nominee, between a word and the thing signified, was to shake the whole structure of Elizabethan thought and society' (*ibid.*, 73; cf. 85, 'the word and its referent are two things').

That sounds deconstructionist even before that term was invented. But you will recall from my Introduction that Malcolm Evans (for what the opinion is worth, drawing only on Mahood's introductory chapter) rejects her as 'in retreat from the implications of her own linguistic analyses' because (he claims) she trusts in 'an unproblematized subject and sign', and is confident that a transcendent bard is in the driving seat, not language itself. And Eagleton goes further: if 'positive value in *Macbeth* lies with the three witches' (Eagleton, 1986: 2), this is despite Shakespeare himself and is due to 'their riddling, ambiguous speech' in which they 'signify a realm of non-meaning and poetic play which hovers at the play's margins' (*ibid.*). Language ('the sliding, metaphorical word') is 'cut loose from reality, signifiers split from signifieds' (*ibid.*, 7). Whereas 'a stability of signs – each word securely in its place, each signifier (mark or sound) corresponding to its signified (or meaning) – is an integral part of any social order' (*ibid.*, 1). So that 'official society can only ever imagine its radical "other" as chaos rather than creativity, and is thus bound to define the sisters as evil' (*ibid.*, 3).

I don't think this is a bright idea to apply to the witches. All they ever talk about is what concerns the 'society based on routine oppression and incessant warfare' (*ibid.*, 2) – who can expect this or that promotion and how he's going to get it. But the linguistic implications of Eagleton's case are in themselves huge. A can of worms, endlessly and aimlessly writhing and reproducing in proliferating play, has been opened up.

Deconstruction has prised off the lid and shown that 'texts are
. . . endlessly, like language itself, in free play'. But when
Hawkes wrote that in the mid-1980s, he had to add that 'there
is, as yet, no body of deconstructive analysis of Shakespeare'
(Hawkes, 1986: 292). What Shakespeare critic, even now, has
stuck her/his hands deep into that can?

First be it noted that most recent critics themselves go in for
a perfectly traditional form of wordplay; and like all wordplay
it is variably clever, variably plausible. Hawkes's own essay
'Telmah' calls John Dover Wilson's long influential account of
the play 'smoothed-over (or smooth Dover)' (Hawkes, 1985:
329), but then he is egged on by Wilson publishing one article
under the anagram-pseudonym 'Wildover Johnson' and calling
his autobiography *Milestones on the Dover Road*. That's all good
innocent fun. But later on Hawkes's larger design on us, which
involves analogies between drama, criticism and jazz, leads with
insidious intent to a punning conclusion about which even
Hawkes is bashful: 'It is not inappropriate finally – it is not even
surprising – that within [Fortinbras's] name (since my paper has
spoken so much of nomenclature) we should just discern, if we
ponder it, the name of the greatest black American jazz
trumpeter' (*ibid.*, 331). This is mildly less lame than Elaine
Showalter's little pleasantry, in the same volume (Parker and
Hartman, 1985: 91), that in 1981 Ophelia 'was played by an
actress much taller and heavier than the Hamlet (perhaps
punningly cast as the young actor Anton Lesser)'.

Margaret Ferguson, who immediately precedes Hawkes in
that *Question of Theory* volume, has her own wordplay: e.g.
Hamlet is 'entrapped by others' tropes'; and 'communication
between kings in this play would, indeed, appear to be a grim
illustration of Saint Paul's dictum that the letter killeth'
(Ferguson, 1985: 294, 300). What about her treatment of
Shakespeare's own wordplay and/or that of his characters? I now
turn to look in detail at this article, '*Hamlet*: Letters and Spirits'.

VII

First, our old new friends, signifiers and signified, are set to work
on Hamlet's first line about 'kin' and 'kind'. I think Ferguson

strains to make this fit the current fixed idea about non-fits between words and meanings. And strains unsuccessfully: for she appears to tie to Hamlet's quibble *both* the discrepant ideas I noted in Mahood. On the one hand, we're told Hamlet is demanding that words 'receive their full freight of meaning' in the face of Claudius's wordy attempts at compromise and blur, his linking with a series of 'ands' such incompatibles as funeral and marriage, aspiring and drooping eye, mirth and dole, cousin and son. On the other hand, Ferguson also maintains, Hamlet's wordplay here is 'driving a wedge between words and their ordinary meanings' (*ibid.*, 293; cf. 292 on a 'divorce between words and their conventional meanings'). Surely Hamlet's distinction appeals to the plain, dictionary-verifiable fact that 'kin' and 'kind', the ninth part of a hair's breadth apart in sound and spelling, are also semantically very closely related but not identical. They don't, that is, necessarily mean the same thing – especially, Hamlet conveys to us, in the case of Uncle Smoothie over there, Sir Smile who tries to harmonise all with smoothed-over syntax.

Be that as it may, Ferguson is clearly not groping in a free-playing can of worms but describing verbal play which is under the control of Hamlet (and through him, of Shakespeare). And she herself controls the whole of her challengingly intricate article in which Shakespeare's words combine with Ferguson's own wordplay. For instance, her word 'divorce' in the phrase quoted above wasn't chosen casually, for we're soon reminded (*ibid.*, 294) that by marrying, 'Claudius has yoked not only words but bodies together', bodies that Hamlet would like to separate. But in the interests of reaching at last that scene I said long ago we'd consider as an apparently marginal and certainly marginalised one to set against the prayer and closet scenes, I will jump over the many thought-provoking comments Ferguson makes on the middle stretches of the play and come to Act IV, scene vii. Claudius here persuades Laertes that he himself is innocent of Polonius's death and plots with him to kill Hamlet.

Ferguson's interpretation of this scene is that Hamlet has moved

> towards occupying the place of the king as the play defines it: not in terms of an individual, but in terms of a *role* associated

with the power to kill and with the tendency to justify killing
with lines of argument unavailable to lesser men . . . For
Claudius's letter ordering the king of England to kill Hamlet,
Hamlet substitutes a letter ordering the King to kill
Rosencrantz and Guildenstern. (*ibid.*, 299–300)

Hamlet's further letter, announcing his return home, reaches
Claudius early in his talk with Laertes and Claudius finds it 'an
incentive to kill' Hamlet just as (Ferguson, I think wrongly,
claims) Hamlet found the message from his father. But
Shakespeare, too, sends 'a letter (of sorts)', addressed to the
audience,

> that invites a radically different interpretation from those
> which Claudius and Hamlet take from the messages they
> receive from mysterious places . . . He does so by using
> Claudius as the unwitting spokesman for a greater king, the
> one who will really win the duel in the final scene. This is the
> King, whom Richard II describes in Act III of his play: 'within
> the hollow crown . . . keeps death his court . . .' (*ibid.*, 300–
> 1) [Ferguson quotes lines 160–8 of Richard's speech.]

Here is Claudius's speech: 'two months since',

> Here was a gentleman of Normandy:
> I have seen myself, and serv'd against, the French,
> And they can well on horseback, but this gallant
> Had witchcraft in't, he grew unto his seat,
> And to such wondrous doing brought his horse,
> As had he been incorps'd and demi-natur'd
> With the brave beast. So far he topp'd my thought
> That I in forgery of shapes and tricks
> Come short of what he did.

Here is Ferguson's interpretation:

> 'A Norman was't?' Laertes asks, and then, in one of the
> subtlest non-recognition scenes in all of Shakespeare, Laertes
> tells us the Norman's name: 'Upon my life, Lamord' (l. 91).
> The spirit behind these letters from the text of the Second

Quarto is invisible to Laertes and Claudius; it was also invisible to the compilers of the First Folio, who spelled the Frenchman's name 'Lamound,' and to eighteenth-century editors like Pope and Malone; the former gave the name as 'Lamond,' the latter, citing the phrase which describes the character as 'the brooch and gem of all the nation,' suggested 'Lamode,' fashion. But I contend that Shakespeare meant us to hear or see the word 'death' in and through the letters of this name; 'Upon my life, Death,' is the translation we are invited to make – and for those who are uncertain of their French but willing to suspect that puns which depend on mere changes of letters have metaphorical significance, Shakespeare provides an English pun in the word 'Norman,' which is all too close for comfort to the phrase used by the gravedigger in the next scene; 'What man dost thou dig it for?' Hamlet asks. 'For no man, sir,' is the equivocal reply (V, i, 126–7) . . .

In the description of the mysterious Norman, Shakespeare paradoxically insists on the presence of Death by animating the dead metaphor in the common phrase 'upon my life'; he also creates a new adjective, 'incorpsed,' which editors (and the *OED*, citing this line as the first use of the term) gloss as 'made into one body,' but which may also evoke the image of a dead body if we hear the Norman's name as 'Death.' The lines make us 'see' Death, as it were, in a strangely materialized and emblematic figure: that of the rider sitting on – and controlling – the horse that traditionally represents human passion and ambition. (*ibid.*, 301–2)

This – to recall the start of my chapter – is an outstanding example of the world of difference made by an editor's choice or a critic's stress of 'a little word'. The words 'Lamond' and 'Lamord' are in fact only a little letter apart; but then, so were 'kin' and 'kind'.

Sceptics, and those envious of her insight, might suggest that success leads her to overdo things; that the security of her identification of 'Lamord' with '*La mort*' is menaced by her subsequent argument that the horseman *also* represents '*L'amour*'. Ferguson has earlier called 'overdetermined' Hamlet's desire to separate mother and uncle, and the same term might apply to her own desire to effect a union between apparently opposed meanings. None the less she smoothes this over effectively by an appeal to the traditional *lebestod* trope (only in death is love fulfilled). And with both interpretations Ferguson is commendably concerned to seek support from literary analogue and precedent, from textual as well as lexicographical authority, and from 'intratextual clues' of which she cites far more than I have had space to quote. Here, then, is none of the modern idea that language is in free play, licensing the critic to be correspondingly fancy-free – as is the case with Hawkes's whimsy about Fortinbras and Armstrong, or Showalter's about Lesser, or Derrida's about Ophelia and O-phallus (cited in Parker and Hartman, 1985: 77). Ferguson compares texts and consults dictionaries for what Hawkes and Eagleton by contrast scorn as 'conventional meanings'.

Just as clearly, Ferguson believes that Shakespeare, not as for Evans 'language itself', is in charge. Indeed her whole point about the Lamord speech is that 'with wonderful irony, Shakespeare has Claudius metaphorically describe this king of kings while *thinking* he is pursuing his own aims – devising his own plot – by manipulating Laertes' competitive spirit' (*ibid.*, 301). This is actually more extreme than the kind of 'ironic interplay' between characters' words and author's meanings which Mahood (1957: 41) thought central to Shakespearean wordplay: Ferguson sees Shakespeare speaking nominally through Claudius, effectively over his head. This is the irony of contradiction, not of interplay, between actor's voice and author's pen.

And that points to a drawback in her article. I defended her from any charge of interpretative greediness, of unpacking too much or too many readings from one little word. But on the speech as a whole she errs in the opposite direction, exclusiveness, letting authorial activity cancel out stage business and interaction. And even in interpreting that authorial voiceover she can be exclusive. In the coinage 'incorps'd' she hears, reasonably enough, an allusion to death. But this perception would have gained in point had she also attended to the way that the passage and indeed the whole play bears out the other meaning of incorpsing, suggested by the context: that is, 'incorporating' or 'integrating'. The centaur-like, 'demi-natured' horse and rider embody perfect unity and reciprocity: is there

not a preceding network of what Ferguson herself calls 'intratextual clues' relating this to the play's preoccupation with
relatedness, psychic integration? Hamlet obsessively compares
himself with others in respect of what Coleridge calls his lack of
'a due balance': Claudius himself ruefully wishes for it, too (in
the prayer scene, and perhaps implicitly in a speech I'll look at
soon that follow the present scene). It enriches rather than
dissipates Ferguson's interpretation if we keep in play the idea
that, just as *l'amour* is fulfilled only in *la mort*, so one is
'incorps'd' only when a corpse – only death brings harmony and
integration.

These aspects of the scene are better treated in an older essay
which I recommend as strongly as Ferguson's and which is,
however, usually as overlooked as the scene itself. In Wilson
Knight's *The Wheel of Fire*, 'Hamlet and the Embassy of Death'
is usually cited to the exclusion of the much later 'Hamlet
Reconsidered'. The latter essay, no less than that of Ferguson,
takes the speech about Lamond (so Knight spells the Norman's
name) as the culmination of much that precedes it. The essay
deserves reading, on all those preceding parts, and especially for
its outstanding analysis of Hamlet's soliloquy 'To be, or not to
be . . .' as 'the central speech in the world's most discussed work
in the world's literature' (Knight, 1967: 308). But from that
central speech, and from Hamlet's advice to the players, Knight
sees 'groped after' the 'one positive to which the unresolved
conflicts of this . . . drama point'; Hamlet 'is continually feeling,
through various approaches, towards this elusive ideal' (*ibid.*,
311–12). One of Shakespeare's own attempts at defining the
ideal is the presentation of Lamond's horsemanship as 'a perfect
unity, a magical skill, beyond technique which baffles all
attempts at definition' (*ibid.*, 319). You see that Knight un-
questioningly adopts the textual reading 'Lamond' (and the
traditionally suggested single meaning of 'incorps'd' as incorporated). He thus doesn't explicitly anticipate Ferguson's
interpretation. But neither does he clash with or implicitly
exclude it. Indeed he keeps alive in our minds the idea caught
in the cross-currents of the 'To be . . .' soliloquy (and about to
be floated again in the graveyard scene): the idea that only in a
post-mortem state of not-being can we really *be*.

While thus alert to what Ferguson called the letter from

Shakespeare in Claudius's speech, Knight gets much more than she does out of the immediate dramatic context, the dialogue between two men. He asks us to note what precedes the speech we've dwelt on, 'the King's crisp dialogue with Laertes on the latter's entry, suggesting that they can do business since they speak the same language, are of the same world' (*ibid.*, 318); and having quoted the Lamond/Lamord speech, Knight says that

> after the grim middle action and its talk of worms and death, our contrasting series of bright, life-charged incidents reaches a climax in this pure dialogue of club-room conversation, the quintessence of healthy-mindedness . . . it forms an apt preliminary to what follows. For soon we return to Hamlet again – in a graveyard . . . from the fine flowers of chivalry and courtesy to the skull. (*ibid.*, 319–20)

Now this has the drawback of appearing positively to exclude thoughts of death in the Laertes–Claudius scene, not least by a partial reversion to the over-generous view of Claudius which has made Knight's earlier essay 'Hamlet and the Embassy of Death' so notorious. But it has the advantage of being both about one person interacting with another *and* about the author communicating with his audience.

Knight's case also gains strength from being followable-through, buildable-on. In the later scenes of the next act 'Hamlet's words witness a new poise. His manners too have changed.' Manners 'are a kind of acting, an attempt if not to live at least to express something of the artistic grace and balance' (*ibid.*, 321). Of course Laertes's and Claudius's mutual courtesies and Hamlet's newfound manners 'are superficial, since on both sides hostility lurks beneath; but that is, precisely, the whole point of manners'. Hamlet is 'at last willing to stop being profound', and thereby 'has accepted not only his surroundings, but himself' (*ibid.*, 322). This done, '*everything falls into line for him*' (*ibid.*, 323; Knight's stress). A very similar case, developed by Barbara Everett in her *Young Hamlet*, is much less phlegmatic about this final adjustment: she calls her essay 'Growing Up' and views the process as a societal version of our fading into the light of common day, common daily compromise standards, and common lowered expectations. But Wilson Knight wittily

challenges us to evaluate the alternatives. 'How should we
ourselves, if we had the choice, end the play?' Have Hamlet
remain bitter like Timon? Go magical like Prospero? Or 'wash
his hands of the whole nasty business and write a Ph.D. thesis at
Wittenberg on satiric literature?' (*ibid.*, 320). So much for the
usual present-day caricature of Knight as a mystical-metaphysical
Mad Monk.[5]

A final point of comparison between the by now traditional
Knight and the 1980s Ferguson: which is the greater moraliser?
The whole aim of Knight's essay (which begins by inviting
us to compare Claudius and Hamlet with a war-profiteer gone
respectable and a volunteer broken and bitter) is to problema-
tise ethics and to transcend both the sentimentalisation of
Hamlet (renewed of late, as we saw, by Ryan) and the dia-
metrically opposite view which dominated Knight's own earlier
essay. Ferguson's essay, while making its way via wordplay,
not only accepts but keeps pressing the moral absolute that
Thou Shalt Not Kill. Its view of Hamlet is to that extent
an elegant variation on the old motif of Noble Hero dragged
down to his opponent's level by flouting that Commandment.
And her essay is full of traditional moralistic disapproval,
for instance of Hamlet 'dwelling with obsessive, disgusted
fascination on his mother's unseemly lust' (Ferguson, 1985:
293). Johnson's 'we are perpetually moralists' is perpetually
true.

VIII

Before leaving our sample scene from Act IV, let me throw
down my own widow's mite. This modest coin lands on a passage
that attracts no comment from Ferguson or Knight, although it
invites scrutiny because, like the speech about Lamord, it goes
beyond any immediate dramatic pretext. This may be why the
Folio severely cut it. Claudius suddenly asks

> Laertes, was your father dear to you?
> Or are you like the painting of a sorrow,
> A face without a heart?
>
> (107–9)

This passes muster in the context, challenging Laertes about whether or not he's up to the fencing plan Claudius is about to unveil. It also echoes Hamlet on 'the trappings and the suits of woe' (I, ii, 86) and on 'eyes without feeling, feeling without sight' (III, iv, 78). But Claudius elaborates:

> Not that I think you did not love your father,
> But that I know love is begun by time,
> And that I see, in passages of proof,
> Time qualifies the spark and fire of it.
> There lives within the very flame of love
> A kind of week or snuff that will abate it,
> And nothing is at a like goodness still,
> For goodness, growing to a plurisy,
> Dies in his own too much. That we would do,
> We should do when we would; for this 'would' changes,
> And hath abatements and delays as many
> As there are tongues, are hands, are accidents,
> And then this 'should' is like a spendthrift's sigh,
> That hurts by easing.
>
> (110–23)

Does this elaboration earn its keep?

First in its defence is that it forms a reprise of many moments in the play: of Hamlet who, three scenes earlier, did not know 'Why yet I say, "This thing's to do",/ Sith I have cause, and will, and strength, and means/ To do't'; and to Claudius who cannot pray 'though inclination be as sharp as will'. Then, some readers manage to find a personal relevance in Claudius's reflections: Michael Hattaway thinks that he is 'musing on the way that his own feelings for his new wife have turned to ashes', while Harley Granville-Barker suggests that Claudius has one drooping eye on a lessening in Gertrude's affection for him since the closet scene – but her almost comic defence of him from Laertes and the mob in IV, v (on which see Sanders and Jacobson, 1978) hardly bears this out.[6] A further defence of such leisurely reflection might be the correspondingly swift return to plotting: immediately after my quotation just now, Claudius snaps out of it:

> But to the quick of th' ulcer:
> Hamlet comes back. What would you undertake
> To show yourself indeed your father's son
> More than in words?

> (123–6)

That first half-line pauses to pick up a recurring image in the play, just as did Claudius's initial question to Laertes. But 'Hamlet comes back' is as brisk and plain as 'The Cat Came Back'; and to the challenge 'What would you do . . .' Laertes flashes back as briskly and plainly, 'To cut his throat i' th' church'.

But none of this can disguise the fact that the main part of Claudius's speech holds up what is an already leisurely scene. I would like to suggest, however, that Shakespeare maintains momentum and expectation, in what could otherwise become another case of Act IV Doldrums, by countering all the regretful retrospects and all the 'would's and 'should's of Claudius's reflective speech with a strong sequence of future tenses. Thus for Laertes my revenge 'will come' (l. 29); 'I shall live and tell him to his teeth' (l. 56); 'I will do't' (l. 139). Claudius 'will work him' (l. 63) so that 'he shall not choose but fall' (l. 65; 'shall' again in ll. 66 and 67). Hamlet's letter to Claudius has three 'shall's. Equally insistent is the future tense in the earlier meeting of Claudius and Laertes (IV, v): where the crowd twice call 'Laertes shall be King!' Laertes urges that 'I'll not be juggled with, I'll be revenged'. And soon after IV, vii comes Hamlet's 'readiness' in 'if it be now, tis not to come; if it be not to come, it will be now; if it be not now, yet it will come' (I, ii, 220–2).

There would be other ways of describing this to-and-fro, two-steps-forward-and-one-step-back rhythm of the play's last two acts. You could talk of onward surge of action with obstructions and setbacks (for Claudius, the setbacks are Ophelia's death and Hamlet's return from the dead). And you could see Hamlet's backward half-looks alternating with forward-looking thoughts.

Knight finds 'the secret of the play's fascination, and its lack of unified and concise poetic statement', to lie in Hamlet's personality, 'wavering, oscillating'; and in a plot which reflects this see-saw motion; it lacks direction, pivoting on Hamlet's uncertitude, and analysis holds the 'fascination of giddiness'

(Knight, 1989: 41). The final episode, the duel, 'sums up the play's general quality of indecision and oscillation, of insecure balance' (*ibid.*, 323). We in turn have to balance the widespread response to this play as a thriller – *what next*??! – against the equal and oddly coexisting consensus that it does not sweep forward like *Lear*. 'So powerful is the current of the poet's imagination,' said Johnson of *Lear* (Johnson, 1969: 125), 'that the mind which once ventures within it is hurried irresistibly along.' This is roughly what Coleridge felt about *Macbeth*, to which he thought *Hamlet* offered a direct contrast because of Hamlet's 'lingering and vacillating': 'the one proceeded with the utmost slowness, the other with breathless and crowded rapidity' (Coleridge, 1989: 76). What I've been trying to suggest is that *Hamlet* is often oddly at once dragging its feet as it looks over its shoulder, *and* pushing firmly forward. Act IV, scene vii is one local instance of this, if we think of Laertes's and Claudius's forward planning being checked equally by the deadly turn of events and by Shakespeare's smuggled 'letter' to us which Ferguson summarises thus: 'the future is death'.

IX

That leads us back to think again about an overarching concern of this book in general – detail and design – and of this chapter on *Hamlet* in particular – generalisations and particulars. *Idiotic* generalisations, *minute* particulars, insisted Blake, rejecting the neoclassical preference for 'the grandeur of generality' (Johnson, 1968, I: 29) that runs through Johnson's criticism. But you may have come to grasp what could be a spanner in the works of Blake's own grand generalisation (for such it is). Are all generalisations about *Hamlet* idiotic? Perhaps the truth lies in minute particulars only when they aren't trivial or incidental and when they contribute (in my earlier phrase) their widow's mite to a larger design.

A writer may of course build on particulars in a way that we find obtrusive or over-anxious. This is for me true of Shakespeare in IV, vii, possibly with the Lamord passage (in any interpretation), probably with the speech about love cooling, certainly with the officious reiterating of iterative images immediately before and at the end of that speech. Equally, a critic may claim that details are reflecting a design in a way that leaves us unconvinced. Such, for me, though not perhaps for you, is Coleridge's view that in the graveyard scene 'Shakespeare seems to mean *all* Hamlet's character [Coleridge's stress] to be brought together before his final disappearance . . . his meditative excess in the grave-digging – his yielding to passion – his love for Ophelia blazing out – his tendency to generalize on all occasions in the dialogue with Horatio – his fine gentlemanly manners with Osric' (Coleridge, 1989: 88). In Ferguson (to refer to valuable parts of her article I've neglected) I find persuasive the pattern she traces through the intricate network of wordplay (e.g. 'spirits'–'letters'–'mother'–'matter') running through the play – here her method works like a diagnostic dye revealing the play's internal organic connections. Much less so is her post-Freudian interpretation of Hamlet as the more like his uncle the more he protests difference; a pattern of 'latent meaning' produced by stealthy escalation from speculation to assertion to assumption, and by appealing to a formidable but wobbly pyramid of the latest approved theorist-authorities.[7]

Whatever does persuade you yourself in Ferguson's essay will, I think, have the effect of chipping away at Blake's stark opposition. But think also of how the essay bears on the equally sweeping, deconstructive claims for absolute free-sliding or free-writhing play of linguistic detail. There's plenty about that in Ferguson's opening pages on Hamlet's 'disjunctive verbal techniques' as he 'disjoins words from their conventional meanings' and thus 'breaks the social contract necessary to ordinary human discourse' (Ferguson, 1985: 294). Yet as I suggested earlier, these pages also see him putting words and true meanings back together again after Claudius has tried to wriggle his way out of them. Likewise, Ferguson's own critical activity may break with the meanings conventionally assigned to the play: but this is all part of her meticulous detailed assembly of what she thinks is Hamlet's true meaning. And this truth, while made up of minute particulars, amounts to a pattern, a design – even one with a moral message (Thou Shalt Not Kill). Hers is no case of a deconstructive can of worms.

To repeat my earlier question, then: who has stuck their hands in that canful? Following Ferguson's essay in *The Question of*

Theory, and clearly meant to be the book's climax, is Terence Hawkes's 'Telmah'. You'll remember Eagleton telling us that 'the witches' subversiveness moves within cyclical time, centred on . . . verbal repetition, inimical to linear history'. (See Introduction above, pp. 10, 11 and 83.) Hawkes expands this idea to cover the whole play of *Hamlet*, finding 'not linearity, but circularity: a cyclical and recursive movement wholly at odds with the progressive, incremental ordering' (the ordering prioritised by Western society and by most traditional accounts of the play including that of Dover Wilson, the essay's main target) (Hawkes, 1985: 312). But Hawkes does not thereby escape what he perceives to be the trap of mounting a distinct alternative interpretation. His evidence for the sheer wrongness of the 'smooth Dover' reading (as distinct from his case about the political motives behind it) pivots on this: why doesn't Claudius react to the dumb show in the mousetrap scene? A recurrent answer of past critics has been simply that he doesn't see it: Hawkes thinks his non-reaction shows we can't rely on the ghost's account of the murder – an account usually taken as a 'given' for any interpretation of the play – or, therefore, on any simple account of Claudius. Thus, at the moment when 'Hamlet the prince, like the play which bears his name, seems committed, purposive, moving inexorably to a predetermined end . . . it all goes wrong . . . *Hamlet* "turns" decisively. It turns into *Telmah*' (*ibid.*, 317). Yet Hawkes doesn't thereby see the whole of *Hamlet* thrown into the melting pot rather than held, as it were, in front of a mirror and made to appear a palindrome writ large – a whole-play equivalent of those artfully symmetrical verses I analysed in earlier Shakespeare. Indeed he talks of 'symmetries' (*ibid.*, 311, 312). This reminds us of Hartman's reference, in this same volume, to rigour consisting in 'having the local reading undo an established symmetry' (Parker and Hartman, 1985: 39; see above, p. 7). Hawkes simply undoes one established symmetry to replace it with another.

* * *

Appendices to Chapter Two

2A: *Hamlets and Lears in the Oxford Edition: alternatives and excisions for your appraisal*

(i) HAMLET

SEVERAL references from 1589 onwards witness the existence of a play about Hamlet, but Francis Meres did not attribute a play with this title to Shakespeare in 1598. The first clear reference to Shakespeare's play is its entry in the Stationers' Register on 26 July 1602 as *The Revenge of Hamlet Prince [of] Denmark*, when it was said to have been 'lately acted by the Lord Chamberlain his servants'. It survives in three versions; their relationship is a matter of dispute on which views about when Shakespeare wrote his play, and in what form, depend. In 1603 appeared an inferior text apparently assembled from actors' memories; it has only about 2,200 lines. In the following year as if to put the record straight, James Roberts (to whom the play had been entered in 1602) published it as 'newly imprinted and enlarged to almost as much again as it was, according to the true and perfect copy'. At about 3,800 lines, this is the longest version. The 1623 Folio offers a still different text, some 230 lines shorter than the 1604 version, differing verbally from that at many points, and including about 70 additional lines. It is our belief that Shakespeare wrote *Hamlet* about 1600, and revised it later; that the 1604 edition was printed from his original papers; that the Folio represents the revised version; and that the 1603 edition represents a very imperfect report of an abridged version of the revision. So our text is based on the Folio; passages present in the 1604 quarto but absent from the Folio are printed as Additional Passages because we believe that, however fine they may be in themselves, *Shakespeare decided that the play as a whole would be better without them*. [My emphasis – H.M.]

Additional Passages

A. Just before the second entrance of the Ghost in 1.1 (l. 106.1) Q2 has these additional lines.

BERNARDO
   I think it be no other but e'en so.
   Well may it sort that this portentous figure
   Comes armèd through our watch so like the king
   That was and is the question of these wars.
HORATIO
   A mote it is to trouble the mind's eye.   5
   In the most high and palmy state of Rome,
   A little ere the mightiest Julius fell,
   The graves stood tentantless, and the sheeted dead

Did squeak and gibber in the Roman streets
At stars with trains of fire, and dews of blood,   10
Disasters in the sun; and the moist star,
Upon whose influence Neptune's empire stands,
Was sick almost to doomsday with eclipse.
And even the like precurse of feared events,
As harbingers preceding still the fates,   15
And prologue to the omen coming on,
Have heaven and earth together demonstrated
Unto our climature and countrymen.

B. Just before the entrance of the Ghost in 1.4 (l. 18.1), Q2 has these additional lines continuing Hamlet's speech:

This heavy-headed revel east and west
Makes us traduced and taxed of other nations:
They clepe us drunkards, and with swinish phrase
Soil our addition; and indeed it takes
From our achievements, though performed at height,   5
The pith and marrow of our attribute.
So, oft it chances in particular men
That, for some vicious mole of nature in them—
As in their birth, wherein they are not guilty,
Since nature cannot choose his origin,   10
By the o'ergrowth of some complexion,
Oft breaking down the pales and forts of reason,
Or by some habit that too much o'erleavens
The form of plausive manners – that these men,
Carrying, I say, the stamp of one defect,   15
Being nature's livery or fortune's star,
His virtues else be they as pure as grace,
As infinite as man may undergo,
Shall in the general censure take corruption
From that particular fault. The dram of evil   20
Doth all the noble substance over-daub
To his own scandal.

C. After 1.4.55, Q2 has these additional lines continuing Horatio's speech:

The very place puts toys of desperation,
Without more motive, into every brain
That looks so many fathoms to the sea
And hears it roar beneath.

D. After 3.2.163, Q2 has this additional couplet concluding the Player Queen's speech:

Where love is great, the littlest doubts are fear;
Where little fears grow great, great love grows there.

E. After 3.2.208, Q2 has this additional couplet in the middle of the Player Queen's speech:

> To desperation turn my trust and hope;
> An anchor's cheer in prison be my scope.

F. After 'this?' in 3.4.70, Q2 has this more expansive version of Hamlet's lines of which F retains only 'what devil . . . blind'):

> Sense sure you have,
> Else could you not have motion; but sure that sense
> Is apoplexed, for madness would not err,
> Nor sense to ecstasy was ne'er so thralled
> But it reserved some quantity of choice   5
> To serve in such a difference. What devil was't
> That thus hath cozened you at hoodman-blind?
> Eyes without feeling, feeling without sight,
> Ears without hands or eyes, smelling sans all,
> Or but a sickly part of one true sense   10
> Could not so mope.

G. After 3.4.151, Q2 has this more expansive version of Hamlet's lines of which F retains only 'refrain . . . abstinence'):

> That monster custom, who all sense doth eat,
> Of habits devilish, is angel yet in this:
> That to the use of actions fair and good
> He likewise gives a frock or livery
> That aptly is put on. Refrain tonight,   5
> And that shall lend a kind of easiness
> To the next abstinence, the next more easy—
> For use almost can change the stamp of nature—
> And either in the devil, or throw him out
> With wondrous potency.   10

H. At 3.4.185, Q2 has these additional lines before 'This man . . .':

HAMLET
> There's letters sealed, and my two schoolfellows—
> Whom I will trust as I will adders fanged—
> They bear the mandate, they must sweep my way
> And marshal me to knavery. Let it work,
> For 'tis the sport to have the engineer   5
> Hoised with his own petard; and't shall go hard
> But I will delve one yard below their mines
> And blow them at the moon. O, 'tis most sweet
> When in one line two crafts directly meet.

I. After 'done' in 4.1.39, Q2 has these additional lines continuing the King's speech (the first three words are an editorial conjecture):

So envious slander,
Whose whisper o'er the world's diameter,
As level as the cannon to his blank,
Transports his poisoned shot, may miss our name
And hit the woundless air.   5

J. Q2 has this more expansive version of the ending of 4.4:

CAPTAIN   I will do't, my lord.
FORTINBRAS
    Go softly on.   *Exit with his army*

    Enter Prince Hamlet, Rosencrantz, Guildenstern, etc.
HAMLET (*to the Captain*) Good sir, whose powers are
these?
CAPTAIN
    They are of Norway, sir.
HAMLET   How purposed, sir, I pray you?
CAPTAIN
    Against some part of Poland.
HAMLET   Who commands them, sir?
CAPTAIN
    The nephew to old Norway, Fortinbras.   5
HAMLET
    Goes it against the main of Poland, sir,
    Or for some frontier?
CAPTAIN
    Truly to speak, and with no addition,
    We go to gain a little patch of ground
    That hath in it no profit but the name.   10
    To pay five ducats, five, I would not farm it,
    Nor will it yield to Norway or the Pole
    A ranker rate, should it be sold in fee.
HAMLET
    Why then, the Polack never will defend it.
CAPTAIN
    Yes, it is already garrisoned.
HAMLET
    Two thousand souls and twenty thousand ducats
    Will now debate the question of this straw.
    This is th'imposthume of much wealth and peace,
    That inward breaks and shows no cause without
    Why the man dies. I humbly thank you, sir.   20
CAPTAIN
    God buy you, sir.   *Exit*
ROSENCRANTZ   Will't please you go, my lord?
HAMLET
    I'll be with you straight, Go a little before.
                              Exeunt all but Hamlet

How all occasions do inform against me
And spur my dull revenge! What is a man
If his chief good and market of his time   25
Be but to sleep and feed? – a beast, no more.
Sure, he that made us with such large discourse,
Looking before and after, gave us not
That capability and god-like reason
To fust in us unused. Now whether it be   30
Bestial oblivion, or some craven scruple
Of thinking too precisely on th'event—
A thought which, quartered, hath but one part wisdom
And ever three parts coward – I do not know
Why yet I live to say 'This thing's to do',   35
Sith I have cause, and will, and strength, and means,
To do't. Examples gross as earth exhort me,
Witness this army of such mass and charge,
Led by a delicate and tender prince,
Whose spirit with divine ambition puffed   40
Makes mouths at the invisible event,
Exposing what is mortal and unsure
To all that fortune, death, and danger dare,
Even for an eggshell. Rightly to be great
Is not to stir without great argument,   45
But greatly to find quarrel in a straw
When honour's at the stake. How stand I, then,
That have a father killed, a mother stained,
Excitements of my reason and my blood,
And let all sleep while, to my shame, I see   50
The imminent death of twenty thousand men
That, for a fantasy and trick of fame,
Go to their graves like beds, fight for a plot
Whereon the numbers cannot try the cause,
Which is not tomb enough and continent   55
To hide the slain. O, from this time forth
My thoughts be bloody or be nothing worth!   *Exit*

K. After 'accident' at 4.7.67, Q2 has these additional lines:

LAERTES   My lord, I will be ruled,
The rather if you could devise it so
That I might be the organ.
KING CLAUDIUS   It falls right.
You have been talked of, since your travel, much,
And that in Hamlet's hearing, for a quality
Wherein they say you shine. Your sum of parts
Did not together pluck such envy from him
As did that one, and that, in my regard,
Of the unworthiest siege.

LAERTES   What part is that, my lord?
KING CLAUDIUS
A very ribbon in the cap of youth,   10
Yet needful too, for youth no less becomes
The light and careless livery that it wears
Than settled age his sables and his weeds
Importing health and graveness.

L. After 'match you' at 4.7.85, Q2 had these additional lines continuing
the King's speech:

        Th'escrimers of their nation
He swore had neither motion, guard, nor eye
If you opposed them.

M. After 4.7.96, Q2 has these additional lines continuing the King's
speech:

There lives within the very flame of love
A kind of wick or snuff that will abate it,
And nothing is at a like goodness still,
For goodness, growing to a plurisy,
Dies in his own too much. That we would do   5
We should do when we would, for this 'would' changes,
And hath abatements and delays as many
As there are tongues, are hands, are accidents;
And then this 'should' is like a spendthrift's sigh,
That hurts by easing. But to the quick of th'ulcer—   10

N. After 'Sir' at 5.2.107, Q2 has these lines (in place of F's 'you are not
ignorant of what excellence Laertes is at his weapon'):

here is newly come to court Laertes, believe me, an absolute gentleman,
full of most excellent differences, of very soft society and great showing.
Indeed, to speak feelingly of him, he is the card or calendar of gentry, for
you shall find in him the continent of what part a gentleman would see.   6
HAMLET Sir, his definement suffers no perdition in you, though I know to
divide him inventorially would dizzy th'arithmetic of memory, and yet
but yaw neither in respect of his quick sail. But in the verity of
extolment, I take him to be a soul of great article, and his infusion of such
dearth and rareness as, to make true diction of him, his semblable is his
mirror, and who else would trace him his umbrage, nothing more.
OSRIC Your lordship speaks most infallibly of him.   15
HAMLET The concernancy, sir? Why do we wrap the gentleman in our more
rawer breath?
OSRIC Sir?
HORATIO Is't not possible to understand in another tongue? You will to't,
sir, rarely.   20
HAMLET What imports the nomination of this gentleman?

OSRIC Of Laertes?

HORATIO (*aside to Hamlet*) His purse is empty already; all 's golden words are spent.

HAMLET (*to Osric*) Of him, sir. 25

OSRIC I know you are not ignorant—

HAMLET I would you did, sir; yet, in faith, if you did it would not much approve me. Well, sir?

OSRIC You are not ignorant of what excellence Laertes is.

HAMLET I dare not confess that, lest I should compare with him in excellence. But to know a man well were to know himself. 32

OSRIC I mean, sir, for his weapon. But in the imputation laid on him by them, in his meed he's unfellowed.

O. After 5.2.118, Q2 has the following additional speech.

HORATIO (*aside to Hamlet*) I knew you must be edified by the margin ere you had done.

P. After 5.2.154, Q2 has the following (in place of F's 'HORATIO You will lose this wager, my lord'):
   Enter a Lord

LORD (*to Hamlet*) My lord, his majesty commended him to you by young Osric, who brings back to him that you attend him in the hall. He sends to know if your pleasure hold to play with Laertes, or that you will take longer time. 5

HAMLET I am constant to my purposes; they follow the King's pleasure. If his fitness speaks, mine is ready, now or whensoever, provided I be so able as now.

LORD The King and Queen and all are coming down.

HAMLET In happy time. 10

LORD The Queen desires you to use some gentle entertainment to Laertes before you fall to play.

HAMLET She well instructs me. *Exit Lord*

HORATIO You will lose, my lord.

(ii) THE HISTORY OF KING LEAR

The Quarto Text

King Lear first appeared in print in a quarto of 1608. A substantially different text appeared in the 1623 Folio. Until now, editors, assuming that each of these early texts imperfectly represented a single play, have conflated them. But research conducted mainly during the 1970s and 1980s confirms an earlier view that the 1608 quarto represents the play as Shakespeare originally wrote it, and the 1623 Folio as he substantially revised it. He revised other plays, too, but usually by making many small changes in the dialogue and adding or omitting passages, as in *Hamlet*,

Troilus and Cressida, and *Othello*. For these plays we print the revised text in so far as it can be ascertained. But in *King Lear* revisions are not simply local but structural, too; conflation, as Harley Granville-Barker wrote, 'may make for redundancy or confusion', so we print an edited version of each text. The first, printed in the following pages, represents the play as Shakespeare first conceived it, probably before it was performed.

(iii) THE TRAGEDY OF KING LEAR

The Folio Text

THE text of *King Lear* given here represents the revision made probably two or three years after the first version had been written and performed; it is based on the text printed in the 1623 Folio. This is a more obviously theatrical text. It makes a number of significant cuts, amounting to some 300 lines. The most conspicuous ones are the dialogue in which Lear's Fool implicitly calls his master a fool (Quarto Sc. 4, 136–51); Kent's account of the French invasion of England (Quarto Sc. 8, 21–33); Lear's mock-trial, in his madness, of his daughters (Quarto Sc. 13, 13–52); Edgar's generalizing couplets at the end of that scene (Quarto Sc. 13, 97–110); the brief, compassionate dialogue of two of Gloucester's servants after his blinding (Quarto Sc. 14, 97–106); parts of Albany's protest to Goneril about the sisters' treatment of Lear (in Quarto Sc. 16); the entire scene (Quarto Sc. 17) in which a Gentleman tells Kent of Cordelia's grief on hearing of her father's condition; the presence of the Doctor and the musical accompaniment to the reunion of Lear and Cordelia (Quarto Sc. 21); and Edgar's account of his meeting with Kent in which Kent's 'strings of life|Began to crack' (Quarto Sc. 24, 201–18). The folio also adds about 100 lines that are not in the Quarto – mostly in short passages, including Kent's statement that Albany and Cornwall have servants who are in the pay of France (3.1.13–20), Merlin's prophecy spoken by the Fool at the end of 3.2, and the last lines of both the Fool and Lear. In addition, several speeches are differently assigned, and there are many variations in wording.

The reasons for these variations, and their effect on the play, are to some extent matters of speculation and of individual interpretation. Certainly they streamline the play's action, removing some reflective passages, particularly at the ends of scenes. They affect the characterization of, especially, Edgar, Albany, and Kent, and there are significant differences in the play's closing passages. Structurally the principal differences lie in the presentation of the military actions in the later part of the play; in the Folio-based text Cordelia is more clearly in charge of the forces that come to Lear's assistance, and they are less clearly a French invasion force. The absence from this text of passages that appeared in the 1608 text implies no criticism of them in themselves. The play's revision may have been dictated in whole or in part by theatrical exigencies, or it may have emerged from Shakespeare's own dissatisfaction with what he had first written. Each version has its own integrity, which is distorted by the practice, traditional since the early eighteenth century, of conflation.

(From William Shakespeare, *The Complete Works*, eds S. Wells and G. Taylor (the Oxford Shakespeare, Compact Edition), 1988, Oxford University Press. Reproduced with permission.)

2B: *Hamlet's Soliloquy in the Prayer Scene*

RIVERSIDE

Enter HAMLET.

Ham. Now might I do it pat, now'a is a-praying;	
And now I'll do't – and so 'a goes to heaven,	
And so am I reveng'd. That would be scann'd:	75
A villain kills my father, and for that	
I, his sole son, do this same villain send	
To heaven.	
Why, this is hire and salary, not revenge.	
'A took my father grossly, full of bread,	80
With all his crimes broad blown, as flush as May,	
And how his audit stands who knows save heaven?	
But in our circumstance and course of thought	
'Tis heavy with him. And am I then revenged,	
To take him in the purging of his soul,	85
When he is fit and season'd for his passage?	
No!	
Up, sword, and know thou a more horrid hent:	
When he is drunk asleep, or in his rage,	
Or in th' incestious pleasure of his bed,	90
At game a-swearing, or about some act	
That has no relish of salvation in't—	
Then trip him, that his heels may kick at heaven,	
And that his soul may be as damn'd and black	
As hell, whereto it goes. My mother stays,	95
This physic but prolongs thy sickly days.	*Exit.*

FIRST QUARTO

enters Hamlet

Ham.   I so, come forth and worke thy last,
And thus hee dies: and so am I revenged:

No, not so: he tooke my father sleeping, his sins brim full,
And how his soule stoode to the state of heaven
Who knowes, save the immortall powres,
And shall I kill him now,
When he is purging of his soule?
Making his way for heaven, this is a benefit,
And not revenge: no, get thee up agen,
When hee's at game swaring, taking his carowse, drinking drunke,
Or in the incestuous pleasure of his bed,
Or at some act that hath no relish
Of salvation in't, then trip him
That his heeles may kicke at heaven,
And fall as lowe as hel: my mother stayes,
This phisicke but prolongs thy weary dayes.   *exit Ham.*

2C: *Wilson Knight on Claudius*

Set against this lovely prayer – the fine flower of a human soul in anguish – is the entrance of Hamlet, the late joy of torturing the King's conscience still written on his face, his eye a-glitter with the intoxication of conquest, vengeance in his mind; his purpose altered only by the devilish hope of finding a more damning moment in which to slaughter the King, next hastening to his mother to wring her soul too. Which then, at this moment in the play, is nearer the Kingdom of Heaven? Whose words would be more acceptable of Jesus' God? Which is the embodiment of spiritual good, which of evil? The question of the relative morality of Hamlet and Claudius reflects the ultimate problem of this play.

Other eminently pleasant traits can be found in Claudius . . . (*The Wheel of Fire*, p. 36)

Chapter Three

Speeches

I

This chapter develops a passing remark in the Introduction, about the double sense in which Shakespeare 'articulates' detail: bolts one unit to another (as with articulated trucks), or in a more continuous, chainlike connection gives a character sustained 'articulate speech'. I can best get into that subject via a joint postscript to the two previous chapters: a brief reference back to Claudius's speech on love cooling that I was considering late in Chapter Two, and a commentary on a *Romeo and Juliet* speech postponed from Chapter One.

The Prologue to *Troilus and Cressida*, you recall, speaks of his relation to 'author's pen or actor's voice'. I saw a wavering balance between those alternatives in Claudius's speech. With Capulet, I traced an unsteady alliance between an individual voice and an all-purpose early-to-middle-Shakespearean patterned style. My new example here brings in a hybrid style: the matter, and intermittently the manner, is appropriate to the speaker and comes across as his own, but is only half-harmonised with a thematic voiceover from the author. In I, ii Capulet encourages Paris to woo Juliet and to that end invites him to the ball:

PARIS
Younger than she are happy mothers made.
CAPULET
And too soon marr'd are those so early made.
Earth hath swallowed all my hopes but she;
She's the hopeful lady of my earth.

> But woo her, gentle Paris, get her heart,
> My will to her consent is but a part;
> And she agreed, within her scope of choice
> Lies my consent and fair according voice.
> This night I hold an old accustom'd feast,
> Whereto I have invited many a guest,
> Such as I love, and you, among the store
> One more, most welcome, makes my number more.
> At my poor house look to behold this night
> Earth-treading stars that make dark heaven light.
> Such comfort as do lusty young men feel
> When well-apparell'd April on the heel
> Of limping winter treads, even such delight
> Among fresh fennel buds shall you this night
> Inherit at my house; hear all, all see;
> And like her most whose merit most shall be;
> Which on more view of many, mine, being one,
> May stand in number, though in reckn'ning none.
> Come go with me. [*To Servant*] Go, sirrah, trudge about
> Through fair Verona, find those persons out
> Whose names are written there, and to them say,
> My house and welcome on their pleasure stay.
>
> (12–37)

For Coleridge this was one of the passages 'where the poet forgets the character and speaks in his own person'. And he thought the speech thus symptomatic of a play in which poet and dramatist, author's pen and speaker's voice, don't always get together.

But perhaps Coleridge here implies too simple an opposition of poetry and drama, in part because he also implies too straightforward an identification of drama with characterisation. Think, rather, of drama as animating fundamental conflicts, and Capulet's speech is cramful of the main matter of this play: the contrast of 'made' and 'marr'd' ('too soon' the one, 'so early' the other); dark and light; love and hate (the latter term unstated here but already well established in I, i and glanced at in the opening lines of this scene). One early-repeated word links several strands: 'earth' is first the creating womb then the swallowing tomb; it indicates heritable family property – 'lands' (*fille de terre* is an old French term for heiress) – and more deeply family 'roots' and reproduction and transmission into further growths of the family tree. Perhaps even more broadly it indicates earthly existence: Riverside glosses 'the hopeful lady of my earth' as 'the hope round which my world revolves' as well as 'heiress of my wealth'.

Shakespeare steers clear of the actual cliché-rhyme 'womb'– 'tomb' here (although it comes in the friar's speech on 'the earth' which opens II, ii). But still, a good deal of the contrasting I've just described is mechanical antithesis, both in I, ii and as it recurs in the entire play. Not so, however, with the theme of youth and age. Coleridge saw this, but with too much sanctimonious sermonising about the purity of young love, and it was his contemporary Hazlitt who responded best to the play's spirited and robust treatment of this theme:

> This play presents a beautiful *coup-d'oeil* of the progress of human life. In thought it occupies years, and embraces the circle of the affections from childhood to old age. Juliet has become a great girl, a young woman since we first remember her a little thing in the idle prattle of the nurse. Lady Capulet was about her age when she became a mother, and old Capulet somewhat impatiently tells his younger visitors,
>
> > – I've seen the day,
> > That I have worn a visor, and could tell
> > A whispering tale in a fair lady's ear,
> > Such as would please: 'tis gone, 'tis gone, 'tis gone.
>
> Thus one period of life makes way for the following, and one generation pushes another off the stage. One of the most striking passages to show the intense feeling of youth in this play is Capulet's invitation to Paris to visit his entertainment. [Hazlitt quotes I, ii, 24–30.] The feelings of youth and of the spring are here blended together like the breath of opening flowers. Images of vernal beauty appear to have floated before the author's mind, in writing this poem, in profusion. (Hazlitt, 1957: 251)

I called Shakespeare's treatment of this theme spirited and robust because, in spite of Coleridge's stress on purity, the play

is frank about sexual desire, and equally accepting of the way
that (in Hazlitt's words) 'one generation pushes another off the
stage'. 'Lusty young men' take over as they take up with young
'fresh fennel buds',[1] while oldsters turn into wallflowers (cf. the
start of the ball discussed in Chapter One), just as 'well-
apparell'd April on the heel/ Of limping winter treads' (cf.
Capulet's little joke at the ball about having your corns trodden
on). This idea of youth giving age the push is so pervasive that
Shakespeare draws on it for imagery when talking of Juliet
supplanting Rosaline in Romeo's affections: the Prologue to Act
II begins:

> Now old desire doth in his deathbed lie,
> And young affection gapes to be his heir.

And there is a reverse example of such cross-reference in this
same scene of Act I; when Benvolio, entering with Romeo hard
on the heels of Capulet and Paris, remarks that 'one fire burns
out another's burning;/ One pain is lessen'd by another's
anguish', and that 'the old will die' and the 'new' take over, he
unwittingly predicts not only Rosaline's replacement by Juliet
but the old family feud being burnt out by desperate grief at the
young lovers' deaths.

Satisfyingly interrelated as the imagery of youth versus age
thus may be, does it mean that Capulet's speech to Paris – no less
than the Prologue to Act II – sounds like a sort of thematic
chorus from the author's pen? No: I think there's a compromise
whereby character half-pushes author off the stage before the
speech is out. And I can get at this through the speech's
fluctuating busy-ness in pattern-weaving.

Once more (as with our recurrent examples in Chapter One)
rhyming in couplets sparks off insistent verbal patterning. Paris's
cue-line and Capulet's opening response interlock with not only
a rhyme but an identical word, 'made'. That word sounds like,
but contrasts in meaning with, another word in Capulet's first
line, 'marr'd': 'maid' and 'married' may hover in our minds,
while Paris has just been speaking of 'mothers'. Besides capping
Paris's line, Capulet's first line itself assumes antithetical form by
its positioning of the echo-words 'marr'd'–'made' which are
preceded by 'too early' and 'so soon'. His next two lines are the

only ones that don't rhyme but they are still intricately symmetrical, with one line's sequence 'Earth'–'my'–'hopes'– 'she' reversed into the other's 'She's'–'hopeful'–'my'–'earth'. Couplets now resume; but 'heart' at the end of Capulet's fourth line is not only a rhyme for the next line's 'part' but amounts to a para-rhyme (and para-anagram or even para-palindrome) for the preceding line's 'earth'. (I concede that this shades off into speculation. Do Capulet's words 'hopes' and 'hopeful' intentionally pick up Paris's 'happy'? Can I hear, even if Shakespeare doesn't actually 'sound', 'hearth' lying between 'heart' and 'earth'?) Further evidence of intent to bind lines together lies in the possessive pronouns which provide virtually identical line-ending and -beginning ('she'/'She's'), contrasted start and end ('She's'–'my'), contrasted ends ('my earth'/'. . . her heart') and contrasted end and start ('her heart'/'My will'). This kind of sewing-machine busy-ness persists when 'light' rhymes with 'night' and contrasts with 'dark', 'earth' contrasts with 'stars' and 'heaven', while alliteration is laid on with a trowel in 'house'– 'behold'–'heaven'.

I can't quite talk of a speech being static when I've just called it busy. What I mean is that all the activity of symmetry and antithesis keeps our minds and eyes alert but makes them rove back as much as forward. Or, we look down from above on a pattern, rather than moving through it with any onward rhythmic push.

Except, that is, in one brief passage. The human 'stars' for whom Capulet is throwing a party are 'earth-treading' (just as April treads on winter's heel), and for a while the speech takes off, with dance-momentum and youth-energy:

> Such comfort as do lusty young men feel
> When well-apparell'd April on the heel
> Of limping winter treads, even such delight
> Among fresh fennel buds shall you this night
> Inherit at my house . . .

Here, as in the whole play, Capulet is old in heels ('there was a time . . .', he ruefully reminisces at the ball) but young at heart ('foot it, girls!') And as he here looks forward to the youngsters' display of energy, the hearty rhythm of his voice breaks into a canter, cutting through the mesh of symmetrical patterning and (despite the rhymes) of end-stopping.

Those constricting elements then regain their grip in the last part of the speech, producing the word groupings 'hear all', 'all see', and 'like her most whom merit most . . .' as well as the more sustained sequence 'more'–'more'–'many'–'mine'–'one'–'number'–'none'. (The latter consists mainly of number-words, creating an alliterative pattern which is extended by 'merit most' and 'may'.) True, this resumed patterning isn't entirely self-serving. And several late verbal echoes not only bolt together or 'articulate' the whole speech structurally, but also knit together the dramatist's thematic with the character's personal concerns. Thus 'inherit' is an odd enough choice for its context ('even such delight/. . . shall you this night/Inherit at my house') to remind us of this particular old man's preoccupation with passing on his 'earth' to the next generation – the concern that dominated the start of his speech. This is a particularly happy instance of the terms of Capulet's speech being appropriately his, whereas the pattern into which those terms are arranged constrict any impression of this young-spirited old man's voice and eagerness, although Shakespeare briefly lets him loose in the middle stretch of the speech.

II

So far I've talked of *pattern* as static and self-serving, a drag on dramatic animation. I now go on to talk more positively about *structure*, in speeches where it helps propel an argument or an animus.

By way of transition, I'll contrast briefly two speeches from *Richard II*, both assigned to Bolingbroke but hardly in the same voice. In the first, he prepares at Flint Castle to meet Richard:

> Methinks King Richard and myself should meet
> With no less terror than the elements
> Of fire and water, when their thundr'ing shock
> At meeting tears the cloudy cheeks of heaven.
> Be he the fire, I'll be the yielding water;

The rage be his, whilst on the earth I rain
My waters – on the earth, and not on him.
(III, iii, 54–60)

The 'drag' here lies partly in the imagery that is so predictable by now in the play but is nevertheless so spelt out, and partly in the routine coupling of adjective and noun. But it lies also in the conundrum element which requires us to linger and tease out such links as 'water', 'rain', and 'tears' (the last noun isn't actually present but is strongly suggested by the verb 'tears'), and such contrasts as 'rage' versus 'rain' (with a punning hint of 'reign'). Such decorative intricacy blunts the primary opposition of pronouns 'I' versus 'he', in the last three lines.

By contrast, in the same speaker's accusation of Bushy and Green back in III, i, opposed pronouns join forces with relentless verbs to give punch and forward propulsion – as well as to provide a fairly long speech with milestones or structural landmarks for actor and hearer. There's a *he* again and, this time, a *she* – the absent king and queen. But the main clash is between *I* and *you*: Bolingbroke has the caterpillars of the commonwealth pinned and wriggling at his feet. I'll point up the emphases and structural units in its main part; with pronouns in italics and verbs in bold:

You **have misled** a prince, a royal king,
A happy gentleman in blood and lineaments,
By you unhappied and disfigured clean;
You **have** in manner with *your* sinful hours
Made a divorce betwixt *his queen and him*,
Broke the possession of a royal bed,
And stain'd the beauty of a fair queen's cheeks
With tears drawn from *her* eyes by *your* foul wrongs;

Myself, a prince by virtue of *my* birth,
Near to the King in blood, and near in love
Till *you* **did make** *him* misinterpret *me*,
Have stoop'd *my* neck under *your* injuries
And sigh'd *my* English breath in foreign clouds,
Eating the bitter bread of banishment,

Whilst *you* **have fed** upon *my* signories,
Dispark'd *my* parks **and fell'd** *my* forest woods,

From *my* own windows **torn** *my* household coat,
Ras'd out *my* imprese, **leaving** *me* no sign,
Save *men's* opinions and *my* living blood.
To show the world *I* am a gentleman.

This and much more, much more than twice all this,
Condemns *you* to the death.

(III, i, 8–29)

The opening doesn't bear too much looking at in terms of plot consistency (the play otherwise ignores these broad hints of homosexuality, and we've seen Bushy for one being solicitous to the queen back in II, ii). Nor will I deny the occasional wordiness, the unsubtle alliteration and the over-busy word-echoes I didn't mark up (e.g. the 'happy gentleman' being 'unhappied' and the 'foul wrongs to a fair queen'). None the less the excerpt shows how contrasting pronouns and chains of active verbs can both hold a speech together and push it energetically forward. That Shakespeare himself realised he was on to a good thing is suggested by the repeated exploitation – and sophistication – of this structural technique in the *Henry IV* plays.

Introducing Richard on 'the hollow crown' in Chapter One, I suggested that such long speeches often act as a cue for chocolate-unwrapping and throat-clearing until something starts to happen on-stage. In Acts IV and V of *Henry IV, Part One* we have good cause to accuse Shakespeare of holding up the onward movement with repeated and elaborated mutual recriminations between court and rebels. He has realised he'll be hard-pushed to reach Henry's death and Hal's coronation in just one play, so he decides to hang about and play for time in order to make the battle of Shrewsbury the grand finale of a Part One. This need to tread water means that the scene between Henry and Worcester in V, i chews over the same bones of contention as the IV, iii confrontation between Hotspur and Blount (and, for that matter, as the plenary session of I, iii and each camp's rehearsal of the arguments to themselves in subsequent episodes). So that the King understandably breaks into Worcester's long list of grievances with 'These things you have indeed articulate[d] . . .' – 'so you keep claiming as you go hoofing round the hustings'. Such altercations are a drawback in the strict sense that they contain more reminiscence than anticipation: we are in danger of the Act IV Doldrums I saw Shakespeare only just escaping with the Claudius–Laertes scene in *Hamlet*. In *Henry IV* he amply compensates by the combined devices of pronoun-contrast and relentless volley of punchy verbs. Worcester's, Henry's and Blount's speeches all do this, but Hotspur (characteristically) overdoes it. 'My father *and* my uncle *and* myself', he tells Blount (IV, iii, 54ff.), 'Did give *him* [Henry] that same royalty he wears', and the ensuing lines include these openings: 'we/ Did give him', 'My father gave him', Swore him' (that is, promised help), 'Met him', 'Attended him', 'Laid gifts before him', 'Gave him'. (Ample reinforcements stand in mid-line: 'perform'd', 'proffer'd', 'stood', 'followed'.) And with what thanks? – Hotspur compensates for all this reminiscence by switching to the immediate present tense: 'He [Henry still] steps . . .' 'takes on him . . .' 'Gives out . . .' 'seems to weep'. The tense then reverts to the past but the verbs still come fast and furious as Hotspur, as hotheadedly headlong as Hamlet racing past his mother's pleas, overrides in mid-line Blount's 'Tut, I came not to hear this.' A welcome element of variation now comes by placing the verbs in mid-line ('depos'd', 'depriv'd', 'task'd', 'suffered') before returning them to the start for added punch ('Disgrac'd', 'Sought', 'Rated', 'Broke'); and by such variations in phrasing as 'In rage dismiss'd'. I think you'll see and hear all this without any typographical nudges on my part.

> In short time after, he depos'd the King,
> Soon after that, depriv'd him of his life,
> And in the neck of that, task'd the whole state;
> To make that worse, suff'red his kinsman March
> (Who is, if every owner were well plac'd,
> Indeed his king) to be engag'd in Wales,
> There without ransom to lie forfeited,
> Disgrac'd me in my happy victories,
> Sought to entrap me by intelligence,
> Rated mine uncle from the Council-board,
> In rage dismiss'd my father from the court,
> Broke oath on oath, committed wrong on wrong,
> And in conclusion drove us to seek out

This head of safety, and withal to pry
Into his title, the which we find
Too indirect for long continuance.
                    (IV, iii, 90–105)

All this and more, much more than twice all this, could be dwelt
on and delighted in here: for instance, the discreet alliteration of
many verbs with each other and with other words; and the
sequence of phrases that give growing emphasis as well as
structure because they build up not only a chronological
sequence but a mounting pile of outrages: 'In short time
after . . .' 'Soon after that . . .' 'And in the neck of that . . .'
'To make that worse . . .' 'And in conclusion . . .'. At the same
time, anyone with an eye on imagery and theme rather than
structure could find plenty to link with other parts of this and
other plays. For instance, the accusation of hypocrisy or
camouflaged motives in 'this face, This seeming brow of justice'
gets flung back (V, i) when the King calls the grievances
'things . . ./ To face the garment of rebellion/ With some fine
colour that may please the eye'. And Hotspur's gibe about
Bolingbroke 'angling' for hearts (compare our modern phrase
'fishing for compliments') hooks up both with Richard (*Richard
II*, I, iv) saying his opponent 'dived' into men's hearts, and with
Henry's own admission (*Henry IV, Part One*, III, iii) that he 'did
pluck allegiance from men's hearts' (as well as 'dressed myself in
such humility'). Such relevances of image and theme wouldn't
keep us awake without Hotspur's sarcasm, colloquialisms (e.g.
'came in with cap and knee'; 'in the neck of that . . .') and table-
thumping repetitions (e.g. 'Broke oath on oath, committed
wrong on wrong'). But my overriding point is about the
cumulative force of Hotspur's verbs which gather round a binary
opposition of pronouns. Thus the skeleton of his speech is, '*We*
did this for *him*. And look what *he* did to *us*!' This structural
method leaves us in no doubt about his indignation. It ensures
that the speech reinforces character as well as rehearses plot and
theme. An added advantage is that character expression (by a
character much given to spluttering, disproportion, digression,
forgetfulness and reluctance to conclude) is given shape and
closure as well as sustained punch. I think it thus gives some

support to my working distinction between static patterning and onward-moving structure.

Although they help verbs build Hotspur's speech, the play of pronouns is restricted to the collective 'we' and to the use of 'he' to indicate sometimes Henry and sometimes Hotspur's father. But when Henry confronts his son in III, ii of Part One, his second speech (ll. 29–91) is built on triangular comparisons of three figures indicated by the first-, second-, and third-person pronouns. Henry contrasts himself with, but likens Hal to, King Richard: *you*, son (he complains) are behaving not like *me* but like *him*; the previous King made an ass of himself, 'and in that very line, Harry, standest *thou*'. ('Line' of conduct or style of behaviour, but also linear descent – 'you carry on as if you're *his* son, not mine!') And despite the Prince's protestation that '*I* shall hereafter, *my* thrice-gracious lord, be more *myself*', the King insists that 'as *thou* art to *this* hour was *Richard then*'.

To make matters worse, 'even as *I* was *then* is *Percy now*'. And this Percy, the other Harry – Harry Hotspur – forms an immediate standard of comparison with Hal: 'if only *he* were *my* son, and not *you*!' This present-day third person replaces Richard as Henry makes Hal's ears ring with a relentless series of *he* versus *thou* ('Look upon this son and on this', to adapt Hamlet on his two fathers). He rams home the odious comparison with a pretence of arresting it:

> But wherefore do *I* tell these news to *thee*?
> Why, Harry, do *I* tell *thee* of *my* foes,
> Who art *my* nearest and dearest enemy?
> (III, ii, 121–3)

(With such sons, son, who needs enemies? – the normally propitious epithets 'nearest and dearest', which we often turn into quasi-nouns and let stand as a phrase in themselves, redouble the sting in the tail of 'enemy').

Hal's responding speech picks up pronouns with a vengeance:

> *I* will redeem all this on Percy's head
> And, in the closing of some glorious day
> Be bold to tell *you* that *I* am *your* son . . .

I will leave you to trace the details of this speech (ll. 129–155), and will move on to illustrate more fully an even more developed use of pronouns for speech-constructing purposes, in Part Two of *Henry IV*.

If Part One played for time with some semi-repetition on the road to Shrewsbury, Part Two as a whole has elements of a rerun of Part One; as R. W. David puts it, a replay against a second eleven.[2] Hotspur is permanently off the field (or rather, under it – providing 'food for worms'; Northumberland has sent in a sick-note (a 'crafty-sick' note); but the reserve team rebels carry on rebelling while Hal carries on revelling, even though each side has less heart for it. So when in IV, v father again reproaches son Shakespeare has to work hard not to repeat the Part One up-and-downer I just now sketched. So this time he piles on the urgency and the complications. The King is on his death-bed and gives his heir 'the very latest [i.e. last] counsel/ That I shall ever breathe'. But Hal is still behaving more like Richard than like either Henry or Hotspur: the first thing he does on turning up belatedly at the paternal sick-bed, a touch loud and joky after an evening at the pub, is to grab the crown from the drowsing but still-living King. Given his own uneasy conscience, Henry is especially touchy about crown-snatchers (it takes one to know one). Transmission, however, is the name of the game for which Henry anxiously goes on to outline a strategy. Hal, who should be the future big scorer, is acting as if he were in the other team – or is scoring own goals. Safe forward-passing of the crown will be tricky enough with the rebels trying to grab the ball on one side, without Falstaff and company tugging at Hal on the other. There is the distinct feel of a football match in all this talk of hazardous passes and threatened interceptions ('to me!' then 'to you!' – 'watch out for *them* – AND *them*'). The crown is the ball, the 'it' that bobs between 'him', 'me', 'you' and 'them': I will mark up Henry's speech to highlight these pronouns and related structural bolts.

O my son,
God put it in *thy* mind to take it hence,
That *thou* mightst win the more *thy* father's love,
Pleading so wisely in excuse of it!

Come hither, Harry, sit *thou* by *my* bed,
And hear (*I* think) the very latest counsel
That ever *I* shall breathe. **God knows, my son**,
By what by-paths and indirect crook'd ways
I met this crown, and *I myself* know well
How troublesome *it* sate upon *my* head.
To thee it shall descend with better quiet,
Better opinion, better confirmation,
For all the soil of the achievement goes
With me into the earth. **It seem'd in me**
But as an honor snatch'd with boist'rous hand,
And *I* had many living to upbraid
My gain of *it* by their assistances,
Which daily grew to quarrel and to bloodshed,
Wounding supposed peace. **All these bold fears**
Thou seest with peril *I* have answered;
For all *my* reign hath been but as a scene
Acting that argument. **And now my death**
Changes the mood, for what *in me* was purchas'd
Falls *upon thee* in a more fairer sort;
So *thou* the garland wear'st successively.
Yet though *thou* stand'st more sure than *I* could do
Thou art not firm enough, since griefs are green,
And all *my* friends, which *thou* must make *thy* friends,
Have but *their* stings and teeth newly ta'en out;
By whose fell working *I* was first advanc'd,
And by whose power *I* well might lodge a fear
To be again displac'd; which to avoid,
I cut *them* off, and had a purpose now
To lead out many to the Holy Land,
Lest rest and lying still might make *them* look
Too near unto *my* state. **Therefore, my Harry**,
Be it *thy* course to busy giddy minds
With foreign quarrels, that action, hence borne out,
May waste the memory of the former days.
More would I, but *my* lungs are wasted so
That strength of speech is utterly denied *me*.
How *I* came by the crown, O God forgive,
And grant *it* may with *thee* in true peace live!
                                   (IV, v, 177–219)

And Hal clinches all this with one exultantly reassuring line locking together three vital pronouns, and four stages of transmission in four active verbs, all in single syllables:

You **won** *it*, **wore** *it*, **kept** *it*, **gave** *it* **ME**

– 'OK, I've *got* it!'

In isolating that line I've played down a more traditional way of structuring and linking speeches that takes over towards the end of the King's speech: rhyme ties together his last two lines, continues through Hal's brief rejoinder and returns in Henry's last two lines that conclude the scene. This lends an apt formality and solemnity. But it also intensifies by contrast that structural principle which runs through Henry's whole long speech to Hal and into Hal's triumphant reply. What the nuts and bolts of verbs and pronouns build up is not formality but urgency and anxiety. The ball is far from safely in the net and we could borrow a famous phrase from Henry earlier in this scene and say that, in Hal's reassurance that he's firmly 'got it', the wish is father to the thought. This again is what I mean by a kind of structuring that lends its hand to momentum rather than boxes it in.

III

You should check for yourself whether pronouns really have a special prominence in those *Henry IV* episodes. After all, it's in the very nature of dramatic dialogue for an *I* to address a *you*, often about *her*, *him* or *it*. If I exaggerated, it was because I had one eye on speech structure and the other on the speeches' transmission of the plays' running concerns. I'll let you size up my case further by trying my hand at a new play, *Measure for Measure*, where content or concerns are inseparable from questions of structure.

In the opening scene the Duke of Vienna awards himself sabbatical leave and appoints as deputy Angelo, whose entry prompts this exchange:

DUKE

       Look where he comes.

ANGELO
Always obedient to your Grace's will,
I come to know your pleasure.
DUKE
                              Angelo:
There is a kind of character in thy life,
That to th' observer doth thy history
Fully enfold. Thyself and thy belongings
Are not thine own so proper as to waste
Thyself upon thy virtues, they on thee.
Heaven doth with us as we with torches do,
Not light them for themselves; for if our virtues
Did not go forth of us, 'twere all alike
As if we had them not. Spirits are not finely touch'd
But to fine issues; nor Nature never lends
The smallest scruple of her excellence,
But like a thrifty goddess, she determines
Herself the glory of a creditor,
Both thanks and use. But I do bend my speech
To one that can my part in him advertise.
Hold, therefore, Angelo:
In our remove be thou at full ourself.

                                        (I, i, 24–40)

The elements I will summarise are: (a) the directive '*Look* where
he comes'; (b) Angelo looks to the Duke for a lead ('your',
twice); (c) the Duke counters by breaking into Angelo's second
line with the single word, the call to attention, 'Angelo' – to
anticipate an image we'll meet in a later scene, Angelo's looking
to the Duke is intercepted by a mirror held by the Duke which
turns the look back on to Angelo; (d) that single word, Angelo's
name, is followed by five lines with eight appearances by the
second-person pronoun (thou, thee, thine, thyself); (e) attention then moves to the general 'model' in the form of a précis of
Jesus's parable about using one's talents, which withdraws the
spotlight from Angelo in particular to humanity, Everyman, in
general. (Angelo isn't a special type here, neither a freak of
frigidity nor a suspected 'seemer' as he will be in the Duke's
discrepant description of him in scene iii.) Accordingly the
pronouns are now in the first person plural (we, us, ourselves) –

not 'they': the Duke implicitly includes himself in humanity; (f) we return to the particular human instance on whom the play will centre, with the line (prominent because short) 'Hold therefore, *Angelo*', and the delegation of power is confirmed by the next line, 'In *our* remove be *thou* at full *ourself*'. (*Our* is now, of course, the 'regal plural'.)

The 'I'–'you' pattern continues through this first scene: for instance, '*We* shall write to *you* . . .'/ 'How it goes with *us* and do look to know/ What doth befall *you* here'. But pronouns are wielded most insistently, if with similar point, when Angelo's strict regime has begun to bite. Isabella, a novice nun, visits him to plead for her brother, who is condemned to death for making his fiancée pregnant. Isabella confronts Angelo with comparisons (just as Henry did Hal), ringing the changes on both 'put *yourself* in *his* [her brother's] position' and 'if only *I* were in *your* position!' Such directness of challenge is what distinguishes her pleas from Portia's famous general invocation of Mercy in *The Merchant of Venice*: that, and the fact that Isabella doesn't expend her case in one set speech but keeps coming at Angelo from different directions. Would Angelo, she first asks, issue a pardon to her brother 'If so *your* heart were touched with that remorse [pity]/ As *mine* is to *him*'? Then,

> If *he* had been as *you*, and *you* as *he*,
> *You* would have slipped like *him*; but *he*, like *you*,
> Would not have been so stern.
>
> (II, ii, 64–6)

No wonder he completes that last line with 'Pray you be gone' – but she comes right back with '*I* would to heaven *I* had *your* potency/ And *you* were *Isabel*'; then '*I* would tell what 'twere to be *a judge*/ And what *a prisoner*'. The appeal intensifies when she adds a further third-person pronoun: besides *he*, her brother, we now have *He*. 'How would *you* be,/ If *He*, which is the top of judgment, should/ But judge *you* as *you* are?' (Angelo, incidentally, is equally resourceful with pronouns, seeing the law as an *it* and stating that 'It is the law, not I, condemn your brother'. Perhaps he takes his cue from Isabella who sought to distinguish between *him* and *it*, between her brother and his wrongdoing: 'let it be his fault, and not my brother'.)

This facet of the scene is related to so much else that I must relegate to an Appendix (3A). It is partly because we have jumped ahead, to a play roughly contemporary with *Macbeth*, that dialogue moves quickly and Isabella's plea comes in a flurry of thrusts and stabs. Yet even in the individual short excerpts I have quoted you see how pronouns hold everything together, shaping a speech and propelling the argument.

But any 'part of speech' can do that; even the humble *which*s and *that*s of this world. Listen to Goneril scolding her father, Lear, who has come to stay with her in the company of his court fool and hundred knights:

> Not only, sir, this your all-licens'd Fool,
> But other of your insolent retinue
> Do hourly carp and quarrel, breaking forth
> In rank and not-to-be-endur'd riots. Sir,
> I had thought, by making this well known unto you,
> To have found a safe redress, but now grow fearful,
> By what yourself too late have spoke and done,
> That you protect this course and put it on
> By your allowance; which if you should, the fault
> Would not scape censure, nor the redresses sleep,
> Which, in the tender of a wholesome weal,
> Might in their working do you that offense,
> Which else were shame, that then necessity
> Will call discreet proceeding.
>
> (I, iv, 201–14)

The threat is veiled, but not the complaint. In a manner recalling outbursts by Hotspur and Hamlet, the anger is given vent in the '*not only . . . but also*' opening and followed through with 'carp *and* quarrel', 'rank *and* not-to-be-endur'd riots', 'spoke *and* done', 'protected *and* put on'. So that Lear's 'offense' is (she says) not only rank but flagrant and defiant. It is much less clear what will be Goneril's own 'offense' – that is, her retaliation if and when she goes on the offensive – and the veiling of her threat produces clumsy, rambling syntax, a mixture of bluster and smokescreen. A series of clauses dangle from each other by three *which*s, each of which pairs with some provisional-conditional-hypothetical verb ('Which if you should, the fault/ Would . . .'; 'Which . . . Might'; 'Which . . . were'. But then comes the final slamming down of the verbal trump card in the unambiguous future indicative: 'that . . ./ WILL . . .'. Even that doesn't strip the threat naked but jumps ahead to its justification. Just what she'll do, she's not saying – yet; but people WILL approve of it as right and proper and unavoidable.

I hope to have alerted you to the speech's strategy and punch, why it has to be that length and shape (even why it has to seem shapeless or rambling before the final slam), and why words come where they do. All this will be reinforced by comparing the version I've used (which Riverside derives mainly from the Folio) with the Quarto version which is in prose, and with the truncated version in Nahum Tate's adaptation. (See Appendix 3B.) Of course the speech also cries out to be related to the rest of the play. The way it develops makes it a microcosm of the particularly startling escalation and acceleration of this tragedy: 'It is terrible in its accumulation – like a great big wave coming up – and then crash!'[3] And it helps bear out Coleridge's comparison: 'Of all Shakespeare's plays *Macbeth* is the most rapid, *Hamlet* the slowest, in movement. *Lear* combines length with rapidity, – like the hurricane and the whirlpool, absorbing while it advances. It begins as a stormy day in summer, with brightness; but that brightness is lurid, and anticipates the tempest.'[4] More specifically, it asks to be linked with the wayward syntax of Lear's own later veiled threat – veiled in his case because, unlike Goneril, he has nothing to threaten with:

> I will have such revenges on you both
> That all the world shall – I will do such things –
> What they are yet I know not, but they shall be
> The terrors of the earth!
> (II, iv, 279–82)

But to keep our attention on how Shakespeare used various parts of speech to structure speeches, here are conjunctions signalling the old man's veerings between patriarchal-tyrannical and self-pityingly childish ways of addressing his daughters (conjunctions in bold, other structural steps in italics).

I prithee, daughter, do not make me mad.
I will not trouble thee, my child; farewell:
We'll no more meet, no more see one another.
But yet thou art my flesh, my blood, my daughter –
Or rather a disease that's in my flesh,
Which I must needs call mine. Thou art a bile,
A plague-sore, or embossed carbuncle,
In my corrupted blood. **But** I'll not chide thee,
Let shame come when it will, *I do not* call it.
I do not bid the thunder-bearer shoot,
Nor tell tales of thee to high-judging Jove.
Mend when thou canst, be better at thy leisure,
I can be patient, *I can stay* with Regan,
I and my hundred knights.

(II, iv, 218–31).

Note, after all those swivellings, the way he tries to smuggle in his hundred knights in that last dangling phrase, one of three beginning with 'I'. Regan, however, promptly squashes that with her dry rejoinder, 'Not altogether so'.

IV

This chapter on speech structure began by looking for both flexibility and momentum emerging from Shakespeare's early concern with insistent patterning. As my illustrations moved on through his work, and certainly as we reached *King Lear*, my subject has about-faced or turned inside-out, so that I'm pointing out welcome structural devices in what could have been merely shapeless outbursts. Goneril and Lear express disordered or rapidly oscillating feelings, and so Shakespeare avoids static, symmetrical patterning, but equally he chooses not simply to write large the disjointed, confused effect of (to refer back to examples from Chapter One) York at 'sixes-and-sevens' or of Capulet distracted by Tybalt. I'll bring this veering of my direction more into the open by considering the reactions of one critic to Shakespeare's later verse; reactions that are themselves disturbed and oscillating.

I have two reasons for choosing A. C. Bradley as that one

critic. First, this passage from his *Shakespearean Tragedy* (Bradley, 1905: 66–9) usually goes unnoticed because he is pigeonholed as a character-critic who neglects the plays' verse. More important, he goes against the still prevailing current of modern ideas about Shakespeare's development. In T. S. Eliot's 1920s rehabilitation of Shakespeare's near-contemporaries the Metaphysical poets, key terms were 'compressed', 'complex' and 'difficult' (which modern poetry also, Eliot maintained, 'must be') (Eliot, 1975: 66). These terms soon got carried over to Shakespeare commentary, so that R. D. Altick's still current article on 'Symphonic Imagery' reflects the common view that after early 'diffuseness' Shakespeare distinguished himself by 'the ultimate condensation, the compression of a universe of meaning into a single bold metaphor' (Altick, 1947: 365). Bradley offers not an opposite view but a mixed, hesitant one. At the start of his third chapter, before focusing on *Hamlet*, he sees that play as Shakespeare's stylistic turning point. He speaks of 'the fullness of its eloquence', tracing continuity with leisurely lyrical passages in *Romeo and Juliet*. (Eliot, equating maturity with compression, was to cite such links as evidence that *Hamlet* incorporates relics of an earlier, less 'mature' writing (Eliot, 1975: 47).) But after this play, Bradley goes on, 'this music is heard no more'. What supplants it is 'more concentrated, rapid, varied, and, in construction, less regular, not seldom twisted and ellyptical'. This later verse is 'deficient in charm', but 'always full of life and movement, and produces sudden, strange, electrifying effects rarely found in earlier plays'. You see how this bears on my concern with the changing compromises Shakespeare makes, in individual speeches, between what Bradley himself calls 'construction' on one hand and, on the other, 'life and movement'.

For examples, Bradley turns to *Antony and Cleopatra*, concluding his expression of ambivalent feelings by quoting Enobarbus's comment on Antony's last-ditch stand, his desperate challenge to Caesar to come and slug it out face-to-face, one-to-one. Deluded as well as desperate, exclaims Antony's so-far faithful right-hand man:

> [*Aside*] Yes, like enough! high-battled Caesar will
> Unstate his happiness, and be stag'd to th'show

Against a sworder! I see men's judgments are
A parcel of their fortunes, and things outward
Do draw the inward quality after them,
To suffer all alike. That he should dream,
Knowing all measures, the full Caesar will
Answer his emptiness! Caesar, thou hast subdu'd
His judgment too.

(III, xiii, 29–37)

Bradley speaks of 'the impatient throng of thoughts not always completely embodied' on Shakespeare's part, and for us 'an astonishing variety of ideas and experiences' to 'live through'. So is this a case of rapid 'life and movement' at the expense of 'construction'?

A first reply is that the tone of this outburst is what both carries it along and makes it cohere. That tone is incredulous scorn. It's one thing to be down on your luck, Enobarbus tells himself, another to talk as if you're still on top! Not surprisingly Enobarbus, like the doctor near the end of *Macbeth*, is soon measuring the distance to the door and intent on getting 'away and clear'. This is what Bradley *ought* to have had in mind when he followed his misgivings about this passage by conceding that, while 'less poetic' than that of *Hamlet*, this later style is 'invariably more dramatic'. For the speech is dramatic not just in the sense of wild or explosive but in conveying a voice and tone prompted by a specific turn of events.

Certainly compression (that is, held-in explosiveness) characterises the phrasing: thus 'high-battled' and 'sworder', the 'full Caesar' and 'answer his emptiness'. But the speech is firmly organised in clear contrasts and parallels; as those last two phrases exemplify. They are immediately clinched by the speech's conclusion, its final sentence, about Antony's 'subdued judgement' which in turn echoes an earlier point ('I see men's *judgments* are/ A parcel of their *fortunes*'). And that point is itself virtually repeated in the ensuing link of opposites, 'things outward' and 'inward quality' (note how symmetry is secured by reversing the noun–adjective word-order). Sound, too, plays its part in pulling things together as well as pushing them forward: thus the near-alliteration in 'answer his emptiness'; the end-of-word echoes of 'all' – 'full' – 'will'; and the sustained sequence 'Caesar' – 'unstate' – 'stag'd' – 'show' – 'sworder' (the s-hisses of which are echoed in 'happiness' and 'against'). And the nearly identical sounds at both front and end of 'Caesar' and 'sworder' reinforce their opposition in meaning.

By this stage in Shakespeare's development – our speeches from *Henry IV* some pages back were transitional examples – we aren't thrown by a speaker starting a fresh sentence and point (and indeed an entire speech) in mid-line. We no longer look for parallel or contrast simply between the first and second half of a line or between one line and the next. And so we'll appreciate the metrical arrangement of one particularly trenchant contrast, between self-delusion and realism, when Enobarbus is appalled that Antony 'should *dream / Knowing* . . . !' That contrast is initially disguised by straddling the line-break, but is thereby actually intensified by the stress and prominence which always come as a bonus to words which begin and end lines.

Structure aplenty, then; even symmetrical antitheses and near-repetition to make sure we haven't missed the main point. But 'charm'? – indeed no. Aptly not; the scorn is meant to grate, even if grating isn't unique to that passage, or to Enobarbus. In a comment on the roughly contemporary *Coriolanus*, Frank Kermode refers back to *Henry IV, Part One* where Hotspur 'would "rather hear a brazen canstick turn'd,/ Or a dry wheel grate on the axle-tree" than have his teeth set on edge by "mincing poetry"; and some of the verse of *Coriolanus* has this grating vigour'.[5] So does that of *Antony and Cleopatra*.

Here's another gratingly vigorous passage, from the opposite military camp:

MESSENGER
Thy biddings have been done, and every hour,
Most noble Caesar, shalt thou have report
How 'tis abroad. Pompey is strong at sea,
And it appears he is belov'd of those
That only have fear'd Caesar; to the ports
The discontents repair, and men's reports
Give him much wrong'd.
CAESAR
                                I should have known no less:
It hath been taught us from the primal state

That he which is was wish'd, until he were;
And the ebb'd man, ne'er lov'd till ne'er worth love,
Comes dear'd by being lack'd. This common body,
Like to a vagabond flag upon the stream,
Goes to and back, lackeying the varying tide,
To rot itself with motion.
MESSENGER
                              Caesar, I bring thee word
Menecrates and Menas, famous pirates,
Makes the sea serve them, which they ear and wound
With keels of every kind. Many hot inroads
They make in Italy; the borders maritime
Lack blood to think on't, and flush youth revolt.
No vessel can peep forth, but 'tis as soon
Taken as seen; for Pompey's name strikes more
Than could his war resisted.

                              (I, iv, 34–54)

The messenger may be dismissed as routine rough-and-ready
exposition, a feed for 'most noble Caesar'. But Shakespeare
takes care over even this basic bread and butter. The first speech
holds together by interlocking sound sequences: 'report' – 'ports'
– 'reports', and 'appears' – 'fear'd' – 'repair' – 'reports' –
'wronged'. The messenger's second speech has 'sea' – 'serve' –
'ear', 'wound' – 'kind', and (more tenuous) 'Menecrates and
Menas' – 'makes the sea serve'. Words are also marshalled in
contrasts of meaning: thus 'Pompey belov'd' – 'fear'd Caesar',
and 'Pompey's name strikes more/ Than could his war resisted'.
That last contrast again looks across the line-break, as does ' 'tis
as soon/ Taken as seen', where meaning-contrast also plays
against sound-similarity.

Shakespeare clears a space between these admittedly knotty
as well as breathless news flashes to let Caesar point a moral. But
the style hardly changes. We have the same compression of
wording ('the ebb'd man'; 'dear'd') and of aphorism ('ne'er lov'd
till ne'er worth love'), and a return to early-Shakespearean
tongue-twisting in 'he which is was wish'd, until he were').
Words form chains, whether of meaning or sound ('ebb'd'–
'dear'd' – 'lack'd' – 'flag' – 'back' – 'lackeying'; 'lackeying' –
'varying'). We even have a palindrome in 'to rot', very

appropriate in its forward-and-backness for the to-and-fro
vacillation of the populace that Caesar is talking about.

We don't often linger on these chainlike echoes and
constructive webs when we hear or even when we read the play.
We think of the dialogue as an occasion for Caesar's monologue,
and of that in turn as Shakespeare's opportunity to re-sound the
play's linked refrains: Absence Makes the Heart Grow Fonder,
fondness and fidelity are as insubstantial as clouds, and hearts
hesitate and rot themselves with vacillation. It's entirely valid for
a long-celebrated essay by John Danby (reprinted in Signet) to
use Caesar's reflections as a microcosm of the whole play's
outlook. What I myself hope to counter in this chapter on speech
structures, and especially on what Bradley saw as the later
stylistic phase, is the temptation to take the expression as a
means only of interest through, or only justified by, the thematic
end. For this would be what Gary Taylor called looking through
plays rather than at them. In a poem of reminiscence ('The Dry
Salvages'), T. S. Eliot laments having an experience but missing
its meaning. I want rather to head off students from the more
usual habit of having the meaning and missing the experience.

When critics compare *Antony and Cleopatra* with *All for Love*
– John Dryden's adaptation of some sixty years later – it is
usually in larger terms of the plays as indexes of changed cultural
assumptions (F. R. Leavis is a distinguished exception).[6] Here,
by contrast, is a stylistic comparison, an example of what
happens when the compression about which Bradley was
understandably ambivalent is 'expanded to perspicuity and
polished to elegance'.[7] Perhaps taking up Caesar's brief phrase
'the ebb'd man', Dryden lets Antony play with the image at
length, in the explicit and decorative way of early Shakespeare:

Thou hast what's left of me;
For I am now so sunk from what I was,
Thou find'st me at my lowest water-mark.
The rivers that ran in and raised my fortunes
Are all dried up, or take another course;
What I have left is from my native spring.
I've still a heart that swells in scorn of fate
And lifts me to my banks.

(Act III, 127–34)

For a further excerpt from *All for Love*, see Appendix 3C.

We'll return to *Antony and Cleopatra* in the next chapter, but the subject of this one now leads us on to an example from Shakespeare's last plays.

V

'*The Winter's Tale*, it is generally agreed, is difficult to read,' says Russ McDonald (1985: 315).

> To move from *Macbeth* or *Antony and Cleopatra* into the world of Sicilia is to enter strange territory where a peculiar dialect is spoken. When Leontes steps apart from Hermione and Polixenes, turns to the audience, and enters his meditation beginning 'too hot, too hot', listeners and readers alike are apt to be mystified. We ought to be disturbed, of course, by the king's logic and conclusions; but more to the point, we are immediately confused by his language, and the trouble encountered in these early speeches is characteristic of the play as a whole and of the romances in general.

To the language problems, add 'the syntactic and prosodic complexity' with which words are organised into speeches. And even an enthusiast for the play like Wilson Knight speaks of Leontes's jealous speeches as 'spasmodic', 'interjectory paroxysms' (Knight, 1967: 80, 82).

The last thing I'd want to do is earth away the electric charge, lay out flat the tensely wound spring of speeches like that in which Leontes first suspects his best friend of seducing his wife. But that speech has none the less a firm structure, as will be shown by a little tugging apart at the seams and stressing of the main link-words:

108b	Too hot, too hot!
109b	To mingle friendship far is mingling bloods.
110	*I have* tremor cordis on me; my heart dances
111a	*But not* for joy; not joy.
111b	*This entertainment*
112	*May* a free face put on, [*may*] derive a liberty

113   *From* heartiness, *from* bounty, fertile bosom,
114a   And [*may*] well become the agent;

114b   't *may* – I grant.

115   *But* to be paddling palms *and* pinching fingers,
116   As now they are, *and* making practic'd smiles
117   As in a looking glass; *and then* to sigh, as 'twere
118a   The mort o' th' deer –

118b   O, *that* is *entertainment*
119   My bosom likes not, nor my brows!
                                         (I, ii, 108–19)

The main structural devices are: (a) the half-line keynote
introduction in l. 108b (a phrase that could apply to the alleged
feverish lovers or to Leontes whose heart dances at the sight
of them); (b) the transitional half-line (l. 114b), which pivots
on the already stressed 'may' and give way to 'but'; (c) the
recurrence, near the start and very near the close (ll. 111b
and 118b), of 'entertainment', which is similarly placed at the
ends of lines but which is framed by contrasting adjacent words
(*this* entertainment *may* . . . *but that* entertainment *is*: 'there's
entertainment and entertainment, and at *that* sort We Are
Not Amused').

More subsidiary is the recurrence of 'bosom' – theirs (l. 113),
then Leontes's own (l. 119). More prominent is the last line's
alliteratively enforced parallelism of 'bosom' and 'brows'. And
that stylistic habit pervades the speech; a Hamlet-like habit of
nervous repetition ('Too hot, too hot' and 'not for joy; not joy' –
cf. 'very like, very like' and 'Fie on't, ah fie' in the first act of the
other play). But in Leontes's speech this expression of jumpiness
paradoxically also provides an element of expansiveness, of
lucid balance to help actor and audience keep secure footholds
in this heated passage. Examples are the parallelism in l. 109 and
l. 110 (neither of them mere repetition: in each case the abstruse
or technical first phrase is made vivid by the second); l. 111a
which mirrors as it were diagonally l. 108b; and l. 115. Now there
are in fact different kinds of Hamlet-repetitions. Some are
purely expansive, elegant doublings (an early example is his
scorn for 'the trappings and the suits of woe') of the kind we
noticed even in Hotspur's speeches. Others convey eagerness or

impatience that can escalate to near-uncontrolled verbal batterings (as in his attack on Gertrude). And that escalation takes over in Leontes's l. 115, its 'and' racing on to 'and' in l. 116 and 'and then' in l. 117, as he piles up the proof and points right at the couple who are allegedly 'at it' right now. ('Deictics' is a damply defusing designation for his urgent phrase 'as now they are', as it is for his later alerting of the audience (I, iii) that someone, somewhere is being cuckolded 'even at this present,/ Now, while I speak this'.)

Get hold of the clearly signalled sentence structure and the linked structural units; see the feature of symmetrical balance being progressively overlaid with or overtaken by increasing certainty, impatience and agitation – do this, and you'll know just where to pause and when to stress; and you'll have no problems here with the 'syntactic and prosodic complexity' about which Russ McDonald and others speak so alarmingly. But as Leontes's jealousy develops, his tortuous illogic and its expression compound themselves (see Appendix 3D). This, too, is part of Shakespeare's double skill – in tracing through a sequence of episodes the escalation of jealousy, and in gradually leading readers/spectators from the relatively lucid to the increasingly elusive.

And then back to the absolutely pellucid, some would say even naïve and thin, in the pastoral scenes of Act IV. This transition, after the figure of Time steps forward and fast-forwards the clock by sixteen years, brings bigger contrasts, and brings up big questions of unity. The first page of Wilbur Sanders's Harvester study notes that

> for some readers the play is a sublime diptych, a two-movement symphony whose music is only made richer by its overt structural diversity. For others, equally flatly, it is a broken-backed drama, written in two distinct modes, where Shakespeare has stymied himself by trying to do two incompatible things at once. (Sanders, 1987: 1)

The 'others' include, most spiritedly and amusingly, Enright (1970: 155–203). McDonald, whose whole enterprise is to discern a congruence of 'poetry and plot', none the less implies a kind of unconformity when, after analysing the stylistic complexities of

the first 'movement', he slips into speaking of the last two acts'
'lyricism and simplicity' (McDonald, 1985: 327).

Certainly it is hard to hold together in this pastoral movement
the two ideally inseparable approaches through stage and page.
Wilson Knight, normally associated with the second angle, here
succeeds remarkably from the first.[8] By contrast, I will put the
primary stress on poetry and poetic thought – although it is
dramatic poetry and thought, in that it speaks of dance and song
in the midst of those very activities. I'll keep off the famous
theoretical discussion of nature and art (IV, iv, 79–103) which
Eagleton (1986: 91–3) is only the latest to chew over, and take an
equally famous and more defensible passage, Florizel's description of Perdita (IV, iv, 135–46). 'Simplicity and lyricism' is
indeed the first impression, and the challenge here is the reverse
of that presented by 'Too hot, too hot . . .'. I hope to bring out
rhythmic pleasures and subtleties concurrent with what at first
may seem all too firm a structure, a merely lucid series of ideas.
Again, a more pointed layout, lighting up that structure, will
help me in my subsequent comments: you'll find a clean copy in
Riverside, pp. 1589–90.

(A)   What you do
             Still betters what is done.
(B) (i)   When you speak, sweet,
             I'ld have you do it ever;
     (ii)   when you sing,
             I'ld have you (a) buy and sell so; (b) so give alms;
             (c) Pray so; and (d) for the ord'ring your affairs,
             To sing them too.
     (iii)   When you do dance, I wish you
             A wave o' th' sea, that you might ever do
             Nothing but that; move still, still so,
             And own no other function.
(C)   Each your doing
             (So singular in each particular)
             Crowns what you are doing in the present deeds,
             That all your acts are queens.

General statement (A) leads to three examples with their
subsections in (B), which in turn prompts the conclusion (C).

There's the movement of a circling dance, both in the whole passage (C virtually repeats A) and in particular sections (A and C are each in themselves circular in idea and phrasing).

The linked ideas are correspondingly clear. Every fresh action of Perdita's surpasses the previous one(s) – but that paraphrase is more wordy than the original, in part (A). By extension, she can enhance or light up the most everyday activities – even settling the household accounts or doing the chores. (Like Cleopatra, Perdita is one 'whom everything becomes', who 'makes defect perfection': Florizel's compliment turns on its head the Queen of Egypt's protest that she is 'no more than e'en a woman, and commanded/ By such poor passion as the maid that milks'). Furthermore each 'particular' thing Perdita does is 'singular' – special, and unique (our modern 'distinguished' has the same double edge: distinctive, and outstanding). Yet each such act is part of an unbroken whole: like a wave, she moves yet remains the same entity. Shakespeare uses here a wordplay that recurs in such diverse writers as Keats, Lawrence and Eliot. 'Still' = motionless (as in 'the air is still') but by extension also = continuing, paradoxically unchanging, carrying on being the same (as in 'the air is still humid').

Apart from the wave imagery and the wordplay on 'singular' and 'still', the passage could hardly be more plain and literal in its language. The stress throughout is on the initially-stated 'What you do', so the words that recur are 'do', 'deeds', 'acts' (members of this extended family make nine appearances in the twelve lines). Hence also the verbs that bear the main weight – beside 'do' we have that trio 'speak', 'sing', 'dance', together with 'betters', all those verbs in the subsidiary parts of (B) (ii), and the climactic 'crowns'. You could call the speech an elaborate compliment to Perdita, but not a flowery one: for there are no flower images (the nature–art discussion that precedes it gives us more than enough of them, thank you very much), and none of the adjectives and adverbs which usually provide the means of elaborating and decorating descriptions. The words are nearly all bare monosyllables. (A notable exception, the last line but two, is a deliberately pulling-back before the renewed punch of the ending: cf. the end of Richard's hollow-crown speech.) And we find none of the compressed metaphors which are commonly touted by critics as the hallmark of later Shakespeare: the wave amounts rather to an extended simile with the parallels quite explicit, while 'crowns' and 'queens' are metaphorical but familiar to us from colloquial use, not ingenious or difficult poetic coinages.

So – to recall McDonald's phrase 'simplicity and lyricism' – the speech may be well 'articulated', indeed spare and muscular, but where is its subtlety? That lies in particular turns in the rhythm which both enforce the meaning and produce a dancelike movement appropriate to the situation, that of a country festival. For instance, in the mirror-like phrasing 'move still, still so', the play on two meanings of 'still' is accentuated by repeating the word immediately after a comma-pause; by linking the first use of it to the word 'move' which conflicts with the second use; and by contrasting 'move' as the phrase's first word with its last word 'so' (= the same; in this same unchanged way). But the phrase pattern here also contributes to the dance: it's like two partners coming close, pausing, and moving apart. Compare the juxtaposition 'so, so' in (B) (ii), and the reversed arrangement of 'so give alms; pray so', whereby that recurrent little word is moved to opposite ends of the double-phrase; or compare the near-repetition and comma-pause in 'speak, sweet'. Another rhythmic effect is that such pauses give way to the momentum which is provided by a line-start, and by light stressing encouraged by ellipsis, in 'A wave o' th' sea . . .'. Similarly, the play on those two balanced polysyllables 'singular in each particular' intensifies the release of energy with 'crowns' at the start of the next line, an energy that in the final line climaxes with 'queens'. This impression of the quickening in a dance-finale counterbalances any incipient static patterning in that last line and a half (that is, the symmetrical positioning of 'Crowns . . ./ . . . queens', which frame a résumé of the key words 'doing', 'deeds', 'acts'). So this speech is dramatic rather than 'lyrical', crying out to be synchronised with the together-and-apart, hestitate-and-relaunch movements of the couple as they dance. (See Appendix 3E for alternative ways of analysing the speech.)

This chapter started with a dancelike movement, in Capulet's voice breaking through authorial pattern-making as he antici-pates the élan of his ball. The devices I've described in Florizel's speech – for example the telling variations in phrasing when apparently innocuous little words recur – could at a pinch be called patterning. But what I've sought to prise out is the ways that a dance movement is inherent in the phrase arrangements themselves rather than asserting itself in spite of them. This means, I think, that the latter speech *is* a late example of Shakespeare's development, not a regression to either what McDonald calls 'simplicity and lyricism' or to the stop-go, patterning-versus-momentum which the early parts of this chapter illustrated from early plays.

The middle stretches of this chapter sought to bring out, not simplicity, but an underlying straightforwardness, in the initially daunting kind of speech about which Bradley had mixed feelings and which culminated in Leontes's jealous outbursts. I developed this in relation to the structure of individual speeches. In the next chapter, which draws again on several of the later plays considered in this one, I will broaden the focus to scenes and sometimes to longer dramatic sequences. And this prompts an apparent about-turn. I will dwell on aspects of later Shakespearean complexity that are often skipped over in the interests of plot paraphrase or character coherence. But these complexities are only incidentally those of language and metaphor with which twentieth-century criticism has been somewhat obsessed.

* * *

Appendices to Chapter Three

3A

More on *Measure for Measure*, II, ii. I'd like to show how persistent is the play of pronouns and how that relates to a use of verbs which recalls Claudius's speech on love cooling.

Isabella's pleas culminate in this image: 'Go to your bosom,/ Knock there, and ask your heart what it doth know/ That's like my brother's fault.' And so he does, in the soliloquy that starts almost before she's out of the door. Her half-line of farewell, 'Save your honor!' is capped by his 'From thee: even from thy virtue.' These pronouns recur as he admits his desire for her: 'Is this her fault, or mine? . . . Not she . . . But it is I . . . What dost thou, or what art thou, Angelo?'

I hasten to reassure that I'm not suffering from pronoun-monomania by adding that a variation of verbs is equally an organising method in this scene; one that also contributes Shakespeare ironic comparisons and connections. Take the lukewarm start to Isabella's pleas:

> There is a vice that most I do abhor,
> And most desire should meet the blow of justice;
> For which I would not plead, but that I must;
> For which I must not plead, but that I am
> At war 'twixt will and will not.
>
> (29–33)

We would find this almost comic if it weren't a mission of life or death – and if it didn't echo central passages of *Hamlet*. You'll remember, from the last chapter, Claudius at prayer as 'a man to double business bound'; his comment to Laertes that 'That we would do/ We should do when we would; for this "would" changes'; and the way that Hamlet's verbs change in the prayer scene ('Now might I do it . . . And now I'll do't . . . and so 'a goes to heaven . . . That would be scanned . . .' so he *will* do it, this year, next year, some time more appropriate). Compare also Lady Macbeth or her irresolute husband: 'What thou wouldst highly,/ That thou wouldst holily; wouldst not play false,/ And yet wouldst wrongly win. Thou'ldst have, great Glamis,/ That which cries "Thus thou *must* do", if thou have it' (*Macbeth* I, v, 18–23; my stress). This play of verbs is also central to his ensuing soliloquy 'If *it were* done when *'tis* done . . .' and to her persuading him to murder Duncan (see especially I, vii, 44 on 'Letting "I dare not" wait upon "I would"', and her speech beginning 'What beast was't then . . . in 47–59).

With *Measure for Measure* II, ii, the verb sequence 'must'–'might'–'can'–'would'–'will' is as vital to the scene's structure, and to the structure of its thought, as the pronouns 'I'–'thou'–'it'–'he'–'He'. And the verbs are picked up in Angelo's second soliloquy, a non-prayer reminiscent of Claudius's, before he propositions Isabella: 'When I would pray and think, I [do] think and pray/ To several subjects . . .' (II, iv, 1ff.).

3B

The second Quarto of *Lear* prints Goneril's speech thus:

> Not only sir this, your all-licenc'd fool, but other of your insolent retinue do hourly carp and quarrel, breaking forth in rank and not to be endured riots. Sir, I had thought by making this well known unto you, to have

found a safe redress, but now grow fearful by what your self too late have spoken and done, that you protect this cause, and put on by your allowance, which if you should, the fault would not 'scape censure, nor the redress sleep, which in the tender of a wholesome weal, might in their working do you that offence, that else were shame, that then necessity must call discreet proceeding.

(Original punctuation; my modernisation of spelling.) Nahum Tate's version reads:

> Sir, this licentious insolence of your servants
> Is most unseemly; hourly they break out
> In quarrels bred by their unbounded riots.
> I had fair hope by making this known to you,
> To have had a quick redress, but find too late
> That you protect and countenance their outrage;
> And therefore, sir, I take this freedom, which
> Necessity makes discreet.

(Original punctuation and spelling, but many capitals reduced.)

3C

'Expanded to perspicuity and polished to elegance': *All for Love*. In this further sample (Act IV, 232–47), Ventidius describes Cleopatra:

>   she's dangerous;
> Her eyes have power beyond Thessalian charms
> To draw the moon from heaven; for eloquence,
> The sea-green Syrens taught her voice their flatt'ry;
> And while she speaks, night steals upon the day,
> Unmarked of those that hear. Then she's so charming
> Age buds at sight of her, and swells to youth;
> The holy priests gaze on her when she smiles,
> And with heaved hands, forgetting gravity,
> They bless her wanton eyes. Even I, who hate her,
> With a malignant joy behold such beauty,
> And while I curse, desire it. Antony
> Must needs have some remains of passion still,
> Which may ferment into a worse relapse
> If now not fully cured. I know, this minute,
> With Caesar he's endeavoring her peace.

This draws on several passages in *Antony and Cleopatra*: Antony's 'Fie, wrangling queen . . .' in I, i; Enobarbus's comments in II, ii that 'age cannot wither her' and that 'priests/Bless her when she is riggish'; and Cleopatra's enjoyment of the asp whose sting 'is as a lover's pinch,/Which hurts, and is desir'd' (V, ii, 295–6). But no 'riggish' or 'wither' or 'pinch' in Dryden; and no 'charm' in the Shakespearean sense of magic spell – Dryden's mention of 'Thessalian charms' gives way to the anodyne modern connotation in 'she's so charming'. Which reminds me of Bradley's complaint that the verse of *Antony and Cleopatra* was 'deficient in charm': he might have turned for satisfaction to *All for Love*.

3D

This passage comes a hundred lines or so after 'Too hot, too hot':

LEONTES

          How came't, Camillo,
That he did stay?

CAMILLO

          At the good Queen's entreaty.

LEONTES

At the Queen's be't; 'good' should be pertinent,
But so it is, it is not. Was this taken
By any understanding pate but thine?
For thy conceit is soaking, will draw in
More than the common blocks. Not noted, is't,
But of the finer natures? By some severals
Of head-piece extraordinary? Lower messes
Perchance are to this business purblind? Say.

In getting the hang of the structural articulation in all this rhythmic syncopation, a comment by T.S. Eliot may be helpful:

> The most interesting verse which has yet been written in our language has been done either by taking a very simple form, like iambic pentameter, and constantly withdrawing from it, or by taking no form at all, and constantly approximating to a very simple one. It is this contrast between fixity and flux, this unperceived evasion of monotony, which is the very life of verse . . . the ghost of some simple metre should lurk behind the arras in even the 'freest' verse; to advance menacingly as we doze, and withdraw as we rouse. ('Reflections on "Vers Libre"', Eliot, 1975: 33–4)

Shakespeare's whole development might be seen in terms of his adopting the 'very simple form' of iambic pentameter and over two decades steadily withdrawing from it. But even at the end of that development, in passages from *The Winter's Tale* as much like 'free verse' as the one I've just quoted, you can still detect the ghost of that simple metre lurking behind the arras of syncopation.

3E

Florizel on Perdita: 'What you do . . .' Here are two alternative methods of analysis, the first by M. M. Mahood:

> The . . . problem of the inferiority or superiority of art to nature teases Keats out of thought when he looks at the Grecian Urn, too cold and motionless to satisfy as a perpetuation of the life it depicts. Is the lifeless permanence of art better than the transience of 'all breathing human passion'? Hokusai can still a breaking wave for the pleasure of many centuries, but his wave does not still move. But here Shakespeare has the advantage over the painter and even over the craftsman whose Chinese jar, in T. S. Eliot's phrase 'Still moves perpetually in its stillness'. As soon as he has shown that the relationship of art to nature cannot be solved by the hen-and-egg argument of Perdita and Polixenes, he gives us one resolution of the problem in Perdita's dance and in Florizel's description of her dancing:
>
> > When you do dance, I wish you
> > A waue o'th Sea, that you might euer do
> > Nothing but that: moue *still, still so:*
> > And owne no other Function.
> > (140–3)
>
> Drama comes nearest to life of all forms of *mimesis* because it is continually reanimated by living actors; and in acknowledgement of this Shakespeare entrusts the weight of the play's meaning at this climax to a boy-actor's silent mimetic art. When Perdita dances, the old antagonism of art and nature disappears, for there is no way in which we can tell the dancer from the dance. (Mahood, 1957: 186, quoting the Folio text)

The second analysis ends an essay on 'Shakespeare's Use of Rhetoric' by Brian Vickers, which begins by reminding us that 'rhetoric was for over two thousand years the most important discipline to anyone interested in literature'. After introducing the main devices and terms of rhetoric, Vickers quotes Florizel's speech and comments:

To anyone with even a smattering of rhetoric it will be evident that much of what modern critics describe as the 'texture' of verse is in fact the product of a skilful use of rhetoric – density, smoothness, recurrence, fluidity. Here are many of the most formal schemes of rhetoric; three sentences are exactly symmetrical in structure ('When you speak . . . When you sing . . . When you do dance') but *anaphora, parison*, and *isocolon* perfectly convey Florizel's awe at her perfection in all her doings. 'Her doings' is the theme of the whole speech, so it is only right that *ploce* should put constant stress on 'you', and that *ploce* and *polyptoton* should wring every variant from the key verb, 'do': 'do, done, do, do, doing, doing, deeds' until she is crowned: 'all your acts are queens.' Other figures express the perfection of Perdita as she is: *anadiplosis* links together 'sell so; so give alms', or if we take it into the next line 'so' also ends that clause (*epanalepsis*). At the comparison of Perdita to a wave, the verse takes on a wave-like motion, as several critics have noted, but it does so largely through rhetoric, by the cyclic repetition of 'you' and 'do', and again by *anadiplosis*: 'move still, still so.' And the figures are subtly played off against the verse-movement, with the symmetry now corresponding (lines 2–4), now diverging, using the line-division to accentuate the break within a symmetry (lines 4–5, 7–8). Here the mature Shakespearian style absorbs the structures of rhetoric to produce new and expressive structures of feeling. The early poetry displays its rhetoric stiffly, the mature style absorbs it: therefore modern criticism has been able to ignore the rhetorical framework in the mature style and discuss the life and feeling direct. But it seems at least likely that an awareness of the forms of rhetoric can enlarge our understanding of the poetry, for in Shakespeare's time and in Shakespeare's poetry rhetoric and feeling were one. (*A New Companion to Shakespeare Studies*, ed. K. Muir and S. Schoenbaum (Cambridge, 1971), pp. 97–8)

Chapter Four

Scenes

This chapter moves outwards from speeches to the larger structural units of scenes and their sequences. But 'structural units' sound like bricks and their steady, mechanical laying, whereas what I aim to show in Shakespeare's scenes is variety of substance, volatile development and surprise in their juxta-position.

Such qualities have long been acknowledged, but not always described in the same terms or located in the same area of Shakespeare's work. Let me give some air and space to this, much as I did with wordplay in the previous chapter, before seeking to tie this volatility of Shakespeare's to his scenic craft.

I

'Who can be wise, amaz'd, temp'rate and furious, loyal and neutral, in a moment?' asks Macbeth (II, iii). His answer is, 'No man.' My own answer is, 'Any man or woman – if they're in a Shakespeare play.'

But not just in there. As with wordplay and metaphor, much needless argument has arisen through treating Shakespeare, if not as uniquely great, then as a special case or self-enclosed area. So forget him for a moment and listen to these:

I am so changeable, being everything by turns and nothing long – I am such a strange *mélange* of good and evil, that it would be difficult to describe me.

So well she acted, all and every part
    By turns – with that vivacious versatility,

> Which many people take for want of heart.
> They err – 'tis merely what is called mobility . . .

She was agitated, happy, miserable, infinitely obliged, absolutely angry, . . . in the utmost confusion of contrary feelings.

He stood smiling in frustration and amusement and irritation and admiration and love. She was so quick, and so lambent, like discernible fire, and so vindictive, and so rich in her dangerous flamy sensitiveness.

. . . One could watch the change in their eyes from laughter to anger, blue, lit-up laughter, to a hard blue-staring anger; through all the irresolute stages of the sky when the weather was changing.[1]

That last passage is akin to Shakespeare's comparison of the first stages of love with 'the uncertain glory of an April day' – the speaker is one of the *Two Gentlemen of Verona* who just happens to be called Proteus. Weather also provides a parallel with Cordelia before her reunion with Lear:

> patience and sorrow strove
> Who should express her goodliest. You have seen
> Sunshine and rain at once; her smiles and tears
> Were like a better way . . .

But the dramatist's main work is not to describe but – to dramatise. In the previous chapter we saw how Lear's speech 'I prithee, daughter, do not make me mad . . .' swivels in mood between 'but yet', 'or rather' and again 'yet'. Earlier in that scene (II, iv, 88ff.) a similar swivelling follows Gloucester's excuses for Regan and her husband the Duke of Cornwall not coming to the front door to welcome Lear: they're tired, and the Duke is stubborn and 'fiery'. Lear first reacts fierily: 'Vengeance! plague! death! confusion!/Fiery?' Implicit self-knowledge then checks him: 'Tell the hot Duke that –/No, but not yet, may be he is not well/ . . . we are not ourselves/When nature, being oppress'd, commands the mind/To suffer with the body.' But he again looks at his servant Kent in the stocks and resumes his rage: 'Death on my state! wherefore/Should he sit here? . . . /Go tell the Duke, and's wife, I'ld speak with them –/ Now, presently.'

That must have been one of the speeches which the director and critic Harley Granville-Barker had in mind when he discussed the vivacious versatility of Shakespeare's 'strongest weapon, blank verse', its 'suppleness' and 'malleability', and its demands on the actor who 'must master the gymnastics of it' (Granville-Barker, 1972, I: 266, 178). It is not surprising that, already in 1664, an actor in his company (Richard Burbage, whose roles included Othello, Lear and Hamlet) was called 'a delightful *Proteus*, so wholly transforming himself into his part, and putting off himself with his clothes, as he never (not so much as in the tiring-house) assumed himself again until the play was done.'[2]

Increasingly, however, the locating of this 'suppleness' was pushed back even further to first causes: from suppleness of scene or speech, beyond actor's impersonation, to a chameleon quality in the creator. Two years before that tribute to Burbage, Margaret Cavendish exclaimed of Shakespeare himself that 'so well he hath expressed in his plays all sorts of persons, as one would think he had been transformed into every one of those characters', and that with Cleopatra 'one would think he had been metamorphosed from a man to a woman'.[3] This unhelpful attitude of awe in the face of magic ran riot in the Romantic age. Shakespeare, for Keats 'the chameleon poet' who could 'as easily conceive an Iago as an Imogen',[4] was compared to the versatile god 'Proteus, who now flowed a river; now raged a fire; now roared a lion' (Coleridge, 1989: 24). 'This Proteus of the human intellect', added Hazlitt, was forever 'transforming himself at will into whatever he chose'.[5] If recent critics smell bardolatry in all this Romantic veneration, I have it in my nose too: there is an uncomfortable link with Garrick's phrase for Shakespeare, a generation earlier: 'the god of our idolatry'.[6] It is therefore unwise for Ryan to revive the term 'protean', even if for other purposes.

Those other purposes are developed more fully in two recent critics, Robert Weimann and Graham Holderness, whom I'll consider in the final sections of this chapter. Before that, I want to show why a safer and more fertile term would be 'mercurial'. Mercury, too, is the name of a god. But the adjective with its small *m* (and its mouthful-of-a-noun 'mercuriality') directs us rather to the physical substance mercury – quicksilver, which happens to be precious as well as poisonous, but which above all has what Byron called 'mobility'. Keeping well this side of idolatry, let us see with what 'vivacious versatility' one might usefully apply the word 'mercurial' to samples of Shakespeare's writing, especially to the development and linking of scenes.[7] The task I set myself parallels one that occupied me in the previous chapter when analysing speeches from middle-to-late plays: in Bradley's terms, how do Shakespeare's scenes combine 'construction' with 'life and movement'?

II

Mercuriality is what Coleridge thought to be the essence of Richard II: 'throughout his whole character may be noticed the most rapid transitions from insolence to despair, from the heights of love to the agonies of resentment, and from pretended resignation to the bitterest reproaches' (Coleridge, 1989: 120). That is why, 'were there an actor capable of representing it, the character of Richard 2nd would delight us more than any other of Shakespeare's masterpieces, with perhaps the single exception of King Lear' (*ibid.*). But the part of Lear is much more demanding for an actor and much more rewarding for us. 'The most rapid transitions' are here even more mercurially swift, within individual speeches rather than (as is usual with Richard) between them.

So much so that it is tempting to think of a passage like the one I quoted a couple of pages back ('Fiery? What quality?' etc.) as a single flash of lightning from Lear's overcharged mind. Some such analogy is encouraged in the same scene by Lear's invocation of 'nimble lightnings' to 'dart your blinding flames' into Regan's eyes, and is elaborated in the next scene by his 'contending with' (both struggling against and competing with) the 'to-and-fro-conflicting' and 'fretful elements'. But we shouldn't overlook the structural function of external provocations in building up a sustained scene. Lear's lightning glance bounces to and fro between the blank unwelcoming castle door and the stocked Kent. Then Shakespeare moves the scene on with turns of event that twist the knife further. In what I think Granville-Barker was the first to call a rapid volley of blows, Lear's persistent 'Who stocked my servant?' is punctuated by the entrance of Oswald, and of Regan, and of Goneril's cordial welcome of her. This is followed immediately by Cornwall unrepentantly saying he ordered Kent's punishment, reducing Lear to a gasp of 'You? Did you?' which Regan caps coolly with 'I pray you, father, being weak, seem so.' Her suggestion that he return to Goneril with retinue cut to fifty prompts the scene's last section, the grimly grotesque game of human ping-pong or piggy-in-the-middle in which Lear bruises himself against the stonewalling sisters as they steadily chip away at the acceptable number of knights from a hundred to fifty to Goneril's 'What need you five and twenty? ten? or five' and Regan's 'What need one?' A better analogy would be that Lear first runs, then wriggles, then is squashed, between the stone walls that, as in many a horror story, close in on Lear and that (to borrow a word from another context) extrude him on to the heath.

Shakespeare, then, has ordered this scene's development as a twist-by-twist tightening of the vice. Yet he arrests this with a surprise which opens out the perspectives just when the vice is tightest. To 'What need one?' Lear responds with his speech 'O reason not the need . . .' which begins by challenging the terms of this Dutch auction in much the way that Cordelia has challenged his love auction. But the speech splinters into self-pity ('You see me here, you gods, a poor old man'), self-righteousness ('touch me with noble anger') and ludicrous impotence:

> I will have such revenges on you both
> That all the world shall – I will do such things –
> What they are yet I know not, but they shall be
> The terrors of the earth!

This in turn collapses into something that distinguishes Lear's mercuriality entirely from Richard's. Overall, Lear is more truly like mercury in racing off freely in all kinds of unpredictable directions rather than oscillating between the stably identifiable extremes of what Coleridge calls a 'preserved' character; he finds 'no other character preserved with such unequalled chastity as that of Richard 2nd' (Coleridge, 1989: 121). Typical of Lear is the way that the present speech ends with

> I have full cause of weeping, but this heart
> Shall break into a hundred thousand flaws
> Or ere I'll weep. O Fool, I shall go mad!

So much for the dramatist's 'preservation' of character, or the character's own preservation of integrated identity: Lear splits, as the psychologists would put it, splintering like spilt mercury that hurries this way and that away from cohesion.

Who or what am I? – this question has already risen to Lear's lips, at the climax of an especially swift section of I, iv. By looking at this section, we can see in its scenic context a speech of Goneril's which we inspected in the previous chapter, and of which I now quote only the opening line:

LEAR
How now, daughter? what makes that frontlet on? You are too much of late i' th' frown.
FOOL
Thou was a pretty fellow when thou hadst no need to care for her frowning, now thou art an O without a figure. I am better than thou art now, I am a Fool, thou art nothing. [*To Goneril*] Yes, forsooth, I will hold my tongue; so your face bids me, though you say nothing.
> Mum, mum:
> He that keeps nor crust nor crumb,
> Weary of all, shall want some.
[*Pointing to Lear*]   That's a sheal'd peascod.
GONERIL
Not only, sir, this your all-licens'd Fool . . .
FOOL
> For you know, nuncle,
> 'The hedge-sparrow fed the cuckoo so long,
> That it had it head bit off by it young'.
So out went the candle, and we were left darkling.

LEAR

Are you our daughter?

GONERIL

I would you would make use of your good wisdom
(Whereof I know you are fraught) and put away
These dispositions which of late transport you
From what you rightly are.

FOOL

May not an ass know when the cart draws the horse?
[*Sings*]   'Whoop, Jug! I love thee.'

LEAR

Does any here know me? This is not Lear.
Does Lear walk thus? speak thus? Where are his eyes?
Either his notion weakens, his discernings
Are lethargied – Ha! waking? 'Tis not so.
Who is it that can tell me who I am?

FOOL

   Lear's shadow.

Lear's leap is swift from 'you've been looking a touch grumpy recently, dear' to that last question (one of the play's sublime sequences of plainest monosyllables). That question, like the earlier 'Are you our daughter?', is partly a concern about power and status, hoping in vain for the answer 'You, honoured Sir, are my father the King' (he's about to refer to his 'marks of sovereignty'). But the Fool's immediate reply, the knife-thrust punchline 'Lear's shadow', shows he understands the other point of Lear's question: Lear has swiftly come to the verge of losing all bearings on his basic identity – on 'who I am'.

That sequence is mercurial in its unpredicted swiftness of escalation. Equally mercurial is the play of tones through Lear's alternations of sarcasm, self-righteousness and bewilderment, Goneril's quasi-parental scolding and, ducking and weaving between them, the Fool's stinging scurrilous backchat. Such effects led Wilson Knight to dwell on 'The Comedy of the Grotesque' in this play, calling its blend of comic and tragic 'a new sublime incongruity': 'in no tragedy of Shakespeare does incident and dialogue so recklessly and miraculously walk the tight-rope of our pity over the depths of bathos and absurdity'. So we have in Lear himself 'greatness linked to puerility'

(Knight, 1989: 160–2, 168). If we now connect the two scenes we've been drawing on (I, iv and II, iv) and take them in the entire sequence of scenes that make up the play's first 'movement' (Acts I and II), we find such incongruities exploited as structural principles.

One incongruity, as Knight observes, is that 'so storm-furious a play as *King Lear* should have so trivial a domestic basis' (*ibid.*, 161). Perhaps Wilson Knight overstresses the family element of the 'who loves me most?' game in I, i to the neglect of the formal, even ritual staging and the national implications of dividing the kingdom. But certainly a slump into considerations nearer home – how to cope with a childish but headstrong elderly father when he sells up and moves in with you – begins with the prose dialogue between Goneril and Regan which ends that opening scene and is picked up in the next entries of both Goneril (I, iii) and her father (I, iv). The former asks her steward about some tit-for-tat scuffle between Lear and her domestic staff; Lear, whom we've just heard declaring he'll 'unburdened crawl toward death', comes sweating in from hunting with a hearty appetite and 'won't stay a jot for dinner'. What a rapid leap from that to 'Who is it that can tell me who I am?'!

'When I read Shakespeare', reflects D. H. Lawrence,

> I am struck with wonder
> that such trivial people should muse and thunder
> in such lovely language.

If Wilson Knight has succeeded in making a virtue of that incongruity – between 'so storm-furious a play' and 'so trivial a domestic basis' – what about Lawrence's second complaint?

> Lear, the old buffer, you wonder his daughters
> didn't treat him rougher,
> The old chough, the old chuffer!

The answer to Lawrence is that Shakespeare insists it was six of one and half a dozen of the other, and the first two acts are constructed so as to keep open the question, Was Lear pushed or did he jump? The question is far from settled by a matter-of-fact prose passage at the end of I, i where Goneril warns Regan that, given Lear's treatment of his *favourite* daughter, *they* had better watch out. When Regan remarks that 'we shall further think of it', Goneril presses that they must *do* something pre-emptive and be quick about it. At this stage one sister resembles and one contrasts with Edmund who, immediately after (I, ii), declares his intention to take all the initiative in his own family situation. When we next meet Goneril (I, iii) she immediately lists an already long if so far trivial sequence of provocation and retaliation – 'Did my father strike my gentleman for chiding of his Fool?' When Oswald confirms this, I hear in her angry response no factitiousness, no working herself up or protesting too much: she feels real grievances, and it's time to put her foot down. I'll stress the direct everyday phrases (most monosyllables; mostly there for emphasis), the conjunctions, and the punchy end-of-line phrases:

> *By day and night* he wrongs me, **every hour**
> He *flashes into one* gross crime *or other*
> That *sets us all at odds.* **I'll not endure it.**
> His knights grow riotous, **and** himself upbraids us
> *On every trifle.* When he returns from hunting
> I will not speak with him; **say I am sick.**
> If you come slack of former services,
> You shall do well; the fault of it I'll answer.

So push comes to shove in the next scene (I, iv): Oswald snubs Lear, the disguised Kent trips up Oswald, Goneril reproves Lear ('Not only, sir . . .'), Lear's knights may well (as in the Brook–Scofield version) kick the furniture about before Lear calls them 'men of rare and choicest parts', Goneril tells him to grow up and act his age, he delivers a bloodcurdling curse and packs his bags to throw himself on Regan. The tit-for-tatting continues: in II, i Kent, sent ahead to prepare the ground, runs into Oswald whom Goneril has in turn sent ahead, dusts him up and so gets put in the stocks, which infuriates Lear when *he* arrives; which in turn . . . but we know the rest from our earlier look at II, iv, the scene from which Lear after increasing escalation half hurls himself out, and is half pushed, into the storm.

The scenes of Acts I and II, then, are arranged so as to balance the blame. Does the play's tone, or our attitude to Lear, settle once he is a defenceless old man in the storm?

Granville-Barker is particularly attentive to the abrupt tonal modulations of those first two acts. For instance, he suggests that Lear's curse late in II, iv should not be yelled but arrest us by 'its deadlier quiet, lodged between two whirlwinds of Lear's fury' (Granville-Barker, 1972, I: 288). But Granville-Barker tidies up the overall direction of the play by speaking of Lear's 'transition from malediction to martyrdom: when Act II ends he is now at the nadir of his fortunes; the tragic heights are at his command' (*ibid.*, I, 290). He is referring to the storm scenes in Act III (ii, iv and vi), whirlwinds effectively separated by the quiet of i, iii and v. Certainly Lear in these scenes sees himself – except fleetingly – as tragically wronged, 'a poor, infirm, weak and despis'd old man' who is 'more sinned against than sinning'. But then he would, wouldn't he? Those self-exonerations are put in contexts designed to raise our resistance; and when after yet another tirade he resolves to be 'the pattern of all patience: I will say nothing' we may well react as we do when Polonius promises to keep his mouth shut behind Gertrude's arras. Between a Lear as sinner or martyr, and a Lear of titanic stature or in his second childhood, Shakespeare walks a tightrope right to the end of the play. This dictates the pattern of contrasts within and between scenes; as is brought out strongly by comparison with Nahum Tate's version, of which Appendix 4A reprints Act I.

III

For many, the danger is not of endowing Lear with spurious grandeur but of diminishing him entirely to an 'old buffer' (Lawrence's phrase), or 'an old man tottering about . . . with a walking-stick' (as Lamb feared was the case with any stage representation). Diminishment becomes an acute problem in the later stages of several other tragedies. By the middle of *Antony and Cleopatra*, Enobarbus is already muttering about 'a diminution in our captain's brain', while a critic sees Macbeth subjected to 'a series of diminutions'. In my present sampling of these plays I'll suggest how the mercurial quality of Shakespeare's scenic construction by turns aids and counteracts that shrinkage.

We last heard Enobarbus, in our previous chapter, scoffing at his leader's single-combat challenge to Caesar. By late in Act IV he's no longer available to point out a moral, having decided that enough is enough, deserted and died guilt-ridden in a ditch. But as things go from bad to worse, Antony himself can't avoid drawing the right conclusions:

```
9                         All is lost!
      This foul Egyptian hath betrayed me.
      My fleet hath yielded to the foe, and yonder
      They cast their caps up and carouse together
      Like friends long lost. Triple-turn'd whore! 'tis thou
      Hast sold me to this novice, and my heart
15    Makes only wars on thee. Bid them all fly;
      For when I am reveng'd upon my charm,
      I have done all. Bid them all fly, be gone.
                    [Exit Scarus]
      O sun, thy uprise shall I see no more,
      Fortune and Antony part here, even here
20    Do we shake hands. All come to this? The hearts
      That spannell'd me at heels, to whom I gave
      Their wishes, do discandy, melt their sweets
      On blossoming Caesar; and this pine is bark'd,
      That overtopp'd them all. Betray'd I am.
25    O this false soul of Egypt! this grave charm,
      Whose eye beck'd forth my wars and call'd them home,
      Whose bosom was my crownet, my chief end,
      Like a right gipsy, hath at fast and loose
      Beguil'd me to the very heart of loss.
                                        (IV, xii)
```

Before I resume this chapter's broader focus and place it in context, I will pause to look at this speech in itself.

I could have used it in my previous chapter as an illustration of speech articulation of firm structure even though the speaker is beside himself with anger and despair. Note the regular series of sentence states in the second parts of lines 9, 13, 15, 20, and 24; the repeat of 'Bid them all fly' (ll. 15 and 17); and the weaving together of earlier key phrases – 'All is lost' (l. 9); 'heart' (l. 14); and 'the hearts' (l. 20); 'betrayed me' (l. 10) and 'betrayed I am' (l. 24) – in the concluding line 'Beguil'd me to the very heart of loss'.

So it's firmly bolted together. But in another way it slips and slides. Most mecurial are the metaphors. It's as if we run over a series of precarious stepping stones, hardly touching down. In lines 19–24 Fortune and Antony 'shake hands'; then 'hands' suggests 'hearts' as shorthand for the devoted friends who take their cue from Fortune and desert him; 'hearts' in turn suggests 'heels' – those who now turn on their heels were 'at heel', followers who flattered and fawned like spaniels (in the interests of speed Shakespeare coins a verb from that noun).[8] Antony gave them something like sweets or candies which they licked up like dogs, but their hearts now 'discandy', which means to melt or dissolve (they melt away, make themselves scarce) but which gets extended into 'melt[ing] their sweets' in the sense of dribbling with fawning affection over Caesar. 'Blossoming' Caesar, that is, whereas Antony is now a 'pine' (line 1 of the scene arranged an after-battle rendezvous at an actual pine tree). The pine is tall (it 'overtopp'd them all') but is about to topple because it's been stripped of bark; but such is the volatile association of sounds and ideas in this passage that one also hears an echo, so to speak, of dogs barking.

Judging from his remarks quoted in the last chapter, you can imagine Bradley's mixed feelings about these mercurial metaphors spilling swiftly all over the place. To give fair hearing to such misgivings, against a twentieth-century orthodoxy that treats Lady Macbeth's dog's breakfast of mixed metaphors 'Was the hope drunk wherein you drest yourself?' as the height of poetic force, let me quote Johnson on Shakespeare's 'fulness of idea', 'which might sometimes load his words with more sentiment than they could conveniently convey, and that rapidity of imagination which might bring him to a second thought before he had fully explained the first' (Johnson, 1969: 53). And here is a 1988 work on Shakespeare and metaphor which thinks that the taste for 'compression' in Donne has a lot to answer for in the assumption that 'fawning dogs are a commonplace metaphor for flattering people and melting sweets are not exactly a novel metaphor for the favours of such people, but together the "cluster" is distinctly Shakespearean'.[9] Acceptable or not, the imagery of Antony's speech is matched by the mercurial idiom and correspondingly mercurial tone. Johnson, talking about 'propriety' of style, praises Shakespeare for habitually using a language 'level with life' that was 'above grossness and below refinement' (*ibid.*, 8). But in fact Shakespeare rarely keeps level-toned for more than a line or two any more than his protagonists keep level-headed. He likes to play agilely up and down the scale even in one speech, mercurially mingling (in Eliot's phrase) 'the oratorical, the conversational, the elaborate and the simple'. In Antony's outburst, the oratorical comes in 'O sun, thy uprise shall I see no more' and in the inversion 'Betrayed I am'; the conversational, downright slangy, in 'a right gipsy' and 'play'd at fast and loose' (the second phrase, and that particular sense of 'right' in the first, are still colloquially current). These stylistic extremes converge in the final phrase, 'the very heart of loss', with both nouns 'simple' but 'heart' making palpable and human the abstract 'loss'. (For contrast, see Dryden's version in Appendix 4B.)

How are these impressions extended by resuming this chapter's wider focus and seeing the speech in context? Immediately before in this scene, Scarus (Enobarbus's replacement) has warned us that Antony

Is valiant, and dejected, and by starts
His fretted fortunes give him hope and fear
Of what he has, and has not.

(7–9)

That would fit Richard II and, as we'll see, Macbeth who is frequently said to start and fret. But to find those oppositions in Antony, we have to look more broadly at the rapid sequence of scenes to which IV, xii belongs. We find a contrast between this scene of despair with his extreme elation in IV, viii. A further contrast is with his steely calm antagonist, Octavius Caesar, whose chillingly steady voice has just been heard in the four-line preceding scene. This is part of a recurrent scenic opposition that Shakespeare exploits elsewhere, as with Richard writhing and thrashing helplessly on a pin held steadily by the Octavius-like Bolingbroke, Lear nailed down by Goneril and Regan, and Macbeth as the avenging forces steadily close in.

Within this scene in itself, Granville-Barker finds ample 'change and variety' after Antony's big speech:

His fury soon begins to work again; it is like yeast in him; and
when he turns, expectant of Eros coming to his call, to find
Cleopatra herself, he chokes for a moment, long enough for
her smooth incongruity,

> Why is my lord enrag'd against his love?

to give a fresh twist to his torture. In this babyish line, and in
her flabbergasted, tongue-tied, sudden, very unqueenlike
bolting, in his frenzied pursuit of her, Shakespeare again
skirts the ridiculous; and closely enough this time to provoke
in us a sort of half-hysteria which will attune us to his next shift
of key – into the delirium which brings Antony, exhausted, to
a pause. We must picture the actor, transfigured to the terms
of

> The shirt of Nessus is upon me; teach me,
> Alcides, thou mine ancestor, thy rage.
> Let me lodge Lichas on the horns o' the moon . . .

and storming from the stage. While we still hear him we see
Cleopatra with her scared women and her sapless eunuch
scurrying across like rabbits. And as they vanish he follows,
vertiginous, insensate! It is a wild, roundabout chase,
hazardously raised to poetic power. (Granville-Barker, 1972,
I: 398)

Having made the most of the aforesaid grave charm's barefaced
injured innocence ('what seems to be the trouble, my dear?')
Granville-Barker might also have dwelt, in Antony's retort, on
the threat which is equally 'incongruous' and 'skirts the
ridiculous'. Antony, who tends to feel for his wives a little
belatedly, unconvincingly threatens Cleopatra with 'patient
Octavia' being incited by her brother Octavius to 'plough thy
visage up/With her prepared nails' (ll. 38–9). Now *that's* a one-
to-one fight to place bets on!

When the flailing and lashing becomes this ludicrous, on a
level with Lear warning he'll do such things that shall be the
terrors of the earth, Antony is surely a diminished figure. The
threat is comically implausible because the sparse stage

appearances of the 'still and silent' Octavia have never shaken off the report with which jealous Cleopatra was comforted:

> She creeps;
> Her motion and her station are as one;
> She shows a body rather than a life,
> A statue, than a breather.
>
> (III, iii, 18–21)

– not exactly what you'd call mercurial. Whereas mobility and 'undiminishability' are central to the conception of Cleopatra – even if they arguably exist in description more than being projected into scenes. Enobarbus sums up his account of her hopping forty paces through the public street: 'she did make defect perfection/ And breathless, pow'r breathe forth . . . Age cannot wither her, nor custom stale/ Her infinite variety . . . she makes hungry/ Where most she satisfies; for vildest things/ Become themselves in her' (II, ii, 228–39). This very idea came up in the play's first scene:

> Fie, wrangling queen!
> Whom every thing becomes – to chide, to laugh,
> To weep; whose every passion fully strives
> To make itself (in thee) fair and admir'd.
>
> (I, i, 48–51)

It is a paradox echoed in all corners of the play: the first section of the barge description ends with the cupid-like boys with fans 'whose wind did seem/ To glow the delicate cheeks which they did cool/ And what they undid did' (II, ii, 203–5)

This is a quality that lets Cleopatra defy the danger of diminution. It is, by contrast, only early on and in passing that she attributes the same immunity to Antony – 'O heavenly mingle! Be'st thou sad or merry,/ The violence of either thee becomes,/ So does it no man's else' (I, v, 59–61). His own most arresting speech, in the scene immediately following the one we have inspected closely, looks into loss's mercurial processes, beyond diminution to dissolution:

ANTONY
Eros, thou yet behold'st me?
EROS
                              Ay, noble lord.
ANTONY
Sometime we see a cloud that's dragonish,
A vapor sometime like a bear or lion,
A tower'd citadel, a pendant rock,
A forked mountain, or blue promontory
With trees upon't that nod unto the world,
And mock our eyes with air. Thou hast seen these signs,
They are black vesper's pageants.
EROS
                              Ay, my lord.
ANTONY
That which is now a horse, even with a thought
The rack dislimns, and makes it indistinct
As water is in water.
EROS
                              It does, my lord.
ANTONY
My good knave Eros, now thy captain is
Even such a body.

                              (IV, xiv, 1–13)

Soon, as if to cap Scarus's remark that 'what he has, and has not', what Antony was, he is not. 'Here I am Antony,' he says, 'but cannot hold his visible shape.' The precious substance disperses, and as Cleopatra says in the next scene, 'All's but nought.'

On all these threads of paradox that I have picked out, I will now recommend and quote from a classic essay (happily reproduced in full in the Signet edition of this play). If Bradley's stress falls on the 'marvellously swift' Cleopatra, John Danby's theme is the mercurial swiftness of *Antony and Cleopatra* as a whole; and this passage, which follows a quotation of Antony's speech about dragonish clouds, is another way of describing what I have likened to the volatility of mercury.

There is something deliquescent in the reality behind the play. It is a deliquescence to the full display of which each judgment, each aspect pointed to, and each character, is necessary, always provided that no single one of these is taken as final . . . The pigments vividly opposed to each other on the canvas have to mix in the spectator's eye.

Underlying, however, the bewildering oscillations of scene, the overlapping and pleating of different times and places, the co-presence of opposed judgments, the innumerable opportunities for radical choice to intervene, there is, I think, a deliberate logic. It is this which gives the play its compact unity of effect and makes its movement a sign of angelic strength rather than a symptom of febrility. It is the logic of a peculiarly Shakespearean dialectic. Opposites are juxtaposed, mingled, married; then from the very union which seems to promise strength dissolution flows. It is the process of this dialectic – the central process of the play – which we must trace if we wish to arrive anywhere near Shakespeare's meaning.[10]

IV

By contrast, *Macbeth* is what Enright calls 'a single-minded play',

> uniquely so among Shakespeare's works, and there would seem to be little for the commentator to say about it at this time; very little indeed, compared with *Lear* and *Antony and Cleopatra*, two plays where the 'total situation' involves a more complicated arithmetic. Everyone admires *Macbeth*; nearly everybody has written about it. (Enright, 1970: 121)

Among the 'nearly everybody', Hazlitt still provides the best antidote to the idea of *Macbeth* as a sleek, streamlined piece of engineering. He combines larger dramatic contrasts with detailed linguistic effects in this comment:

> *Macbeth* . . . is done upon a stronger and more systematic principle of contrast than any other of Shakespear's plays. It moves upon the verge of an abyss, and is a constant struggle between life and death. The action is desperate and the

reaction is dreadful. It is a huddling together of fierce extremes, a war of opposite natures which of them shall destroy the other. There is nothing but what has a violent end or violent beginnings. The lights and shades are laid on with a determined hand; the transitions from triumph to despair, from the height of terror to the repose of death, are sudden and startling; every passion brings in its fellow-contrary, and the thoughts pitch and jostle against each other as in the dark. The whole play is an unruly chaos of strange and forbidden things, where the ground rocks under our feet. Shakespear's genius here took its full swing and trod upon the farthest bounds of nature and passion. This circumstance will account for the abruptness and violent antitheses of the style. (Hazlitt, 1957: 191)

That is stirred and stirring, its metaphors rising to the occasion. For something cooler, in manner and in judgement, try this summary by Anne Barton:

This is a play which begins with the most intense individual focus, a searching light directed into the dark places of the protagonist's mind, and ends with generality. It starts out as a tragedy, and finishes as a history play. Macbeth himself is not even accorded the honour of an on-stage death, as Richard III was, let alone any encomium of the kind that Mark Antony speaks over the body of his enemy Brutus, in which some of the good qualities which this man once possessed might be remembered. The brave soldier, the man of imagination and valour who earned golden opinions from his peers, is forgotten as though he had never been. Macbeth makes his last entrance as an object, a head ignominiously rammed on to a pole. It is only the last in a series of diminutions, the gradual reduction of a complex and tormented human being painfully aware of the nature and significance of his own actions, first to an hysteric, next to a psychopathic killer, then to an automaton mechanically propelled and finally, at Dunsinane, to a cornered animal distinguished only for the savagery of its last defence.[11]

That's a usefully brief, firm generalisation which students can question by looking in detail at the latter stages of the play. From individual focus to generality; tragedy to history; hero to beast? Is the play this 'single-minded' in development? In particular, has Macbeth shrunk so far (to 'a dwarfish thief') by what Barton calls 'a series of diminutions'? Before Barton, Rossiter (1989: 228) found 'a terrible shrinking', 'a human mind dwindled down' in the Macbeth of Act V. Let us, then, look at a sequence of scenes in that act and see whether Shakespeare's mercurial art complicates any single-minded, one-track development or relentless diminution.

The changes of focus have been startling. The general choric scene about Scotland (IV, vi) assumes an intense, individual focus when Macduff is told of his family's murder by Macbeth's agents. Next (V, i) we return to Macbeth's castle – not yet to Macbeth himself, but to the wife who in preceding scenes has been increasingly set aside. This sleepwalking episode's individual focus is without question as intense as anything in earlier acts.

But now all tension drops as we go (V, ii) to the opposite camp and hear from a miscellany of semi-anonymous Scottish characters – I've heard them called Extras in Kilts – about whom we know little and care less, and who simply co-operate in an antiphonal chorus. This makes us scan the scene listlessly for (a) factual exposition – what's the military situation? and (b) yawn, yawn, our old friend 'iterative imagery' – disease images, picked up from the sleepwalking scene and transmitted to scene iii. This is, on the face of it, another standard off-the-peg fifth-act scene, which Shakespeare brushes down and starts up whenever he needs avenging forces advancing with choric cries of 'rhubarb, rhubarb: image-pattern, image-pattern'. A routine early example is V, ii in *Richard III*.

But a comparison with that scene brings out how the focus, and focal length, varies *within* this scene of *Macbeth*. I will give the latter scene in instalments: here is the opening.

MENTETH
The English pow'r is near, led on by Malcolm,
His uncle Siward, and the good Macduff.
Revenges burn in them; for their dear causes
Would to the bleeding and the grim alarm
Excite the mortified man.

ANGUS
                              Near Birnan wood
Shall we well meet them; that way are they coming.
CATHNESS
Who knows if Donalbain be with his brother?
LENNOX
For certain, sir, he is not; I have a file
Of all the gentry. There is Siward's son,
And many unrough youths that even now
Protest their first of manhood.

This is the distant-outside-military situation as English converge
with Scots: 'The English power is near . . . Near Birnan wood /
Shall we well meet them' (interest flickers as the rendezvous
reminds us of one of the witches' promises to Macbeth, that he's
safe till Birnham wood do come to Dunsinane).

MENTETH
                              What does the tyrant?
CATHNESS
Great Dunsinane he strongly fortifies.
Some say he's mad; others that lesser hate him
Do call it valiant fury; but for certain
He cannot buckle his distemper'd cause
Within the belt of rule.
ANGUS
                              Now does he feel
His secret murthers sticking on his hands;
Now minutely revolts upbraid his faith-breach;
Those he commands move only in command,
Nothing in love. Now does he feel his title
Hang loose about him, like a giant's robe
Upon a dwarfish thief.

This passage switches attention back to Macbeth's fortress. But
that attention is still external – hostile, using conflicting reports
and rumours to assess likely resistance. 'Those he commands
move only in command, Nothing in love' is the exact equivalent
of the Act V scene in *Richard III* where the tyrant 'hath no
friends but what are friends for fear'. Pretty routine speech

assembly here ('Some say' . . . 'others' . . . 'but for certain' and 'Now does' . . . 'now' . . . 'now does . . .'). As for imagery, that of a 'dwarfish thief' is striking, but it threatens a drastically diminished view of Macbeth.

But that danger is counterbalanced by 'Now does he feel/His secret murders sticking on his hands'. This might pass as a dead metaphor in any other context. But we've just watched Lady Macbeth frantically trying to rub dried blood off her hands. And 'stick' has surfaced again and again in the play, an apparently innocuous little word whose meanings have crept up on us: to be firm ('screw your courage to the sticking place', urged Lady Macbeth); to penetrate ('our fears in Banquo stick deep', reflected Macbeth, so Banquo like Duncan is stuck like a pig); to adhere (as with sticky or congealed blood). Menteth (ll. 22–5) takes up that cue to probe inside Macbeth, using the enemy's pestered, guilty followers as a metaphor for his psychological state which is (to quote *Julius Caesar*) like a little kingdom, suffering the nature of an insurrection:

MENTETH
                    Who then shall blame
His pester'd senses to recoil and start,
When all that is within him does condemn
Itself for being there?

Enough of that – it's time we got down to business, says Cathness gruffly, the pronoun 'we' closing choric ranks and closing that intimate view of the enemy:

CATHNESS
                    Well, march we on
To give obedience where 'tis truly ow'd.
Meet we the med'cine of the sickly weal,
And with him pour we, in our country's purge,
Each drop us.
LENNOX
                    Or so much as it needs
To dew sovereign flower and drown the weeds.
Make we our march towards Birnan.

So we end with fairly leisurely, predictable soundings of recurrent imagery – metaphorical laxatives and weedkillers – and *Exeunt, marching*. But, note how, in the construction of this last section, Lennox's last line repeats Cathness's first half-line, but with a key addition, so that the scene ends with 'Birnan' ringing in our ears. (Similarly, at the start of this scene, line 1 is repeated but augmented by line 5: 'The English power is near' . . . 'Near Birnan wood').

The place-name is picked up immediately in the scene that follows, of which this is the opening:

Enter Macbeth, Doctor, and Attendants.

MACBETH
Bring me no more reports, let them fly all.
Till Birnan wood remove to Dunsinane
I cannot taint with fear. What's the boy Malcolm?
Was he not born of woman? The spirits that know
All mortal consequences have pronounc'd me thus:
'Fear not, Macbeth, no man that's born of woman
Shall e'er have power upon thee.' Then fly, false thanes,
And mingle with the English epicures!
The mind I sway by, and the heart I bear,
Shall never sag with doubt, nor shake with fear.

Macbeth now speaks for himself. And those reports that he's mad, or full of valiant fury, don't seem far wide of the mark. Crazy confidence at first; so secure in the witches' promises (the one about Birnham wood is prominent) that he actually challenges his flattering followers to desert. This false security settled into the stability of a concluding couplet – which, beside the rhyme, has intricate symmetry, the bare bones of which are 'mind'–'heart', 'sway'–'bear', 'sag'–'shake', 'doubt'–'fear', and 'never'–'nor'.

The art of this opening is bold and broad, and may well evoke the pantomime figure who boasts that 'I'm all right *now* – they can't catch me!' while the audience wants to yell 'Watch out! They're right *behind* you!' This broad humour is kept up by the next stage of the scene, the corresponding collapse of stoutly self-assured party into dwarfish dismay:

Enter Servant.

MACBETH
The devil damn thee black, thou cream-fac'd loon!
Where got'st thou that goose-look?
SERVANT
     There is ten thousand –
MACBETH
                                   Geese, villain?
SERVANT
                                    Soldiers, sir.
MACBETH
Go prick thy face, and over-red thy fear,
Thou lily-liver'd boy. What soldiers, patch?
Death of thy soul! those linen cheeks of thine
Are counsellors to fear. What soldiers, whey-face?
SERVANT
The English force, so please you.
MACBETH
Take thy face hence.   [*Exit Servant*].

We sense displaced or transferred panic fought down as he
jumps down the messenger's throat before he's had time to open
his mouth. The resulting 'dialogue' is at the furthest possible
metrical remove from that preceding couplet, and a throwback
to the nervy chop-chop between the Macbeths immediately after
the murder of Duncan (II, ii, 16–18: eight 'speeches' in three
lines). This mainly confirms at first hand the enemy's view of
Macbeth's relations with both his pestered senses and his
pestered servants. But with what liveliness! What energy of
insult ('loon', 'villain', 'boy', 'patch'), and endlessly resourceful
ways of saying the messenger looks pale and scared ('cream-
fac'd', 'goose-look', 'lily-liver'd', 'linen cheeks' that are
'counsellors to fear', 'whey-face'). No temptation for us to open
a catalogue of colour imagery here, contrasting all those
whitenesses with the opening phrase 'the devil damn thee black'
– we do that when images are boringly predictable or routine,
whereas here we revel in the paradoxical energy of the 'cornered
animal' even when that energy is summoned to fight off
infectious fear and betrays more jumpiness than sturdiness.

Contrast the equivalent moment in that scene from *Richard II* (III, ii) to which we keep returning:

AUMERLE
Comfort, my liege! why looks your Grace so pale?
RICHARD
But now the blood of twenty thousand men
Did triumph in my face, and they are fled;
And till so much blood thither come again,
Have I not reason to look pale and dead?
All souls that will be safe, fly from my side,
For time hath set a blot upon my pride.

No metrical agitation there, or fresh ways of expressing the blood/pale antithesis.

But then Shakespeare springs another surprise. After that transition from Macbeth's opening regular, confident verse to agitated stichomythia, the latter clears a space for and intensifies by extreme contrast the extraordinary calm clarity of a soliloquy.

                    Seyton! – I am sick at heart
When I behold – Seyton, I say! – This push
Will cheer me ever, or disseat me now.
I have liv'd long enough: my way of life
Is fall'n into the sear, the yellow leaf,
And that which should accompany old age,
As honor, love, obedience, troops of friends,
I must not look to have; but in their stead,
Curses, not loud but deep, mouth-honor, breath,
Which the poor heart would fain deny, and dare not.
Seyton!

Enter Seyton
SEYTON
What's your gracious pleasure?

The characteristics I'd stress are: (a) the rapid metaphorical richness of the preceding section with the servant gives way to plain literal statement. (Of the exceptions, the metaphor 'my way of life'–'sear'–'yellow leaf' is leisurely and lucid, almost opening out into a simile; 'mouth-honor', rather than inventive or surprising, is a transparently colloquial idiom as when we still say someone's boasts or promises are 'just mouth'.) (b) the verse moves with measured calm. Stresses sometimes get syncopated on to monosyllables ('*I* must not look to have'; '*mouth*-honor'; '*breath*'), but end-stopping, or at least -pausing, prevails. Overall is a still clarity without the wild and whirling words that came before, and (to go back again to Richard) without the histrionic elaboration of the hollow-crown speech. (I make that point of contrast because Richard's speech and Macbeth's partly run parallel, both ending with irreducible monosyllabic things like want, grief, bread, friends, honour, love, obedience, troops of friends.)

Another helpful comparison is with Macbeth's soliloquy-like rhapsody about sleep (II, ii, 32–40), just after that nervy rapid stichomythia between him and Lady Macbeth, and in the midst of the most pressing urgency – the body is upstairs, blood is sticking on their hands, the relatives are banging on the front gate: a fine time to pause for an Ode to Sleep! The present instance is surely a repeat exploitation of that tense situation and it's important to pick up the soliloquy's integration with what's fore and aft. At each end, contrasting with the flat-toned (perhaps *sotto-voce*) lines, comes a loud yell to his lieutenant, and the opening lines are interrupted by a renewed, impatient 'Seyton, I say!' The solemn intensity of the speech gives way to a return to incipient farce with Seyton's urbane, Jeeves-like get-on line, 'What is your gracious pleasure?' (Remember Cleopatra's emollient entry line after Antony's 'all is lost' speech; and note how 'gracious' gains here by its hilarious inappropriateness, whereas this last act's 'straight' use of the term goes into mechanical overdrive and overkill.) The near-farce continues with putting on and putting off the armour and (after some heavy-handed heightening of disease imagery applied to Lady Macbeth's mind and Scotland's illness) with the doctor humouring Macbeth, whom he thinks as suitable a case for treatment as Lady Macbeth, while wishing he could make a bolt for it. Macbeth's get-off couplet, which reverts to the confidence of that couplet which preceded the cream-faced loon's bad tidings, and which appeals again to the vital promise about Birnham wood, is capped by the doctor's couplet that closes the scene:

'Were I from Dunsinane away and clear, / Profit again should hardly draw me here.' So the scene, which included one passage of 'the most intense individual focus', ends with the viewpoint of 'those he commands' who 'move only in command'.

This alternation between the two military sides and between the external and internal viewpoints, set up in scenes two and three of Act V, is nominally repeated in the next two. The added element is acceleration: of Macbeth's inner break-up (Lady Macbeth dies; the witches' promises start to collapse) and of the breaking into Macbeth's stronghold of the previously external military threat. But it's V, ii and V, iii that provide the last act's most mercurial changes in focus and style. Of those two scenes the latter is more virtuoso-like in the variations in Macbeth's mood, tone, idiom, rhythm and vocal volume. But my broader point was that, while V, ii gives the external view and V, iii the inner (inside Dunsinane, also inside Macbeth), each scene is mercurial and vivaciously versatile enough to include ample elements of the other perspective.

V

'Verse malleable to every diversity of character and mood' is what Granville-Barker (1972, I: 411) finds in *Antony and Cleopatra*. But he issues a warning about dangers ahead by adding that Shakespeare has 'reached in the writing as in the shaping of this play limits of freedom and daring *that he will not, but for the worse, overpass*' (*ibid.*, 423; my emphasis).

I've done a little towards counteracting that concern about such late plays as *The Winter's Tale* by showing, in Chapter Three, a reassuring lucidity in Leontes's opening speech of jealousy. The structure and therefore the direction of that speech is, I suggested, quite clear: such carryings-on could conceivably be innocent, Leontes reflects, but in actual fact they clearly are not, and he concludes by 'settling' into jealousy. But by now going on to relate the speech to the dialogue that follows it, I want to show that his mood remains mercurial and the verse correspondingly malleable. I press this because state-of-the-art critics like Howard Felperin (Parker and Hartman, 1985: 3–18) debate only whether the scene suggests any justification for Leontes's jealousy. What continues unquestioned is the time-honoured assumption that the jealousy flicks on as instantaneously as a light-switch, remaining steadily on until switched off with equal abruptness two acts later.

In my previous chapter I broke off that speech 'Too hot . . .' before the final word of its last full line. Here is how it ends (cf. Macbeth's soliloquy ending with 'Seyton!'):

> O, that is entertainment
> My bosom likes not, nor my brows! Mamillius,
> Art thou my boy?
> MAMILLIUS
> Ay, my good lord.
>
> (118–20)

Leontes responds with half a dozen lines that mingle address to his son with private mutterings. He begins by picking up the question of whether this is his legitimate son and (what is nominally the same question) whether they are like each other. The reassuring evidence of identical facial features is undermined by Leontes's worry about the 'smutch' on his son's nose, and remarks ostensibly addressed to Mamillius become a cover for innuendoes about horns (on cattle or on cuckolds), his fever fed by sidelong glances at the couple who are still behaving smutchily:

> I' fecks!
> Why, that's my bawcock. What? hast smutch'd thy nose?
> They say it is a copy out of mine. Come, captain,
> We must be neat; not neat, but cleanly, captain:
> And yet the steer, the heckfer, and the calf
> Are all call'd neat. – Still virginalling
> Upon his palm?
>
> (120–6)

(Virginalling = nimble fingerwork, as on the keyboard of the virginals, but with a shadow presence of the sarcastic comment that the lovers' behaviour is 'a highly virginal way of carrying on, I don't think!'). Yet Leontes repeats his question to Mamillius: 'art thou my calf?' (l. 127). And he again gets a reassuring answer: 'Yes, if you will, my lord.' The new phrase seems to imply, either 'yes, if you're willing and psychologically able to recognise me as such' or 'yes, if *you'll* be like *me*' (bearing in mind passages about innocence and childhood that come both earlier and later in this scene). And Leontes's ensuing speech at first takes heart from that reassurance or challenge, but then oscillates between one belief and its opposite as well as between reply to his son and quasi-soliloquy or inner debate. I will bring this out by taking the liberty I took with part of Claudius's prayer-scene speech, and also by stressing the connectives (on the pivotal function of which compare Lear's speech quoted above, p. 125).

LEONTES I
Thou want'st a rough pash and the shoots that I have,
To be full like me;
LEONTES II
                  yet they say we are
Almost as like as eggs;
LEONTES I
                women say so –
That will say any thing.
LEONTES II
             But were they false
As o'er-dy'd blacks, as wind, as waters, *false*
As dice are to be wish'd by one that fixes
No bourn 'twixt his and mine, *yet were it true*
To say this boy were like me. Come, sir page,
Look on me with your welkin eye. Sweet villain!
Most dear'st! my collop! . . .
                              (128–37)

What makes this tough going isn't any metaphorical complexity – the excerpt is concrete, monosyllabic, colloquial, proverbial, using everyday similes, not metaphors, except for 'welkin eye' (l. 136) which is immediately clear in showing us a child's eye as deep blue and transparently open as the sky. The difficulty comes in the mercurial manoeuvrability of mood, the swiftly executed, tight-torque U-turns. Paradoxically it is when the psychological direction settles in the continuation of this speech, when 'Leontes I' (or King Leontes the Jealous) seizes the wheel and puts his foot down, that the style clouds to obscurest abstraction (demanding, as Felperin despairingly remarks, three pages of commentary in the Variorum edition). At the start of this passage, the two Leonteses wrestle for the controls, but the jealous one soon wins:

> Can thy dam? – may't be? –
> Affection! thy intention stabs the centre.
> Thou dost make possible things not so held,
> Communicat'st with dreams (how can this be?),
> With what's unreal thou co-active art,
> And fellow'st nothing. **Then** 'tis very credent
> Thou mayst co-join with something, **and** thou dost
> (**And** that beyond commission), **and** I find it
> (**And** that to the infection of my brains
> **And** hard'ning of my brows).
>
> (137–46)

A crescendo of 'and's has replaced the 'yet's and 'but's of the speech's first half.

But the to-and fro-conflicting elements of Leontes's mind still haven't finally settled. The alleged lovers notice him 'unsettled':

POLIXENES
> What means Sicilia?

HERMIONE
> He something seems unsettled.

POLIXENES
> How? my lord?

LEONTES
> What cheer? How is't with you, best brother?

HERMIONE
> You look
> As if you held a brow of much distraction.
> Are you mov'd, my lord?

LEONTES
> No, in good earnest.
> How sometimes nature will betray its folly!
> Its tenderness! and make itself a pastime
> To harder bosoms! . . .
>
> (146–53)

The opening to his reply may be Leontes the Jealous seeking to cover up as Othello does at one point:

IAGO
I see this hath a little dash'd your spirits.
OTHELLO
Not a jot, not a jot
                    (*Othello*, III, iii, 214–5).

What is the 'folly' that Leontes speaks of betraying? Being cuckolded; or being caught humiliatingly 'unsettled' by it? Or letting yourself be misled by fondness, for instance for the boy at your side? But *is* he being misled? – Leontes II now takes over again, convinced afresh that he and Mamillius are indeed as like as eggs.

And this reassurance takes a fresh form: '*he* now *is* exactly as *I was*'.

LEONTES
                    Looking on the lines
Of my boy's face, methoughts I did recoil
Twenty-three years, and saw myself unbreech'd
In my green velvet coat, my dagger muzzled
Lest it should bite its master, and so prove
(As ornament oft does) too dangerous.
How like (methought) I then was to this kernel,
This squash, this gentleman. Mine honest friend,
Will you take eggs for money?
MAMILLIUS
                    No, my lord, I'll fight.
LEONTES
You will? Why, happy man be 's dole!
                    (153–62)

This takes his mind right back to the dialogue with his other 'honest friend', Polixenes, before the onset of jealousy in 'too hot, too hot . . .'; dialogue in which his friend had reminisced about their own childhood (ll. 62–75). And it prompts him now to address Polixenes as 'my brother' as if the last sixty or so anxious lines hadn't existed:

> My brother,
> Are you so fond of your young prince as we
> Do seem to be of ours?
> POLIXENES   If at home, sir,
> He's all my exercise, my mirth, my matter;
> Now my sworn friend, and then mine enemy;
> My parasite, my soldier, statesman, all.
> He makes a July's day short as December,
> And with his varying childness cures in me
> Thoughts that would thick my blood.
> LEONTES   So stands this squire
> Offic'd with me. We two will walk, my lord,
> And leave you to your graver steps. Hermione,
> How thou lov'st us, show in our brother's welcome;
> Let what is dear in Sicily be cheap.
> Next to thyself and my young rover, he's
> Apparent to my heart.
>
> (163–77)

Yet once more the scene unsettles itself: friend and wife somewhat ill-timedly announce that 'you'll find us together in the garden, dear', and Leontes now claims that his conversation with them was all mere 'angling': he retreats into his own mind where the boy has become merely a pretext for obsessed innuendo:

> HERMIONE   If you would seek us,
> We are yours i' th' garden. Shall 's attend you there?
> LEONTES
> To your own bents dispose you; you'll be found,
> Be you beneath the sky. [*Aside*] I am angling now,
> Though you perceive me not how I give line.
> Go to, go to!
> How she holds up the neb! the bill to him!
> And arms her with the boldness of a wife
> To her allowing husband!
>
> [*Exeunt Polixenes, Hermione, and Attendants*]

> Gone already!
> Inch-thick, knee-deep, o'er head and ears a fork'd one!
> Go play, boy, play. Thy mother plays, and I
> Play too, but so disgrac'd a part, whose issue
> Will hiss me to my grave: contempt and clamor
> Will be my knell. Go play, boy, play . . .
>
> (177–90)

But still the boy stays put through the remaining fifteen lines of this outburst, and persists with his precious assurance: 'I am like you, they say' (l. 208). In Leontes's reply, 'Why, that's some comfort', we hear again what D. H. Lawrence called 'the trembling instability of the balance'. But the attendant lord Camillo is called, the boy leaves (dismissed with 'Go play, Mamillius, thou'rt an honest man' – i.e. 'unlike some I could mention'), and from now on Leontes is settled and bends up every mental agent to this terrible belief that he is 'inch-deep, knee-deep a forked one'. Whatever their differences in provocation, Leontes is now like the absolutist or wholehogging Othello for whom 'to be once in doubt/is once to be resolv'd . . . Away at once with love or jealousy'; and whose 'bloody thoughts, with violent pace,/Shall nev'r look back' once he resolves to be jealous (*Othello*, III, iii, 180–1, 192, 457–8). But Othello runs with dismaying swiftness from the knife-edge of uncertainty, in which 'I think my wife be honest, and think she is not;/I think that thou [Iago] art just, and think thou art not' (*Othello*, III, iii, 384–5). Shakespeare constructs I, ii to leave Leontes by contrast far longer on that sickening see-saw.

His child with the welkin eye keeps him there. But modern critics can't stand kids. The 'taboo on tenderness' which a critic commented on some decades ago has returned with a vengeance. Perhaps a touch of hard-heartedness was healthy after Dickens, and after Coleridge's stress on 'Shakespeare's fondness for children' in 'the sweet scene between Lady Macduff and the child', that 'heightens the after pathos', and the (again) 'sweet scene [II, i] in *The Winter's Tale*' between Hermione and Mamillius (Coleridge, 1989: 104). Reactions have ranged from the prim – 'there is much more in the death of young Macduff than "pathos"; the violation of the natural order is completed by the murder' (L. C. Knights) to the cheerfully bloodyminded:

'Mamillius is almost as trying as Macduff's son' whose pathos is ill-prepared for by the child's cuteness and precocity; 'it seems rather less unnatural to kill him than to kill good old Duncan' (Enright, 1970: 171). The 1980s critics are no more kindly. But there's no escaping the play's equation of childhood or youth with innocence. The equation is made, however, in an unsentimental way that the author of *Songs of Experience* wouldn't be ashamed of – seen playfully, then poignantly, through the eyes of adults recalling their own childhood (I, i, 60–75; 153–60). Conversely, the youthful Perdita's speeches in Act IV will be ominous with impending adulthood – and death. There's nothing pious or abstract about all this. When Leontes addresses the child that stands by him throughout the first stages of jealousy I've analysed, with what resourceful energy of phrase does he describe him! – 'my bawcock', 'captain', 'my calf', 'sir page' with 'welkin eye', 'sweet villain', 'most dear'st', 'my collop', 'this kernel', 'this squash', 'this gentleman', 'mine honest friend', 'this squire', 'my young rover', 'apparent to my heart'. There's every reason for Wilson Knight to stress that Mamillius is 'dramatically central. Defined mainly by what is said to, or about, him . . . "my young rover" focalizes the poetry of boyhood and fills the stage' (Knight, 1967: 78). My further defence of 'the poetry of boyhood' in this scene is that Polixenes's description of *his* son (ll. 165–71) gives a totally unidealised picture of youth as very demanding; this lad is more like Coriolanus's son who enjoys tearing butterflies than like Little Lord Fauntleroy or Christopher Robin. The stress is on his multidirectional energies and quick-changing moods: 'he's all my exercise, my mirth, my matter;/Now my sworn friend, and then mine enemy'. The succinct clinching phrase is 'varying childness'. The child himself is, in short, mercurial.

VI

You'll recall that, at the outset of this chapter, I suggested 'mercurial' was a safer as well as more fertile term than 'protean'. But you'll also recall from Chapter One that Kiernan Ryan was happy to use the latter term when speaking of Shakespeare's versatility – of what he also calls 'heteroglossia'.

That last term comes from Mikhail Bakhtin, a belatedly translated Russian critic who has been influential over the last ten or fifteen years (in criticism of fiction as well as of drama). His work on the concepts of Carnival and the Grotesque, in *Rabelais and His World* (1940; translated 1968), complements the study of medieval drama and other social institutions in the German critic Robert Weimann's *Shakespeare and the Popular Tradition in the Theatre* (1967; translated 1978). You'll repeatedly find these two cited as the most seminal Shakespeare critics of recent decades (see for instance Holderness, below, or Evans's *Signifying Nothing*). In what follows I sample Weimann direct because he applies his historical research directly to Shakespeare's scenes. Bakhtin I present at second hand for it is Graham Holderness who, after giving an extremely lucid and reliable summary of the Russian's ideas, tries them out in detail with Falstaff.

Weimann is valuable for his account of the Middle Ages; although I would rather recommend to students a book he frequently acknowledges, A. P. Rossiter's *English Drama from Early Times to the Elizabethans*, a third the length and thrice as agile, drawing on wider traditions (including the visual arts) and in no danger of burying you under ponderous erudition. But here is a substantial sample of Weimann bringing that erudition to bear on Shakespeare.

He speaks of a tension between 'illusionistic and non-illusionistic' dramatic modes, correspondingly flexible use of the platform stage and an 'astonishing variety and richness of language' which conveyed the 'interplay between realistic and stylized modes of expression'. Instances are provided by such monologues as this one, seen in its context of Act III scene ii:

> When, for example, an angry and distracted Lear challenges the forces of nature – 'You cataracts and hurricanoes, spout' – he uses a stylized and elevated diction. His apostrophe to lightning and thunder is grandiose and rhetorical:
>
>> You sulph'rous and thought-executing fires,
>> Vaunt-couriers of oak-cleaving thunderbolts,
>> Singe my white head. And thou, all-shaking thunder,
>> Strike flat the thick rotundity o' th' world;

Crack nature's moulds, all germains spill at once,
That makes ingrateful man.

(III, ii, 4–9)

But this is immediately followed by a most ordinary kind of
prose:

O nuncle, court holy water in a dry house is better than this
rain-water out o'door.

(III, ii, 10–11)

The contrast between elevated metaphor and simple, everyday speech here sharpens the effect of both. But the
difference in metre, assonance, and style produces more than
a formal contrast; for it signalizes the distance between two
basically different themes and two widely divergent attitudes.
No sooner has the raging King adjured the 'all-shaking
thunder' to flatten the earth and 'Crack nature's moulds' than
'natural' common sense comes to the fore in the person of the
pragmatic Fool, who would rather compromise principles
than face the torrent.

But even within Lear's own speech we find a similar range
of expressive modes. Whereas here he uses elevated rhetoric
to command the elements, when he awakes to find Cordelia in
Act IV his tone and speech change:

Where have I been? Where am I? Fair daylight?
. . . I know not what to say.
I will not swear these are my hands. Let's see.
I feel this pin prick.

(IV, vii, 51–5)

These words are especially moving when compared with
Lear's previously exalted speech. (Weimann, 1987: 216–17)

Having given Weimann that hearing, I now append a few
notes of doubt and dissent.

His critical vocabulary, to judge from the translation, is a
rather blunt instrument: thus the undifferentiated 'grandiose',
'rhetorical', 'stylized', 'elevated', 'exalted'. The contrasts he
draws are correspondingly broad. While he writes of 'the range of

expressive modes' not only between King and Fool but '*within
Lear's own speech*' (my stress), this turns out to mean between
one speech of Lear's and another. Incidentally the choice of the
contrasting speeches suggests a covert dependence on what he
himself (*ibid.*, 224) has castigated as the 'speculative concerns of
character analysis', and on time-honoured sentimental concerns
too that see Lear as undergoing a purgatorial pilgrimage from
arrogant defiance to humility. A more adequate reading of
Lear's III, ii speech (it runs straight through to line 24, despite
the Fool's unheeded interruption) would point out that it does
not end as it begins. What Weimann calls 'the grandiose and
rhetorical' gives way to 'Here I stand, your slave,/A poor,
infirm, weak, and despis'd old man' (ll. 19–20). The change, like
others I discussed earlier, is perilously near to humour.
Although he has a section which purports to be on comedy,
Weimann is throughout unwaveringly earnest, and therefore
unable to detect the possibility of humour.

In the analysis I have quoted, the load of research which
Weimann's preceding two hundred pages has wheeled alongside
Shakespeare is quite irrelevant. The paragraph which 'introduced' that analysis invokes stage conditions, but the actual
analysis is purely about 'variety and richness of language'.
Previous comments about the inherently downstage, audience-
friendly types like the Fool are not picked up here – if only
because Weimann's acknowledgement of heteroglossia *within*
characters makes *everyone* potentially upstage – downstage.
Thus, immediately after my previous excerpt, he continues:

> Similar, if not such striking, examples can be found in the
> language of almost all of the tragic heroes. The rhetorical and
> stylized language of Macbeth, Othello, Cleopatra, and
> Hamlet is mixed with everyday syntax and diction in remarks
> like Macbeth's 'I have done the deed,' or 'I am afraid to think
> what I have done' (II, ii, 14, and 51), Othello's 'Soft you; a
> word or two before you go' (V, ii, 341), Cleopatra's 'Will it eat
> me?' or 'What should I stay –' (V, ii, 269 and 311), and
> Hamlet's frequent use of popular images and proverbs.

Surely we have long known this. But then comes a reprise of the
book's investigation of staging:

This extremely effective alternation between rhetorical and mundane language, stylization and directness, presupposed and helped to perpetuate specific stage conditions such as those offered by the large and variable platform. A downstage position, for instance, allowed for a smoother transition from dialogue to monologue and facilitated the delivery of wordplay and proverbs directly to the audience – a mode of delivery with obvious precedents in the popular theatre. Such transitions abound in Shakespeare's plays, as, for example, in Hamlet's conversation with his mother (III, iv). (*ibid.*, 217)

And with the closet scene he takes his cue from '*the dramatic representation* of leave-taking' (his emphasis) to detect in Hamlet's speech 'O throw away the worser part of it . . .' (III, iv, 157–79) a generalised chorus-like monologue addressed directly to the audience. But only in bits of that speech – he specifies snippets of three, three and two lines. So that if an actor were more convinced than I am by Weimann's ear for those lines and wanted to adopt the correct stage position, he'd have to hop to and fro with dizzying dexterity.

Weimann continues with the scene between Lear and Gloucester in *Lear* IV, vi, claiming that what he calls the visionary lines, of Lear's admonition to 'Thou rascal beadle' (ll. 160 ff.), 'dissolve the illusion of conversation with Gloucester; since they are abstract – generalized – they are addressed less to a partner in dialogue than to a general listener (perhaps even to an individual in the audience singled out by an icy stare or accusing finger)' (*ibid.*, 220). It may be so, perchance . . . and I myself have suggested that, for instance, Leontes may point to a spectator in the front row when he urges that 'many a man there is (even this present,/Now, while I speak this) holds his wife by th' arm,/That little thinks she has been sluic'd in's absence'. But Weimann ought first to notice that, if Lear points to the front row, he *thinks* he's pointing at an actual beadle; the speech is 'visionary' in the sense that he's seeing things, fantasising his position of regal power again as he did in the trial on the heath. And if the speech is what Weimann broadly calls 'abstract', in one sense it could not possibly be more concrete (in details like 'plate sin with gold'; 'arm it in rags').

I want to make a distinction between the opening four-fifths of Weimann's book, the long medieval and Renaissance run-up to the crease, and his performance when he delivers on Shakespeare. When Weimann finally gets to Shakespeare there is, to reapply a phrase of Rossiter's he often quotes, a 'two-eyedness' about Weimann's analyses. Either he concentrates on language (however inadequately), or he focuses on stage positioning (*figurenposition*). He can't keep both in play without neglecting or distorting one of them. In general statements about their link he wavers: in *Hamlet* I, i the protagonist's position is 'defined verbally as well as spatially' (*ibid.*, 230), then 'certainly by his speech but probably also spatially' (*ibid.*, 231), then 'almost certainly reinforced by a downstage position' (*ibid.*). Any sense that we are being told about visual actualities, movements of body and shoulders if not of feet, something 'objective' to replace what he calls mere 'speculation' about character, is often undercut as *figurenposition* retreats to a mere figure of speech, and 'stance' or some other physically noncommittal word would be more appropriate. In any case, after commenting on an episode in *Timon of Athens*, Weimann concedes that 'such a reconstruction of the scene in performance' (actually it is a speculation) 'explains the flexibility and variability of conventions of speech *immediately apparent from the text*' (*ibid.*, 225; my emphasis).

I came on strong with these misgivings because Weimann is still so extravagantly praised, and because students may be browbeaten into thinking that all that heavy historical plant is necessary to appreciate Shakespeare – or worse, that it provides some tool that obviates the need to attune themselves to the text's flexibility and variability of speech. Studying up 'conventions' of speech, or thinking that stage positions give simple signposts to styles, won't develop a quick ear. It is more likely to make ears less attuned to nuances by positing distinct opposites, as does that commentary of Weimann's on *Lear* III, ii.

I promised an alternative on that scene, from Granville-Barker. He says of 'Blow, winds . . .' (the first nine lines):

This is no mere description of a storm, but in music and imaginative suggestion a dramatic creating of the storm itself;

and there is Lear – and here are we, if we yield ourselves – in the midst of it, Yet Lear himself, in his Promethean defiance, still dominates the scene.

But clearly the effect cannot be made by Lamb's 'old man tottering about the stage with a walking-stick'; and by any such competitive machinery for thunder and lightning as Bradley quite needlessly assumes to be an inevitable part of the play's staging it will be largely spoiled. What actor in his senses, however, would attempt to act the scene 'realistically'? (I much doubt if any one of Lamb's detested barnstormers ever did.) And as to the thunder and lightning, Shakespeare uses the modicum to his hand; but it is of no dramatic consequence, and his stagecraft takes no account of it. Yet if the human Lear seems lost for a moment in the symbolic figure, here is the Fool to remind us of him:

> O nuncle, court holy water in a dry house is better than this rain-water out o' door. Good nuncle, in, ask thy daughters' blessing; here's a night pities neither wise men nor fools.

– and to keep the scene in touch with reality. Yet note that the fantasy of the Fool only *mitigates* the contrast, and the spell is held unbroken. It is not till later – when Lear's defiant rage, having painted us the raging of the storm, has subsided – that Kent's sound, most 'realistic' common sense, persuading him to the shelter of the hovel, is admitted.

But Shakespeare has other means of keeping the human and the apocalyptic Lear at one. Though the storm is being painted for us still – [he quotes lines 14–20] – both in the sense of the words and the easier cadence of the verse the human Lear is emerging, and emerges fully upon the sudden simplicity of

> here I stand, your slave;
> A poor, infirm, weak and despis'd old man.

But the actor is not meant, therefore, suddenly to drop from trenchant speech to commonplace, present us a pathological likeness of poverty, infirmity and the rest, divest himself of all poetic power, become, in fact, the old man with a walking-stick. For if he does he will incontinently and quite fatally cease to be the Lear that Shakespeare has, as we said, conceived and embodied in poetry. In poetry; not, one must again insist, necessarily or simply in verse. And it is no more, now or later, a mere question of a method of speaking than of form in the writing. Verse, prose, and doggerel rhyme, in those strenuous scenes, each has its use, each asks an appropriate beauty of treatment, and the three in harmony are, by dramatic title, poetry. (Granville-Barker, 1972, I: 267–8)

And in analyses of the Dover scene, and in the scenes from *Hamlet* selected by Weimann, Granville-Barker more successfully builds bridges between language and staging. He anticipates Weimann's basic point about Shakespeare's combination of mimetic drama and non-illusionist audience awareness, writing a good paragraph (*ibid.*, I: 310–11) on 'the stage Fool' in *Lear*, 'a-straddle between play and audience'. He also anticipates Weimann's point about the downstage position often adopted by Hamlet and other principals, especially for soliloquy and aside:

With the soliloquy upon the platform stage it is a case – as so often where convention is concerned – of extremes meeting. There is no illusion, so there is every illusion. Nothing very strange about this man, not even the dress he wears, leaning forward a little we could touch him; we are as intimate and familiar with him as it is possible to be. We agree to call him 'Hamlet', to suppose he is what he says he is, we admit that he thinks aloud and in blank verse too. It is possible that the more we are asked to imagine the easier we find it to do. (*ibid.*, I: 16)

But 'thinking aloud' doesn't mean talking to oneself, nor does blank verse necessarily entail elevated philosophising:

For a parallel to its [the soliloquy's] full effectiveness on Shakespeare's stage we should really look to the modern music-hall comedian getting on terms with his audience. We may measure the response to Burbage's *O, that this too too solid flesh would melt . . .* by recalling – those of us that happily can – Dan Leno as a washer-woman, confiding domestic troubles to a theatre full of friends, and taken unhindered to their hearts. The problem is not really a difficult one. If we solve the physical side of it by restoring, in essentials, the relation between actor and audience that the intimacy of the platform stage provided, the rest should soon solve itself. (*ibid.*, I: 17)

This pre-empts pretentious modern talk about illusion. The music hall and Dan Leno have gone, but stand-up comics (and tragi-comics) again flourish. How much less remote and daunting this is than all Weimann's marshalling of traditions which 'explain' Shakespeare's mode of drama but won't make it more accessible or congenial.

VII

A major book of the early 1990s, less cited or respected than Weimann, is Graham Holderness's *Shakespeare Recycled: The making of historical drama* (1992: a revised and expanded version of his *Shakespeare's History*, 1985). It has two linked subjects: 'production' of Shakespeare's historiography, and the plays' 'reproduction' at different stages of British social development. In practice that second concern degenerates into easy bardolatry-bashing; in the words of one British politician about attacking his supine opponent, it's like savaging a dead sheep. The first part of the book, however, is original and needs assimilation by Shakespeare critics. It includes an incisive account of *Richard II*. But the part relevant to my present chapter builds on 'the fine studies of C. L. Barber and Robert Weimann' (Holderness, 1992: 133) about popular traditions and Elizabethan drama, by enlisting Bakhtin's theories on 'carnivalisation', which Holderness ably summarises (*ibid.*, 133–40) and then relates to Falstaff.

Several stages in the summary are close to the New Historicist paradox I presented in Chapter One. Holderness speaks of

this contradiction: from the point of view of the people, carnival is an expression of the independent values, the

humanism of popular culture, a fantasy of equality, freedom
and abundance which challenges the social order; from the
point of view of authority, carnival is a means of incorporating
and controlling the energies and anti-authoritarian emotions
aroused by carnival licence. This cultural contradiction, this
confrontation of popular and authoritarian discourses, will
prove a sound basis for defining the function of Falstaff . . .
Bakhtin's most innovatory and useful emphasis lies on the
oppositional character of popular traditions . . . his various
languages all derive from popular culture – the language of
criminals, the accents of anti-Puritan parody and satire, the
language of tavern and high-road. (*ibid.*, 135–9)

And here we come round to mercurial heteroglossia: 'Falstaff is
. . . a polyphonic clamourer of discourses' (*ibid.*, 139).

Holderness will help students hear those diverse discourses
and how they help build mercurial scenes. But that last sentence
of his, in its full version, goes drastically further: 'Falstaff is not a
coherent individual subject but a polyphonic clamourer of
discourses, a fluid counterfeiter of dramatic impersonations'; a
'variety of dramatic ideas, which bear no coherent relation to
what we call "character", but operate only as part of a specific
relation between actor and audience' (*ibid.*, 139). And Holderness shows how traditional critics have reduced to moral
categories and psychological coherence this 'site of contradictions'; for example, Humphreys acknowledges his 'shotsilk
variety' but none the less ends up saying that 'the king stands for
rule, Falstaff for misrule' (Humphreys, 1967: 155). 'Stands for'
indeed unhelpfully suggests a symbol, or cypher. Yet isn't there
the same difficulty with Holderness's use of the word 'principle'?
'Falstaff *is* Bakhtin's "material bodily principle" writ large', he
says (Holderness, 1992: 139). But if Falstaff's discourses and
roles are mercurial or shot silk, his *person* is too, too solid and
unchanging: what is 'writ large' is the fat man on the stage whom
we agree to call Falstaff, not just the principle. Holderness ought
to be able to drag our attention to the chameleon aspect of
Falstaff without shrinking his stage presence to (in bloodless
modern parlance) 'a site of contradictions' (*ibid.*, 146). Imagine
Falstaff's soliloquy about being reduced to a site!

My second quibble is that Holderness himself is a site of

contradictions. He ought also to be able to do something illuminating with the mercurial discourses of Hotspur. But this is what we get : Hotspur's 'macho antics . . . display the chivalric hero . . . privileging male violence as an absolute virtue . . . This quality of "honour" which has become so aggressively contemptuous towards women, is demystified in Hotspur's and Falstaff's talk of buying and selling maidenheads' (*ibid.*, 162). This illustrates how the most sternly anti-moralistic critics are cowed back into pursed lips, scurrying to make their sexual-political correctness of mind clear whenever a whiff of chauvinism crosses Shakespeare's stage. This leads us on to my next chapter.

*   *   *

Appendices to Chapter Four

4A

For a century and a half, Nahum Tate's 1681 version held the stage as 'the' *King Lear*. It is now out of print, and even more out of mind. I reproduce its first act, the better to notice by contrast the original's mercurial effects.

Tate keeps the tone more steady, and the direction of our sympathies more straightforward, by dispensing with the Fool and excising both Gloucester's speech about 'these late eclipses' and Edmund's trenchantly moral dismissal of such superstition as an excuse for irreponsibility. The dramatic rhythm and dynamics are equally straightforward, with 'big numbers' at the act's start (Edmund's soliloquy – rewritten) and end (Lear's curse). Shakespeare prefers to begin and end both his first scene and the entire act with prose of deceptive casualness. He starts the big 'State occasion' scene with Gloucester gossiping about his bastard son, and winds the scene down from the curse to Cordelia spitting terse words at her sisters who then discuss what's just happened. Most strikingly the original Act I ends with an apparently inconsequential little scene in which Lear half chats to the Fool and half talks to himself. After an act in which he has always been yelling at top volume, and yelling that he's in the right, nothing could be more resounding than his blurted-out phrase here: 'I did her wrong'.

The History of King Lear

Act I.

Enter Bastard *solus.*

Bast.　THOU Nature art my Goddess, to thy Law
　　　　My Services are bound; why am I then
Depriv'd of a Son's Right, because I came not
In the dull Road that Custom has prescrib'd?
Why Bastard, wherefore Base, when I can boast
A Mind as gen'rous, and a Shape as true
As honest Madam's Issue? Why are we
Held Base, who in the lusty Stealth of Nature
Take fiercer Qualities than what compound
The scanted Births of the stale Marriage-bed;
Well then, legitimate *Edgar*, to thy Right
Of Law I will oppose a Bastard's Cunning.
Our Father's Love is to the Bastard *Edmund*
As to legitimate *Edgar*; with Success
I've practis'd yet on both their easy Natures:
Here comes the old Man chaf't with th' Information
Which last I forg'd against my Brother *Edgar*,
A Tale so plausible, so boldly utter'd,
And heightned by such lucky Accidents,
That now the slightest Circumstance confirms him,
And Base-born *Edmund* spight of Law inherits.

Enter Kent *and* Gloster.

Glost.　Nay, good my Lord, your Charity
O'er shoots it self to plead in his Behalf;
You are your self a Father, and may feel
The Sting of Disobedience from a Son
First-born and best-Belov'd: Oh Villain *Edgar*!

Kent.　Be not too rash, all may be Forgery,
And Time yet clear the Duty of your Son.

Glost.　Plead with the Seas, and reason down the
　　Winds,
Yet shall thou ne'er convince me, I have seen
His foul Designs through all a Father's Fondness:
But be this Light and thou my Witnesses,
That I discard him here from my Possessions,
Divorce him from my Heart, my Blood, and Name.

Bast.　It works as I cou'd wish; I'll shew my self.

Glost.　Ha! *Edmund!* welcome Boy; O *Kent!* see here
Inverted Nature, *Gloster's* Shame and Glory,
This By-born, the wild sally of my Youth,
Pursues me with all filial Offices,
Whilst *Edgar*, beg'd of Heaven, and born in Honour,
Draws Plagues on my white Head, that urge me still
To curse in Age the Pleasure of my Youth.

Nay, weep not, *Edmund*, for thy Brother's Crimes;
O gen'rous Boy! thou shar'st but half his Blood,
Yet lov'st beyond the Kindness of a Brother:
But I'll reward thy Vertue. Follow me.
My Lord, you wait the King, who comes resolv'd
To quit the Toils of Empire, and divide
His Realms amongst his Daughters; Heaven succeed
    it;
But much I fear the Change.
   Kent.   I grieve to see him
With such wild Starts of Passion hourly seiz'd,
As render Majesty between itself.
   Glost.   Alas! 'tis the Infirmity of his Age,
Yet has his Temper even been unfixt,
Chol'rick and sudden; hark, They approach
                       [*Exeunt* Gloster *and* Bastard
Flourish.   *Enter* Lear, Cornwall, Albany, Burgundy,
   Edgar, Goneril, Regan, Cordelia, Edgar *speaking to*
   Cordelia *at Entrance.*
   Edgar.   *Cordelia*, Royal Fair, turn yet once more,
And e'er successful *Burgundy* receive
The Treasure of thy Beauties from the King,
E'er happy *Burgundy* for ever fold Thee,
Cast back one pitying Look on wretched *Edgar*.
   Cord.   Alas! What wou'd the wretched *Edgar* with
The more unfortunate *Cordelia*?
Who in Obedience to a Father's Will
Flies from her *Edgar's* Arms to *Burgundy's*?
   Lear.   Attend my Lords of *Albany* and *Cornwall*,
With Princely *Burgundy*.
   Alb.   We do, my Liege.
   Lear.   Give me this Map——Know, Lords, we have
    divided
In Three, our Kingdom, having now resolv'd
To disengage from Our long Toil of State,
Conferring All upon your younger Years;
You *Burgundy*, *Cornwall* and *Albany*,
Long in our Court have made your amorous sojourn,
And now are to be answer'd.—Tell me, my Daughters,
Which of you loves us most, that we may place
Our largest Bounty with our largest Merit.
Goneril, Our Eldest-born, speak first.
   Gon.   Sir, I do love you more than Words can utter,
Beyond what can be valu'd Rich, or Rare;
Nor Liberty, nor Sight, Health, Fame, or Beauty,
Are half so dear, my Life for you were vile,
As much as Child can love the best of Fathers.
   Lear.   Of all these Bounds, e'en from this Line to this,

With shady Forests, and wide-skirted Meads,
We make thee Lady; to thine and *Albany's* Issue
Be this perpetual.——What says our Second Daughter?
    Edg.   My Sister, Sir, in Part, exprest my Love.
For such as Hers, is mine, though more extended;
Sense has no other Joy that I can relish,
I have my All in my dear Liege's Love.
    Lear.   Therefore to thee and thine Hereditary
Remain this ample Third of our fair Kingdom.
    Cord.   Now comes my Trial, how am I distrest,
                                               [*Aside*
That must with cold Speech tempt the Chol'rick King
Rather to leave me Dowerless, then condemn me
To loath'd Embraces.
    Lear.   Speak now Our last, not least in Our dear Love,
So ends my Task of State,——*Cordelia*, speak?
What canst thou say to win a richer Third
Than what thy Sisters gain'd?
    Cord.   Now must my Love, in Words, fall short of
       theirs,
As much as it exceeds in Truth,——Nothing, my Lord.
    Lear.   Nothing can come of Nothing, speak agen.
    Cord.   Unhappy am I that I can't Dissemble,
Sir, as I ought I love your Majesty,
No more, nor less.
    Lear.   Take heed, *Cordelia.*
Thy Fortunes are at stake, think better on't,
And mend thy Speech a little.
    Cord.   O my Liege!
You gave me Being, Bred me, dearly love me,
And I return my Duty as I ought;
Obey you, Love you, and most Honour you;
Why have my Sisters Husbands, if they love you All?
Haply when I shall wed, the Lord whose Hand
Shall take my Plight, will carry half my Love;
For I shall never marry like my Sisters,
To love my Father All.
    Lear.   And goes thy Heart with this?
'Tis said that I am Chol'rick, Judge me, Gods,
Is there not cause? Now Minion, I perceive
The Truth of what has been suggested to us;
Thy Fondness for the Rebel Son of *Gloster*,
False to his Father, as Thou art to my Hopes:
And, oh! take heed, rash Girl, lest we comply
With thy fond Wishes, which thou wilt too late
Repent; for know our Nature cannot brook
A Child so young, and so Ungentle.
    Cord.   So Young, my Lord, and True.

Lear.   Thy Truth then be thy Dow'r;
For by the sacred Sun, and solemn Night,
I here disclaim all my paternal Care,
And from this Minute hold thee as a Stranger,
Both to my Blood and Favour.
    Kent.   This is Frenzy.
Consider, good my Liege,——
    *Lear.*Peace, *Kent*;
Come not between a Dragon and his Rage;
I lov'd her most, and in her tender Trust
Design'd to have bestow'd my Age at Ease:
So be my Grave my Peace, as here I give
My Heart from her, and with it all my Wealth:
My Lords of *Cornwall*, and of *Albany*,
I do invest you jointly in full Right
In this fair Third, *Cordelia's* forfeit Dow'r.
Mark me, my Lords, observe our last Resolve,
Our Self, attended with an hundred Knights,
Will make Abode with you in monthly Course;
The Name alone of King remain with me,
Yours be the Execution and Revenues;
This is our final Will; and to confirm it,
This Coronet part between you.
    Kent.   Royal *Lear*,
Whom I have ever honour'd as my King,
Lov'd as my Father, as my Master follow'd,
And, as my Patron, thought on in my Prayers,——
    Lear.   Away, the Bow is bent, make from the Shaft.
    Kent.   No, let it fall and drench within my Heart,
Be *Kent* unmannerly when *Lear* is mad;
Thy youngest Daughter——
    Lear.   On thy Life no more.
    Kent.   What wilt thou doe, old Man?
    Lear.   Out of my Sight.
    Kent.   See better first.
    Lear.   Now by the God,——
    Kent.   Now by the Gods, rash King, thou swear'st in
vain.
    Lear.   Ha, Traytour!
    Kent.   Do, kill thy Physician *Lear*;
Strike thro' my Throat, yet with my latest Breath
I'll Thunder in thine Ear my just Complaint,
And tell Thee to thy Face that Thou dost ill.
    Lear.   Hear me, rash Man; on thy Allegiance hear me;
Since thou hast striv'n to make Us break our Vow,
And prest between our Sentence and our Pow'r,
Which nor our Nature, nor our Place can bear,
We banish thee for ever from our Sight

And Kingdom; if when three Days are expir'd,
Thy hated Trunk be found in our Dominions,
That Moment is thy Death; Away.
    Kent.   Why fare thee well, King; since thou art
      resolv'd,
I take thee at thy Word, and will not stay,
To see Thy Fall: The Gods protect the Maid
That truly thinks, and has most justly said.
Thus to new Climates my old Truth I bear,
Friendship lives hence, and Banishment is here.   [*Exit.*
    Lear.   Now, *Burgundy*, you see her Price is faln,
Yet if the Fondness of your Passion still
Affects her as she stands, Dow'rless, and lost
In our Esteem, she's your's; take her, or leave her.
    Burg.   Pardon me, Royal *Lear*, I but demand
The Dow'r yourself propos'd, and here I take
Cordelia by the Hand, Dutchess of *Burgundy*.
    Lear.   Then leave her, Sir, for by a Father's Rage
I tell you all her Wealth. Away.
    Burg.   Then, Sir, be pleas'd to charge the Breach
Of our Alliance on your own Will,
Not my Inconstancy.   *Exeunt.*
            Manent Edgar *and* Cordelia.
    Edg.   Has Heaven then weigh'd the Merit of my Love,
Or is't the Raving of my sickly Thought?
Cou'd *Burgundy* forgo so rich a Prize,
And leave her to despairing *Edgar's* Arms?
Have I thy Hand *Cordelia*? Do I clasp it?
The Hand that was this Minute to have join'd
My hated Rival's? Do I kneel before thee,
And offer at thy Feet my panting Heart?
Smile, Princess, and convince me; for as yet
I doubt, and dare not trust the dazling Joy.
    Cord.   Some Comfort yet, that 'twas no vicious Blot
That has depriv'd me of a Father's Grace,
But meerly want of that which makes me Rich
In wanting it; a smooth professing Tongue:
O Sisters! I am loth to call your Fault
As it deserves; but use our Father well,
And wrong'd *Cordelia* never shall repine.
    Edg.   O heav'nly Maid! that art thyself thy Dow'r,
Richer in Vertue than the Stars in Light,
If *Edgar's* humble Fortunes may be grac't
With thy Acceptance, at thy Feet he lays 'em.
Ha, my *Cordelia!* dost thou turn away?
What have I done t' offend thee?
    Cord.   Talk't of Love.
    Edg.   Then I've offended oft, *Cordelia* too

Has oft permitted me so to offend.

   Cord.   When, *Edgar*, I permitted your Addresses,
I was the darling Daughter of a King,
Nor can I now forget my Royal Birth,
And live dependant on my Lover's Fortune;
I cannot to so low a Fate submit;
And therefore study to forget your Passion,
And trouble me upon this Theam no more.

   Edg.   Thus Majesty takes most State in Distress!
How are we tost on Fortune's fickle Flood!
The Wave that with surprizing Kindness brought
The dear Wreck to my Arms, has snatcht it back,
And left me mourning on the barren Shoar.

   Cord.   This baseness of th' ignoble *Burgundy*. [*Aside.*
Draws just Suspicion on the Race of Men;
His Love was Int'rest, so may *Edgar's* be,
And He, but with more Complement, dissemble;
If so, I shall oblige him by denying:
But if his Love be fixt, such constant Flame
As warms our Breasts, if such I find his Passion,
My Heart as grateful to his Truth shall be,
And Cold *Cordelia* prove as kind as He.   [*Exit*

Enter Bastard hastily.

   Bast.   Brother, I've found you in a lucky Minute,
Fly and be safe, some Villain has incens'd
Our Father against your Life.

   Edg.   Distrest *Cordelia!* but oh! more Cruel.

   Bast.   Hear me, Sir, your Life, your Life's in danger.

   Edg.   A Resolve so sudden
And of such black Importance!

   Bast.   'Twas not sudden,
Some Villain has of long Time laid the Train.

   Edg.   And yet perhaps 'twas but pretended Coldness,
To try how far my Passion would pursue.

   Bast.   He hears me not; wake, wake, Sir.

   Edg.   Say ye, Brother?——
No Tears, good *Edmund*, if thus bring'st me Tidings
To strike me dead, for Charity delay not,
That Present will befit so kind a Hand.

   Bast.   Your Danger, Sir, comes on so fast,
That I want Time t' inform you; but retire
Whilst I take Care to turn the pressing Stream.
O Gods! For Heav'n's Sake, Sir.

   Edg.   Pardon me, Sir, a serious Thought
Had seiz'd me, but I think you talkt of Danger,
And wisht me to retire; Must all our Vows
End thus?—Friend, I obey you.—O *Cordelia*.   [*Exit.*

   Bast.   Ha! ha! fond Man, such credulous Honesty

Lessens the Glory of my Artifice;
His Nature is so far from doing Wrongs,
That he suspects none: If this Letter speed,
And pass for *Edgar's*, as himself wou'd own
The Counterfeit, but for the foul Contents,
Then my Designs are perfect.——Here comes *Gloster*.

Enter Gloster

   Glost.   Stay, *Edmund*, turn; What Paper were you reading?
   Bast.   A Trifle, Sir.
.*Glost.*   What needed then that terrible Dispatch of it
Into your Pocket? Come, produce it, Sir.
   Bast.   A Letter from my Brother, Sir, I had
Just broke the Seal, but knew not the Contents;
Yet, fearing they might prove too blame,
Endeavour'd to conceal it from your Sight.
   Glost.   'Tis *Edgar's* Character.   [*Reads.*

     This Policy of Fathers is intollerable, that keeps our
        Fortunes from us 'till Age will not suffer us to
        enjoy 'em; I am weary of the Tyranny: Come to
        me, that of this I may speak more. If our Father
        would sleep 'till I wak't him, you should enjoy
        half his Possessions, and live belov'd of your
        Brother Edgar.

Sleep 'till I wak't him! you shou'd enjoy
Half his Possessions!——*Edgar* to write this
'Gainst his indulgent Father! Death and Hell!
Fly, *Edmund*, seek him out, wind me into him,
That I may bite the Traytor's Heart, and fold
His bleeding Entrails on my vengeful Arm.
   Bast.   Perhaps 'twas writ, my Lord, to prove my
     Vertue.
   Glost.   These late Eclipses of the Sun and Moon
Can bode no less; Love cools, and Friendship fails,
In Cities Mutiny, in Countrys Discord,
The Bond of Nature crackt 'twixt Son and Father:
Find out the Villain; do it carefully,
And it shall lose thee Nothing.   [*Exit.*
   Bast.   So now my Project's firm; but to make sure
I'll throw in one Proof more and that a bold one;
I'll place old *Gloster* where he shall o're-hear us
Confer of this Design; whilst, to his thinking,
Deluded *Edgar* shall accuse himself.
Be Honesty my Int'rest, and I can
Be Honest too: And what Saint so Divine,
That will successful Villany decline?   [*Exit*

Enter Kent *disguis'd.*

   Kent.   Now banisht *Kent*, if thou canst pay thy Duty
In this Disguise, where thou dost stand condemn'd,

Thy Master *Lear* shall find thee full of Labours.

Enter Lear *attended.*

Lear. In there, and tell our Daughter we are here.
Now, What art thou?

Kent. A Man, Sir.

Lear. What dost thou profess, or wou'dst with us?

Kent. I do profess to be no less than I seem, to serve
him truly that puts me in Trust, to love him that's
honest, to converse with him that's wise and speaks
little, to fight when I can't choose; and to eat no Fish.

Lear. I say, what art Thou?

Kent. A very honest-hearted Fellow, and as poor as
the King.

Lear. Then art thou poor indeed.——What canst
thou do?

Kent. I can keep honest Counsel, marr a curious Tale
in the Telling, deliver a plain Message bluntly; that
which ordinary Men are fit for, I am qualified in; and
the best of me is Diligence.

Lear. Follow me; thou shalt serve me.

Enter one of Goneril's *Gentlemen.*

Now, Sir?

Gent. Sir——   [*Exit:* Kent *runs after him.*

Lear. What says the Fellow? Call me the Clatpole
back.

Att. My Lord, I know not; but methinks your
Highness is entertained with slender Ceremony.

Servant. He says, my Lord, your Daughter is not well.

Lear. Why came not the Slave back when I call'd
him?

Serv. My Lord, he answered me i' th' surliest Manner,
That he wou'd not.

Re-enter Gentleman *brought in by* Kent.

Lear. I hope our Daughter did not so instruct him.
Now, who am I, Sir?

Gent. My Lady's Father.

Lear. My Lord's Knave.——   [*Strikes him.*

Goneril *at the Entrance.*

Gent. I'll not be struck, my Lord.

Kent. Nor tript neither, thou vile Civit-box.

[Strikes up his Heels.

Gon. By Day and Night; this is insufferable,
I will not bear it.

Lear. Now, Daughter, why that Frontlet on?
Speak, do's that Frown become our Presence?

Gon. Sir, this licentious Insolence of your Servants
Is most unseemly, hourly they break out
In Quarrels bred by their unbounded Riots,

I had fair hope by making this known to you,
To have had a quick Redress, but find too late
That you protect and countenance their Outrage;
And therefore, Sir, I take this Freedom, which
Necessity makes discreet.
    Lear.   Are you our Daughter?
    Gon.   Come, Sir, let me entreat you to make use
Of your Discretion, and put off betimes
This Disposition that of late transforms you
From what you rightly are.
    Lear.   Does any here know me? Why, this is not *Lear*;
Do's *Lear* walk thus? Speak thus? Where are his Eyes?
Who is it that can tell me who I am?
    Gon.   Come, Sir, this Admiration's much o' th' Savour
Of other your new Humours; I beseech you,
To understand my Purposes aright;
As you are old, you shou'd be staid and wise:
Here do you keep an hundred Knights and Squires,
Men so debaucht and bold, that this our Palace
Shews like a riotous Inn, a Tavern, Brothel;
Be then advised by her that else will take
That which she begs, to lessen your Attendance,
Take half away, and see that the Remainder
Be such as may befit your Age, and know
Themselves and You.
    Lear.   Darkness and Devils!
Saddle my Horses, call my Train together;
Degenerate Viper, I'll not stay with Thee!
I yet have left a Daughter.——Serpent, Monster!
Lessen my Train and call 'em riotous?
All Men approv'd, of choice and rarest Parts
That each Particular of Duty know.——
How small, *Cordelia*, was thy Fault? O *Lear*,
Beat at this Gate that let thy Folly in,
And thy dear Judgment out; Go, go, my People.
              Going off meets Albany *entring.*
Ingratefull Duke, was this your Will?
    Alb.   What, Sir?
    Lear.   Death! fifty of my Followers at a Clap!
    Alb.   The Matter, Madam?
    Gon.   Never afflict yourself to know the Cause,
But give his Dotage Way.
    Lear.   Blasts upon thee,
Th' untented Woundings of a Father's Curse
Pierce ev'ry Sense about thee; old fond Eyes,
Lament this Cause again, I'll pluck ye out,
And cast ye with the Waters that ye lose
To temper Clay.——No, *Gorgon*, thou shalt find

That I'll resume the Shape which thou dost think
I have cast off for ever.
   Gon.   Mark ye that.
   Lear.   Hear Nature!
Dear Goddess hear; and if thou dost intend
To make that Creature Fruitful, change thy Purpose;
Pronounce upon her Womb the Barren Curse,
That from her blasted Body never spring
A Babe to honour her;—But if she must bring forth,
Defeat her Joy with some distorted Birth,
Or monst'rous Form, the Prodigy o' th' Time;
And so perverse of Spirit, that it may live
Her Torment as 'twas born, to fret her Cheeks
With constant Tears, and wrinkle her young Brow.
Turn all her Mother's Pains to Shame and Scorn,
That she may curse her Crime too late, and feel
How sharper than a Serpent's Tooth it is
To have a thankless Child: Away, away.   [*Exit cum suis.*
   Gon.   Presuming thus upon his numerous Train,
He thinks to play the Tyrant here, and hold
Our Lives at Will.
   Alb.   Well, you may bear too far.   [*Exeunt.*
                    End of the First Act.

4B

'All is lost!' – Antony's speech in IV, xii. This is Dryden's version, in which all is indeed lost:

                              My eyes
Are open to her falsehood; my whole life
Has been a golden dream of love and friendship;
But, now I wake, I'm like a merchant roused
From soft repose to see his vessel sinking,
And all his wealth cast o'er. Ingrateful woman!
Who followed me but as the swallow summer,
Hatching her young ones in my kindly beams,
Singing her flatteries to my morning wake;
But now my winter comes, she spreads her wings,
And seeks the spring of Caesar.
                          (Act V, 203–13)

Chapter Five

Gender, Genre, Grabbing

I

How tedious is a guilty conscience, as the Cardinal in Webster's *Duchess of Malfi* puts it. The most anti-moralising critic becomes pious, even priggish, about the Treatment of Women, as we saw just now with Holderness on Hotspur; while the Hotspur-like irreverence of Malcolm Evans turns solemn once he reminds himself that 'with the emergence of a feminist Shakespeare criticism from the mid-1970s on, the text's representations of gender . . . have become a major topic for investigation' (Evans, 1986: 164).

Bradley opened the last section of his lecture on *Antony and Cleopatra* by observing that 'to reserve a fragment of an hour for Cleopatra, if it were not palpably absurd, would seem an insult. If only one could hear her own remarks upon it!' (Signet, 1983: 235). I can imagine the comments of those who write feminist criticism at being relegated to my final chapter. Why do I not, in modern jargon, prioritise them or it?

The question needs a practical context. At a stage in their work with Shakespeare corresponding to the point at which this present chapter appears in the book, students (whether school or university) will have explored some such cross-section of plays as that which my previous chapters have analysed. They will now be ready to try out their confidence and curiosity on some overarching topic. This will typically be in a lightly supervised, independently planned 'long essay', or even in an MA dissertation. And the topic is nowadays very likely to be The Representation of Gender, or Genre-Distinctions, or the activity of Appropriation to which I give the grosser name of

Grabbing. Should the 'light supervisor' stand back and watch – grossly gape on, as Iago puts it – or recommend critical reading that may offer stimulus? And also warn them of intellectual quagmires, dead ends of moral indignation and critical false friends that have often stunted the development of previous years' essays? With Gender, these questions will be especially difficult for a male teacher when most literature students are women. This is the context of my comments on those who write feminist criticism, and of my question, why do I not prioritise them or it?

That last phrase, 'them or it', gives the start of a reason, for it indicates another instance of Heads They Win, Tails You Lose. Suggest that there's only ever criticism, good, bad or indifferent, and you're advised of an emergent body of specifically feminist criticism. Offer to appraise it and with one bound it is free; you're reminded that it is protean, advised that 'it can only be defined by the multiplicity of critical practices engaged in by feminists' (McLuskie, 1985: 88; cf. Lenz *et al.*, 1983: 3).

At the same time no variety, never mind multiplicity, is acknowledged in earlier, male-dominated criticism. And out of this contradiction arises my coolness.

While I question whether criticism by women has yet brought special insights, I fully recognise its specific point of origin. This point is that, in Graham Holderness's words, 'the feminist intellectual not only identifies patriarchal structures in past literature and history, but is also writing out of a cultural situation in which contemporary structures and institutionalized inequality bear directly on her' (Holderness, 1992: 40). Perhaps Holderness is right to conclude that 'her utterance is therefore inevitably polemical, tendentious, political' (*ibid.*). My own reflection is that justified grievance and crusading fervour confer no monopoly of virtue or automatic advantage in perceptiveness. In practice, to avoid being a cosseted hothouse growth, feminist criticism needs to co-operate or compete in the open with the best of previous criticism, swallowing the bitter pill that (for admittedly shameful historical reasons) it was written almost exclusively by men. But feminists have in fact dismissed the whole body of previous criticism with generalising scorn and imperceptive impatience.[1] The effect is to rob students of their intellectual birthright.

In a much-celebrated sustained attempt at open engagement, L. T. Fitz seeks to characterise the persistent attitudes of male critics to *Antony and Cleopatra*. But in her polemical incaution she even says they prefer Octavia to Cleopatra! The accuracy of her attempts at paraphrase may be gauged from her diagnosis of male critics' 'overemphasis on Octavia . . . as a viable alternative to Cleopatra'; so that 'Bradley complains bitterly of Antony's mistreatment of Octavia' (Fitz, 1977: 301–2). Her footnote refers us to what Bradley actually says:

> He [Antony] is in some respects unscrupulous; and while it would be unjust to regard his marriage exactly as if it were one in private life, we resent his treatment of Octavia, whose character Shakespeare was obliged to leave a mere sketch, lest our feeling for the hero and heroine should be too much chilled. Yet, for all this, we sympathise warmly with Antony, are greatly drawn to him, and are inclined to regard him as a noble nature half spoiled by his time. (Signet, 1988: 231)

Note also that Bradley speaks of 'the hero and heroine'; whereas Fitz claims all male critics privilege Antony over Cleopatra. And why? – they fear her with 'an intemperance of language, and intensity of revulsion' (Fitz, 1977: 298). This hardly fits Bradley, who picks up the play's idea that she is a person 'whom every thing becomes', who 'makes defect perfection': 'many unpleasant things can be said of Cleopatra', says Bradley, 'and the more that are said, the more wonderful she appears' (Bradley, 1988a: 236).

'How different, how very different from the home life of our own dear Queen!' – so some Victorian theatregoer is supposed to have said about the play. Bradley, lecturing only a few years after the dear Queen died, revelled in the difference. He points out that 'she lives for feeling. Her feelings are, so to speak, sacred, and pain must not come near her. Her body is exquisitely sensitive, and her emotions marvellously swift . . . She is strong and supple as a leopard' (*ibid.*, 237). This is hardly what Fitz calls 'a grudging or embarrassed tribute', or 'closet prurience' (Fitz, 1977: 303). But again, heads they win: Fitz complains about sexists ignoring her *mind.* Put her mind in your portrait and tails you lose, with accusations of a sexist attack on 'feminine wiles' (*ibid.*, 298ff.).

A related double-bind is that male critics must not presume to interpret women's experience, yet 'the persistent idea that Cleopatra cannot be understood . . . owes much to the notion that women in general are impossible for men to understand' – a notion that Fitz's polemic deems offensively mystificatory (*ibid.*, 315, 316).

'It is most revealing,' Fitz continues, 'to observe with whom Cleopatra has been compared . . . Lear? Macbeth? Othello? No, Cleopatra is compared only with female characters – Viola, Beatrice, Rosalind, Juliet' (*ibid.*, 298). So that Fitz would be even more outraged by Bradley's audacious, amusing and illuminating collocation: 'Cleopatra at times resembles (if I dare say it) Doll Tearsheet sublimated' (Bradley, 1988a: 238). But then Fitz might not be too happy to see Bradley propose this startling trio: 'Cleopatra stands in a group with Hamlet and Falstaff' (*ibid.*, 236). Bradley relishes the atmosphere of a public lecture to develop these comparisons with playful agility. But then, there's no appreciation by Fitz of play or agility in criticism. Witness her tonal deafness to Granville-Barker when he ironically entertains the spirit of Maecenas's praise of Octavia (Fitz, 1977: 302).

So much for Fitz's accuracy, never mind fairness. But her caricature has become gospel truth. It is she herself who invented the phrase 'feminine wiles', but by the time Evans (1986: 166) summarised her ('as Fitz shows . . .', 'as Fitz points out . . .') it is attributed to the critics she has caricatured.

Although it continues to be cited prominently and enthusiastically – Dollimore in 1990 called it 'especially telling' – Fitz's essay dates from 1977. One sign of the guilty male conscience about ten years later was the late 1980s 'New Revised Edition' of the Signet Shakespeares. The only changes to the originals of a quarter-century earlier are at the back: the addition of a survey of performances (a nod at what Gary Taylor called The New Histrionicism), and a token feminist essay. Or at least an essay by a woman; Janet Adelman on *Antony and Cleopatra*, for example, interestingly extends John Danby's interpretation quoted in my previous chapter but in no way reveals the specific form and pressure of a woman's viewpoint. Others hardly help the play's readers male or female, or help the cause of feminist criticism. Carol Neely simply champions the women of *The*

Winter's Tale against the men. The play's 'restorations are achieved by the rich presence and compelling actions of its women' (Signet, *Winter's Tale*, New Revised Edition, 1988: 217). 'They are witty and realistic whereas the men are solemnly fantastic; they are at ease with sex whereas the kings are uneasy about it' (*ibid.*, 221); and 'they take for granted change, difference, separation', whereas the men 'deny themselves the potency, regeneration, and continuity' (*ibid.*, 220), paralysing themselves in nostalgia 'for their innocent, pre-sexual boyhood' and friendship which, 'continued unchanged across time and space, is a protection against women, sex, change, and difference' (*ibid.*, 219). And for good measure, the men go in for 'exaggerated rhetoric and vapid generalisations' (*ibid.*, 224). Those who live in glass houses . . .

That I cannot but find this essay crude, and clumsily dependent on dated terms, will be clear from comparing Neely's comments with my own in the previous chapters. I find moving both Leontes's 'recoil' to his boyhood when 'looking on the lines/Of my boy's face' and Polixenes's portrait of his son's 'varying childness'. I see them as moments of release from the adult ego. Here is Neely: 'The Kings' intimacy with their sons is likewise defensive. They imagine their children as copies of themselves, extensions of their own egos, guarantees of their own innocence. Leontes repeatedly insists that his son is "like me" (I, ii, 129), and Polixenes describes his use of his son to regenerate himself' (*ibid.*, 220). So much for 'cur[ing] in me/ Thoughts that would thick my blood'. And I dwelt on the subtleties and graces of Florizel's description of Perdita (What you do . . .'); here is Neely's bloodless paraphrase of it and its context: 'Florizel . . . delights in her frankness, her beauty, her wit, in her "blood" which "looks out", and praises her unconventionally' (*ibid.*, 224).

To go on to the third of these plays discussed in my previous chapter which are most relevant to my present topic: Linda Bamber's essay selected for the New Signet *King Lear* makes explicit what is also the basis of Neely's. Who can a woman 'identify with' among the goodies and baddies – overbearing father, two wicked sisters and Cinderella Cordelia? Now if, looking on the lines of Fitz's survey, we scan male-dominated criticism of *Lear*, we find that a persistent note is that, in

Granville-Barker's words, 'it will be a fatal error to present Cordelia as a meek saint' (Granville-Barker, 1972, I: 303). This remark echoes Coleridge and Bradley, and pre-echoes most critics of the 1960s and 1970s. It is an equally recurrent habit of feminist criticism to see Cordelia – as 'constituted' by the play before feminist 'intervention' – being part of a black-and-white pattern in which 'the women in tragedy seem to split into two basic types: victims or monsters, "good" or "evil"'. Granted, that last quotation comes from 1980, in an anthology called *The Woman's Part* (Lenz *et al.*, 1980/3: 14), and most of the essays reprinted in the New Signets date back to then or earlier. But the same black-and-white motif persists in a 1985 essay still frequently cited as introducing a new sophistication: Kathleen McLuskie's 'The Patriarchal Bard: Feminist criticism and Shakespeare: *King Lear* and *Measure for Measure*' (in *Political Shakespeare*).

McLuskie is quick to dissociate herself from that strand of earlier feminist criticism which took the texts as 'unproblematically mimetic' (McLuskie, 1985: 89), and saw them as offering authorial attitudes and role models to be co-opted or deplored. Plays should be considered as the products of specific historical conditions – of an all-male 'entertainment industry' (*ibid.*, 92) and of an age without unproblematic ideas on 'the nature of woman' (*ibid.*, 91). These plays are best analysed as 'the sum of their dramatic devices' (*ibid.*, 92), and the feminist way forward is to 'pay attention . . . to the narrative, poetic and theatrical strategies which construct the plays' meanings and position the audience to understand their events from a particular point of view' (*ibid.*).

But the question of strategy is repeatedly begged by McLuskie's use of passive verbs. Thus with *King Lear* 'family relations in this play *are seen as* fixed and determined, and any movement within them *is portrayed as* a destructive reversal of rightful order' (*ibid.*, 98; my emphases, as in following quotations). I am prompted to echo Lady Macbeth's 'O, by whom?' McLuskie's next sentence reads: 'Goneril's and Regan's treatment of their father merely reverses existing patterns of rule and *is seen* not simply as cruel and selfish but as a fundamental violation of human nature – as *is made* powerfully explicit in the speeches which condemn them (III, vii, 101–3; IV, ii, 32–50).' Look up those passages cited, in order to demystify McLuskie's passive constructions by converting them into active verbs with subjects, and you find that in the first a servant condemns Regan only as another has just condemned 'this man' Cornwall. Albany speaks the second passage cited – and in keeping with the play's mobility, Goneril gets in some cutting retorts. But then McLuskie is able to pass off Lear, even in the scene at Dover (IV, vi) that surely damns him in comparison with Gloucester, as a reliable reflector of the play's ideology: 'when Lear in his madness fantasises . . . women's lust *is vividly represented* as the centre and source of the ensuing corruption' (*ibid.*, 99). He is a reliable spokesman because for McLuskie he is presented as a totally sympathetic figure: she believes in 'the transfer of our sympathy back to Lear in the middle of the action. The long sequence of Act II, scene iv dramatises the process of Lear's decline from the angry autocrat of Act I to the appealing figure of pathetic insanity' (*ibid.*, 100). Thus 'the audience's sympathies are engaged by Lear's fury at the insult offered by Kent's imprisonment and by the bathos of Lear's belated attempt at self control (II, iv, 101–4)'; and are further 'secured by his sarcastic enactment [by kneeling and begging] of the humility which his daughters recommend', and by his 'great poetic appeal: "O reason not the need . . ."' (*ibid.*).

Ryan (1989: 45) complains that Knight's essay on '*King Lear* and the Comedy of the Grotesque' has been 'relentlessly reprinted'. He and other 1980s critics, including McLuskie, have got their revenge by leaving it remorselessly unread. But Knight's view of the see-saw, the gingerly balance of our reactions, is much closer to what has long been the prevailing current of interpretation than McLuskie's claim about 'our' one-sided sympathies. That claim involves, of course, selective quotation. She jumps on the 'gendered terms' of Lear's appeal to the gods in his speech 'O reason not the need', but not the near-comic impotence of 'I will have such revenges . . . What they are yet I know not, but . . .' – unless this is covered by her reference to the speech's 'movement from argument to desperate assertion of his crumbling humanity' (McLuskie, 1985: 100).

Not only does McLuskie act innocent of the knowledge of Knight, she seems to be writing about a version of the play that is nearer Nahum Tate's than Shakespeare's. Having offered this simple account of what she claims to be the inherent strategies of the text, McLuskie's own strategy is to produce out of a hat all the elements we've always known about, and to claim feminist credit for discovering them by reading enterprisingly against the grain of the text and its 'reproduction' in performance and criticism. 'The text is tied to misogynist meaning only if it is reconstructed with its emotional power and its moral imperatives intact. Yet the text contains possibilities for subverting these meanings and the potential for reconstructing them in feminist terms' (*ibid.*, 103). So we are startled to realise that II, iv 'could be directed to indicate that the daughters' power over Lear is the obverse of his former power over them'! 'Further potential for comically undermining the focus on Lear is provided by the Fool'! And 'even Cordelia's self-denying love or Gloucester's stoic resignation are denied the status of ideological absolutes'; for instance, 'the grotesque comic lie of Gloucester's fall from Dover cliffs is hardly a firm basis for a belief in the saving power of divine providence'! (*ibid.*, 105–6) As Dr Johnson said in another context, 'surely a man of no very comprehensive search may venture to say that he has heard all this before' – man or, may I venture to say, a woman (Johnson, 1968, II: 227).

'Either you are ignorant, or seem so craftily; and that's not good,' Angelo says to Isabella. When McLuskie refers to 'the extrusion of Gloucester's eyes' (McLuskie, 1985: 103), she may or may not be aware of reproducing Johnson's unforgettably idiosyncratic phrase, which flinches into a near-euphemistic Latinism from the intolerable scene. When, in my previous quotation from her, she speaks of 'the grotesque comic lie of Gloucester's fall', we must conclude that she knows full well Wilson Knight's essay on '*King Lear* and the Comedy of the Grotesque' (in which the suicide fiasco is a prime exhibit), and therefore knows there had been no consensus among male critics to privilege either of the play's patriarchs. Yet in one vital respect McLuskie's eventual reading does differ from the longstanding one of which Knight's is simply an extreme statement. What for most critics overlap or blend are for McLuskie in conflict. She speaks of dialectic: 'a production of the text which would restore the element of dialectic, removing the privilege both from the character of Lear and from the

ideological positions he dramatises, is crucial to a feminist
critique' (*ibid.*, 106). But what she produces is dualism. Thus
'any dispassionate analysis of the mystification of real socio-
sexual relations in *King Lear* is the antithesis of our response to
the tragedy in the theatre' (*ibid.*, 100). When Lear enters with
dead Cordelia in his arms 'the most stony-hearted feminist could
not withhold her pity' even though it is at the expense of her
ideological resistance (*ibid.*, 102). The dualism of response is
still there even when ideologically objectionable elements are
counterbalanced, for 'such a production of meaning [as her
reformed reading proposes] offers the pleasure of understanding
in place of the pleasure of emotional identification' (*ibid.*, 105;
my emphasis). This insistence on the primacy of emotional
identification, and on the separateness of emotional and
intellectual responses, links McLuskie despite herself with such
earlier feminists as Neely and Bamber. Is this the common
element of women's criticism which (in McLuskie's own echo of
Shakespeare) 'bears the form and pressure of their own world'
(*ibid.*, 92)? Certainly it contrasts with the common denominator
of the diverse male critics we have considered in this book –
Johnson, Coleridge, Granville-Barker, Weimann, as well as
Knight.

I will leave McLuskie and Lear with a point arising from
Lear's phrase about 'women's weapons, water drops', which
McLuskie leaps on as sexist. She speaks of Lear's 'crumbling
humanity' but thinks that 'that humanity is seen in gendered
terms' (*ibid.*, 100). But Lear crumbles *into* humanity, and out of
a belief in what his previous line calls 'noble anger'. That belief
was both self-righteous and a self-repressing form of the 'taboo
on tenderness'. Lear has not only believed that right, and the
gods, are on his side, he has resisted giving expression to his
feelings of both hurt and shame. He has resisted weeping,
attributing it – sexist pig as Shakespeare sees he is – to female
weakness or 'feminine wiles'. In I, iv he's ashamed at weeping
(ll. 296–304). In II, iv, as the storm sounds, 'this heart/ Shall
break into a hundred thousand flaws/ Or e'er I'll weep'.
Coriolanus has similar views on weeping: Macduff different ones
('I must also feel it as a man'). In each case, Shakespeare puts us
in mind of the value of weeping or the wrongness of resisting it.
But not too solemnly. No small part of the 'grotesque comedy' of

'O reason not the need . . .' is that the particular women Lear is addressing certainly have no need of, never mind temperamental inclination for, *those* weapons!

McLuskie can serve to introduce another aspect of feminist criticism: its interest in history. One reason for her article being frequently recommended as 'exemplary of an important trend in feminist criticism' (Dollimore, 1990: 417) is that it 'resisted any divorce between feminist theory and historical knowledge' (Holderness, 1992: 41; cf. Kamps 1991: 61 on her 'attack on ahistoricism'). On Shakespeare's theatre she reminds us of the basic facts: the plays 'were the products of an entertainment industry which, as far as we know, had no women shareholders, actors, writers or stagehands' (McLuskie, 1985: 92). On the position of women in Shakespeare's day she summarises the conflicting findings of a few historians, concluding that 'this discussion of social history . . . indicates that the text was produced within the contradictions of contemporary ideology and practice and suggests that similar contradictions exist within the play' (*ibid.*, 104). In the work of later critics, discussion of social history has amounted to little more than that. In weighing the recurrently cited handful of (dated, male) historians, not all have shown the caution of Holderness who speaks of 'those modern historiographical *attempts* to reconstruct the past', in which 'Christopher Hill *speaks of*' this and Lawrence Stone '*has argued for*' or '*believes*' that (Holderness, 1992: 85–6; my emphases). And even if one shares McLuskie's degree of trust in Hill, Stone and Laslett, one should face the problem that they do not concur in discerning contradictions in Shakespeare's age: they simply contradict one another.

At the start of her essay, McLuskie remarks that to the frequent question 'What exactly is feminist criticism?' the only effective reply is, 'I'll send you a booklist.' You'll see by now why my own list of recommendations must be short (see Appendix 5A). As for my foregoing negative comments, it can always be claimed that the life of feminist criticism escapes because of its 'multiplicity of critical practices' (see above, p. 197). But I've selected for comment those essays which are most recurrently recommended by my colleagues, most respectfully cited by later books and surveys, and which students are in any case most likely to pick up because they are especially accessible.

My practical warnings about these essays will be disputed, but should not be dismissed as *a priori* male prejudice. I have in other chapters given extended attention to two women if not feminist critics (Mahood and Ferguson); and I can appeal to the warnings by two others listed in the Appendix about feminist criticism in general (Minogue) and feminist Shakespeareans in particular (Thompson). In any case I'm far from proposing some kind of warfare between male and female critics, because in playing that game too often (making male = chauvinist *and* outdated) several influential female critics have had to suppress their memories of subtler critical essays from the past that happen to be written by men. The result is that, paradoxically and anachronistically, these feminists have been not only anticipated but so to speak superseded in advance by what they offer to go beyond.

genre in form of literary types not tragedy / comedy.

II

My comments on *King Lear* have reflected the twentieth-century wish to carry on with Johnson's good work against the Dramatic Unities and to break down the walls between tragedy and comedy. It will be recalled that I criticised New Historicists for neglecting the comedy in the history plays. And I touched on the humour of *Romeo and Juliet*, the tone and plot of which is nearer comedy until the death of Mercutio.

That last play compares the shades of romantic sincerity, affectation, hypocrisy and cynicism in a way that brings it nearer *As You Like It* or *Twelfth Night* than the later tragedies. But then those two near-turn-of-the-century comedies sometimes tilt over into the tone of those soon-to-follow tragedies. So that on Shakespeare's generic habits one can adapt Eliot's formulation of the 'English compromise' in respect of verse forms (quoted on p. 140). The plays constantly approximate to one distinct dramatic genre, and constantly edge away from it. That is why I felt no need to go out of my way to include any play conventionally labelled a comedy in the selection discussed in this book.

To explore the genre question further, I'll return to a (male) critic we sampled back in Chapter One. Tennenhouse's *Power on Display: The politics of Shakespeare's genres* (1986) reads all Shakespeare's plays, not least the ones we've just considered in relation to feminism, as primarily political in the sense that they continue 'Renaissance debates concerning the nature and origins of political power' (Tennenhouse, 1986: 2). This, he argues, has long been obscured by traditional ways of segregating the plays into dramatic genres. Thus 'the overwhelmingly popular tradition of reading looks at comedy as an utterly apolitical form. Simply because it is about love and courtship, it cannot by definition be political, so the argument goes' (*ibid.*, 3). Equally apolitical is the conventional approach to what are seen as 'the grand metaphysical tragedies of the Jacobean Shakespeare' (*ibid.*, 4).

Paradoxically these false generic distinctions within drama have been encouraged, Tennenhouse says, by a modern tendency to discount the true distinctions between poetic drama as a whole and other literary genres, particularly realist prose fiction. Thus *Antony and Cleopatra* is

> both the easiest and the most difficult of Shakespeare's tragedies for us to read. The language of the play translates so well into modern cultural terms that more than one critic has read the play as if it were a Renaissance version of a modern romance of the order of *Wuthering Heights*. For this very reason, it proves most difficult to understand this play in relation of the Jacobean tragedies and the poetics of display which gave them their form. The sexual relationship between Antony and Cleopatra displaces the political struggles within the Roman empire to the point where sexuality – at least from a modern perspective – appears to transcend politics in the play. Even the most dedicated historical critic feels hard pressed to think otherwise and therefore to maintain his or her concern for the vicissitudes of state power in this play. (*ibid.*, 142)

I will outline his case about that particular play before discussing at some length the general point about literary genre which is indicated by his reference to *Wuthering Heights*: that is, the dangers of confusing play with novel.

'This temptation to say the play is about love rather than

politics is a form of seduction which Shakespeare has built into
Antony and Cleopatra,' Tennenhouse continues. 'Contrary to
novelistic strategies, Shakespeare's drama sets up the possibility
of detaching sexuality from politics only to demonstrate the
preposterousness of thinking of the body this way' (*ibid.*, 143).
Here is a key half-paragraph for your consideration:

> In the Elizabethan plays, union with the aristocratic female is
> always a political act . . . But in Jacobean drama . . . the
> iconic bond between the aristocratic female and the body
> politic is broken. [The former now] has the potential to
> pollute. Nowhere is this clearer than with Cleopatra. [She] is
> Egypt. As such, however, she embodies everything that is not
> English according to the nationalism which developed under
> Elizabeth as well as . . . James. (*ibid.*, 144)

We may romanticise her but, 'in fact', 'the fact is' that she is
represented 'in much the same terms Bakhtin uses to identify the
grotesque – a popular body . . . with all the features of carnival'
(*ibid.*, 144). Popular – but not likely to seduce popular audiences
of the time. 'Any Jacobean audience', claims Tennenhouse's
'historical' trump card, 'would, I think, have recognized
instantly the nature of the delusion in Antony's offer to separate
politics and sexuality in his "let Rome in Tiber melt!"' (*ibid.*,
143–4). With their mind's eye on contemporary England,
audiences would have seen Rome, whatever its 'penury,
harshness, self-denial' (*ibid.*, 144), as the play's real hero. This
may be, if they shared Tennenhouse's view that at the end
Antony and Cleopatra are 'destroyed' and Cleopatra in
particular seen off with an 'elaborate scene of punishment'
which 'purges the world of all that is not Roman' (*ibid.*, 146).
And if they found that 'Shakespeare dwell[s] on the danger of
the offspring of Antony and Cleopatra' (*ibid.*, 145). In case
you'd blinked and missed this, it is Caesar who 'dwells on' it – for
a few lines (III, vi, 1–16). But *he* would, wouldn't he?
      Now back to Tennenhouse's general point, which deserves
more space, about the danger of confusing poetic drama and
prose fiction. It is a long-familiar point. Tennenhouse would
dislike many of Wilson Knight's 'Principles of Shakespeare
Interpretation', not least the claim that 'the "source" of *Antony*

and Cleopatra . . . is the transcendent erotic imagination of the poet' (Knight, 1989: 8). But he would be pleased with the accompanying comment that 'the older critics took psychological analysis to unnecessary lengths'. For Knight in 1930 the principal grey eminence among 'the older critics' was Bradley. But he partly rehabilitates Bradley in a 1947 Prefatory Note: 'my animadversions as to "character" analysis were never intended to limit the living human reality of Shakespeare's people. They were, on the contrary, expected to loosen, to render flexible and even fluid, what had become petrified. Nor was I at all concerned to repudiate the work of A. C. Bradley' (*ibid.*, v). More fully to Tennenhouse's taste, therefore, would be Terence Hawkes's survey of 'Shakespeare and the New Critical Approaches' which opens by asking 'what we mean by "old"', identifies it in 'the approach established by Bradley's monumental *Shakespearean Tragedy* of 1904', and calls this approach 'reductive' in that 'it scales emblematic, non-realist dramas down to the level of quasi-realistic portrait galleries of interesting human specimens: it turns the plays into second-rate novels' (Hawkes, 1986: 207–8).

In my discussion that follows, I am not concerned with the justice of that or other modern claims about the practice of 'older critics'. I want rather to get you thinking about the general issue – about differences and similarities between literary genres. What (to borrow Knight's phrases) is in danger of becoming petrified in present-day criticism is not the alleged old confusion of drama and novel but the new assumption of an absolute difference between them: this is what I'll try to loosen, to render flexible and even fluid.

A preliminary question is to ask how well Tennenhouse is in touch with his students. Judging from my own, 'the nineteenth-century novel' is not at all as familiar and 'transparent' a 'testament to the modern self' as he, datedly, thinks (Tennenhouse, 1986: 13). This is largely because 'the Novel' is an abstraction and all that students are confronted by are extremely diverse individual novels. I've found that a (not always easily won) ease with the procedures and assumptions of *Middlemarch* gets them nowhere with *Anna Karenin*, let alone *Wuthering Heights* or *Shirley*. (Equally, ease with one Shakespeare play doesn't guarantee it with others, or with the plays of, say,

Shirley.) Many elements – class system and geography as much as period gender relations – prevent any identification of these novels' characters with an unchanging reality or an essentialist self. And this defamiliarisation, rapidly increasing as the nineteenth century recedes ever further into the past, is extremely valuable.

But there's much more danger of students being unnecessarily put off Shakespeare by teachers overstressing the differences between plays and novels. This leads to regarding him as a special, separate, area (sanctified territory or otherwise). Let us look at three half-truths about that separation.

(1) Novels Tell: Plays Show

Frank Kermode, introducing the Signet *Winter's Tale* (xxii–xxiii), comments on a speech of Leontes to Camillo ('thus contempt and fear join with sexual disgust and an intolerable sense of his own indignity to crowd and crush the speech'), and invites us to 'measure it against the grave and by no means ill-written opening' of Shakespeare's source, Greene's *Pandosto* (see Appendix 5B). Kermode's own verdict is that Leontes 'is ablaze with the passion of which Greene merely speaks'. This sounds like an echo of Coleridge's remark that 'you seem to be *told* nothing, but to see and hear everything' – see above, p. 25. Now such particular comparisons are fair enough but shouldn't be used as the basis for any general claim that drama 'shows' and fiction 'tells'. Greene's tale isn't a nineteenth-century realist novel (more like a moral fable, and in narrati‧ e virtually devoid of novelistic dialogue). In any case Kermode cites only its generalising introduction; which is like judging *Middlemarch* by its manifesto-essay of a Prologue.

A distinction between showing and telling emerges more clearly from the comparison I sketched in Chapter One, between Richard's hollow-crown speech and a passage from Eliot's *Mill on the Floss*. And emerges more validly, provided we don't take that fictional excerpt as typical of the degree of tact with which Eliot or other novelists habitually use their directing power. The narrator tells us what to think of Maggie, whereas any suspicion of an equivalent pride-in-humility on the part of

Richard is left to surmise and to our speculative deduction from style, tone and context. A symptom of this Shakespeare abstention from 'telling' is that he is frugal with stage directions, none of them making a dead set at directing our interpretation of characters, and the majority incorporated into speeches. (In early work the effect can be heavy-handed, as with the scene-settings in *Richard II*: 'How far is it, my lord, to BERKELEY now?' – 'Believe me, noble lord,/ I am a stranger HERE IN GLOUCESTERSHIRE' and 'BARKLOUGHLY CASTLE CALL THEY THIS AT HAND?' – 'Yea, my lord' (II, iii, III, ii). More interestingly, the hollow-crown passage offers built-in directions that perhaps indicate character interpretation (histrionic traits?) simultaneously with stage instructions: 'For God's sake let us sit upon the ground', . . . and 'Cover your heads . . .' Later in the play this is more sustained, as in the scene where Richard tauntingly challenges Bolingbroke to 'seize' the crown and then compares it to a well (IV, i). Much later in Shakespeare's development, speeches are often little but strings of incorporated stage directions, cues for and/or reactions to a variety of stage business and props small or large, real or in the mind's eye of the speaker. Thus with Lear:

> There's your press-money. That fellow handles his bow like a crow-keeper; draw me a clothier's yard. Look, look, a mouse! Peace, peace, this piece of toasted cheese will do't. There's my gauntlet, I'll prove it on a giant. Bring up the brown bills. O, well flown, bird! i' th' clout, i' th' clout – hewgh! Give the word . . .
> When I do stare, see how the subject quakes. I pardon that man's life. What was thy cause?
>
> (IV, vi, 86–92, 108–9)

and:

> Where have I been? Where am I? Fair daylight?
> I am mightily abus'd . . . I know not what to say.
> I will not swear these are my hands. Let's see,
> I feel this pin prick . . .

(*Cordelia replies*): O, look upon me, sir,
And hold your hand in benediction o'er me.
No sir, you must not kneel.

                                        (IV, vii, 56–8)

and:

Pray you, undo this button. Thank you sir.
Do you see this? Look on her! Look her lips,
Look there, look there!

                                        (V, iii, 310–12)

Such passages (whether in prose or verse) go right out of the frame of reference set by Eliot with his sliding scale of oratory to ordinary speech, rhetoric to conversation.

There's a smart technical term for this element of dramatic writing: *deixis*. Hawkes's survey of new critical approaches gives a succinct summary: drama exploits the way that 'language itself performs actions'; *deixis* is 'the process whereby language establishes the context in which it is taking place and *deictics* are those words, such as the pronouns I and you and the adverbs here and now, whose meaning can only be pinned down by a specific context' (Hawkes, 1986: 294). This can obviously be related to many passages analysed in the present book, from York's or Capulet's twists and turns to Henry addressing Hal in terms of 'you' and 'I' versus 'him' and 'them'; from Hamlet's 'On *him*, on *him*! Look *you* . . . do not look on *me* . . . look *you there*, look how *it* steals away' to Leontes's 'many a man there is (even at this present, Now, while I speak this)' ('yes, you, sir, you in the second row: are you sure you know what your wife's up to while you sit here enjoying the play?') Perhaps this 'deictic thrust' (Hawkes's phrase) is what we should hear in Hamlet's 'Frailty, thy name is woman!' ('Yes, madam, you in the front row with the low-cut dress and inch-thick, knee-deep make-up: I mean *you* as well as the rest of your sort').

So, *deixis* is a speciality if not a monopoly of the drama. It needs a performance like that of Michael Hordern in the BBC *King Lear* to exploit it to the full, picking out and making the most of the implicit cues. Equally it takes an officious critic or an editor with a banal mind to 'make up for' Shakespeare's inexplicitness. Dover Wilson's inserted directions in *Hamlet – the King, very pale, totters to his feet* or *the Queen casts herself sobbing upon the couch* – impose an interpretation.[2] Granville-Barker (1972, I: 448) intrudes equally with the comment that Maecenas's tribute to Octavia's 'beauty, wisdom, modesty' is 'turned . . . to irony with Enobarbus' grimmest smile and shrug', where Shakespeare has the latter say and do nothing (apart from thanking Agrippa for inviting him to be his house guest!) Similarly officious offers to help out the neglectful bard occur in Sanders and Jacobson's *Shakespeare's Magnanimity*: as when they 'see' in *Macbeth* I, iii, 'trudging across' the heath, Banquo and Macbeth 'dwarfed and stoical' (Sanders and Jacobson, 1978: 62) such intrusive inventions are indeed intent on edging the plays towards the mode of novels – or, more often, novelettes.

So much for telling versus showing. Now for a second half-truth about novels and plays.

(2) Novels are Psychologically Realistic: Poetic Drama is Above that Sort of Thing

Or below it, according to the greatest of all novelists, Tolstoy.[3] There is, for instance, 'no possibility of finding any explanation of Hamlet's actions and speeches, and therefore no possibility of attributing any character to him'. So along comes the bardolatrous critic to announce that hereby 'a perfectly new and profound character is most powerfully presented: consisting in this, that the person has no character; and that in this absence of character lies an achievement of genius – the creation of a profound character', on whom commentators 'fill whole libraries' (Tolstoy, 1937: 351).

What alarms me is not Tolstoy's attack but the concessions made by Shakespeareans who have offered to reply. Motives are called trivial, as bones thrown to the rationalists in the audience to keep them occupied with something to chew on while the play proceeds uninterrupted with more important matters.[4]

More helpful would be an acknowledgement that human motivation is more complex than Tolstoy's essay, unlike his novels, seems to assume. If the play in question were not *Hamlet*, or *Lear* (Tolstoy's main example) but *The Winter's Tale*, a start might be made by pointing out that Shakespeare's treatment of jealousy accords with his novelistic source. *Pandosto* opens by announcing its view that jealousy is 'an infectious sore', almost defined by the very fact that unlike 'all other griefs' it refuses 'to be appeased with sensible persuasions, to be cured with wholesome counsel, to be relieved in want'. Furthermore this view, and Shakespeare's, accord with that of Tolstoy's own novel *Anna Karenin*. In Chapter Twenty-three of Part Seven, for instance, the jealous heroine, 'not having as yet an object for her jealousy', was on 'the look-out for one': 'being jealous made her quarrelsome, and she was constantly seeking grounds for her discontent'. 'Even in her partner's rare moments of tenderness . . . she saw a shade of complacency, of self-confidence', and his 'that's right!' about her packing for the country sounds offensively patronising. At one point she is 'ready to forget and forgive everything', but recalls a word of his that had upset her and 'she realized that in her attempt to regain her peace of mind she had only gone the round of the circle completed so often before'. When he explains an innocent reason for needing to delay departure, her partner is embarrassed because 'he felt Anna's eyes fixed on him suspiciously. His embarrassment confirmed her suspicions.' In all the circular mechanisms of groundless jealousy the novel echoes the play. (See Appendix 5C.)

More broadly, Tolstoy's essay complains at the 'inconsistency' of Shakespeare's characterisation. But people constantly surprise not only us but each other and themselves, in a novel as in a play. I want to give this ample space by using as springboard a critic who has written with equal admiration about Shakespeare's tragedies and Tolstoy's novels, John Bayley. On Tolstoy's dislike of Shakespeare, however, Bayley is misleading. The Russian, he says, 'commits the critical fault of attacking a work because it has not the *form* that he prefers, and refusing to understand the form in which it is actually written' (Bayley, 1966: 241–2). The novel form, and Tolstoy's temperament, Bayley goes on, stress characterisation: consistency within and differentiation between individuals. Whereas in a tragedy like *Lear*, Bayley maintains, whatever 'character differentiations that do appear' are 'burnt up in the total human reduction'. This is perhaps an echo of Yeats's distinction between comedy and tragedy, the latter bursting the dykes that separate man from man; and in Bayley's own image of burning up rather than bursting and drowning, there's a pre-echo of his own remark that the Shakespeare who wrote *Lear* 'could have understood and rendered Auschwitz in art: Tolstoy could have not' (*ibid.*, 243). Bayley points out a superficial similarity which turns into a fundamental difference:

> Strangely enough, the openings for *Lear* and *Anna* are by no means so different: we feel we know Gloucester as we know Stiva, but it would be unthinkable for Stiva to surrender his personality in some extraordinary metaphorical climax, to be blinded and driven to despair for his misdemeanours with governesses and ballet-girls. (*ibid.*, 242)

I find these comments suggestive but I think they stop short.

For although he adds that 'we never know where we are with the play' that 'it confounds our desire (which in Tolstoy had become an obsession) to see life steadily and whole' (*ibid.*, 242), Bayley himself is too anxious to know where he is, generically speaking: he makes too drastic a distinction between drama and fiction. The difference narrows with Anna ending up throwing herself under the train for less than 'misdemeanours'; or with Levin's recurring sense of meaninglessness; or with his brother Nikolai's self-destruction. And as for the notion that individual characters in novels are consistent, can't we apply equally to Tolstoy's novel Bayley's words about Shakespeare's play? – 'we never know where we are' in *Anna Karenin*, nor indeed do the characters themselves. At the end of Part One they all go home to their comfortingly familiar surroundings, routines, and standards: 'at home (Tolstoy says) the very walls are a support'. But they have brought home with them things that split those walls apart. And character consistency collapses – people do not know where they are with each other. Already at the ball 'the expression on Vronsky's face [as he dances with Anna] was one Kitty had never seen before', and conversely when 'Vronsky came up against her in the course of the mazurka he did not recognize her at first, so changed she was'. Later, a bewildered Karenin asks, 'Anna, is this you?', while conversely, further on, 'Anna, who thought she knew her husband so well, was amazed at his appearance' and 'in his walk, in his gestures, in the sound of his voice were such determination and firmness as his wife had never seen in him'. One could quote a score of such moments right through to Anna, not long before her suicide, looking in a mirror and asking 'Who is that? Why, it's me!'; or Vronsky, on his way to 'the total human reduction' of war, having a face 'aged and suffering, like a stone' – when he came back from seeing Anna's corpse, his own mother says, 'I shouldn't have recognized him'. So there's plenty in that novel to match the moment when Lear asks 'Who is it can tell me who I am?' and the Fool replies 'Lear's shadow'. It's essential to the effect of this novel that it contains those shocks and transformations as well as that element of circumstantial realistic detail which Nabokov admired – the fact that Tolstoy's trains run to true time and the jam recipes work.

Talk of train timetables and jam-making leads us to a third half-truth.

(3) Novels Thrive on Detail: Plays are Severely Selective

Indeed plays exclude too much, in the interests of a spurious dignity, argues D. H. Lawrence in an amusing, drastic version of this view. In a championing essay on 'The Novel' he claims that

> You can fool pretty well every other medium. You can make a poem pietistic, and it will still be a poem. You can write *Hamlet* in drama: if you wrote him in a novel, he'd be half-comic, or a trifle suspicious: a suspicious character like Dostoevsky's Idiot. Somehow, you sweep the ground a bit too clear in the poem or the drama, and you let the human Word fly a bit too freely. Now in the novel there's always a tom-cat, a black tom-cat that pounces on the white dove of the Word, if the dove doesn't watch it; and there is a banana-skin to trip on; and you know there is a water-closet on the premises. All these things help to keep the balance.[5]

But the excerpts from *Lear* we've inspected are full of mice and toasted cheese, buttons, people sweating in ravenous from hunting who want their dinner pronto, who joke about hard-boiled eggs, and who hourly carp and quarrel and trip each other up. While Gloucester prepares to end it all, people go fishing or harvest cliff-plants: Edgar's description of Dover cliff reminds me of W. H. Auden's observation that 'suffering . . . takes place/ While someone else is eating or opening a window or just walking dully along'. (See Appendix 5D.)

In the previous chapter we saw Weimann and Granville-Barker alike dwell on the circumstance and trivia in between what Lawrence called the musing and thundering. George Orwell goes further.[6] Shakespeare 'loved the surface of the earth' and everything 'that binds us to it'. Hence his 'irrelevancies', the 'products of excessive vitality' (one recalls Coleridge's comment that Shakespeare's wordplay resembles a man flourishing his walking-stick from excess of energy). And Orwell finds in old Tolstoy's impatience with the Fool (who 'runs like a trickle of sanity through the play') a sign that 'at bottom what he probably most dislikes is a sort of exuberance, a tendency to take – not so much a pleasure as simply an interest in the actual process of life'. For Tolstoy's 'main aim, in his later years, was to narrow the range of human consciousness' – to narrow it from the multiplicity and everyday-ness that kept breaking into his own novels earlier in his career and that keep breaking into *King Lear*. Incidentally, a great virtue of Orwell's essay is that, in Lawrence's phrase, it keeps the balance between three aspects of the play: its moral thrust, its haunting quality as tableau or as fable, and its 'belly-to-earth pleasure' in multifariousness.

III

Considerations of genre, as of gender, involve the question of what is nowadays called appropriation. 'Grabbing' is the word I chose to use in the title of this chapter, admittedly in order to enlist alliteration in tying those three topics together. But my word also cuts out the abstraction and politeness of the currently favoured term.

'Acquired for Clients' used to be a common sign over vacant lots of land, 'acquired' being an urbane word that suggested no wheeling-and-dealing or greenbacks changing hands. 'Appropriation' has a similar clean feel. 'The defulting company's funds were appropriated by the court' is nicer than 'seized', 'misappropriated' by employees nicer than 'nicked', 'pocketed' or 'grabbed'. Fine word, 'appropriate'!

Not that the word is always used unthinkingly or, as it were, amorally. Behind recent Shakespearean criticism lies Frank Kermode's classic essay on 'The Survival of the Classic' which replaces the ideas of unchanging greatness and unchanging human nature with a stress on the classics' adaptability, their 'accommodating' nature – 'an openness to accommodation which keeps them alive under endlessly varying dispositions'.[7] In his recent book on the accommodation of Shakespeare in the Augustan and Romantic periods, Jonathan Bate says that 'I endorse Kermode's view . . . but prefer the term "appropriation" because it suggests greater activity on the part of the appropriator – appropriation may slide into misappropriation – and because it has stronger political overtones than "accommodation"' (Bate, 1989: 5). And in her 1991 book on *The Appropriation of Shakespeare* Jean Marsden acknowledges that 'appropriation is neither dispassionate nor disinterested: it has connotations of usurpation, of seizure for one's own uses' (Marsden, 1991: 1).

But that axiom is nowadays applied without discrimination, so that in Marsden's words 'every act of interpretation is an act of appropriation', no less than are textual rewritings such as Tate's or Dryden's – which she calls the 'reinventing' or 'reconstruction of the works'; and no less than are 'advertisements that borrow Shakespeare'. So that *All for Love*, Bradley's lecture on *Antony and Cleopatra*, and a Stratford brewery's bardolatrous beermats all 'appropriate'.

In relating appropriation to the question of literary genre, Tennenhouse is more subtle and resistant. His central example in the Introduction to *Power on Display* is an episode in Charlotte Brontë's novel *Shirley* (Chapter Six) in which the middle-class heroine and her factory-owner friend read aloud and discuss *Coriolanus*. The scene shows 'both what procedures should be used to appropriate Shakespeare for middle-class culture and the very real political interests the reading of literature served' (Tennenhouse, 1986: 8). For example, the heroine appropriates the play to urge that her friend 'renounce one form of power – that which she associates with the imperiously patriarchal nature of Coriolanus – and adopt another one – that which she identifies as a benevolent form of paternalism' (*ibid.*, 9). She does this under cover of 'depoliticising' the play, offering it as the vehicle of perennial human truths.

And this, Tennenhouse argues, is precisely what *novels* are – or what critics make of them: the vicious circle is completed by the fact that Brontë is 'an author whom literary criticism has succeeded in depoliticising more than most' (*ibid.*, 7).

Tennenhouse's analysis hits home, not least because several critics he doesn't mention, including A. P. Rossiter and Wilbur Sanders, have taken at face value the heroine's ostensibly apolitical view of the play as designed not 'to operate like a sermon' but 'to stir you; to give you new sensations. It is to make you feel life strongly.' But isn't this stirring quality none the less one of the play's real attractions? Certainly Bertolt Brecht, the best-known dramatic adapter or 'reinventor' of *Coriolanus*, felt so in his Dialogue about the play.[8]

I end this last chapter with that Dialogue because it will pull together several strands of the present book. It discusses, of course, a play we haven't yet considered. But I've often found students are stimulated by ending a Shakespeare course by testing their confidence on an unfamiliar text. Here is a play which might be compared (in date, subject or style) with the earlier English Histories or the chronologically close *Macbeth* and *Antony and Cleopatra*, but which confounds many expectations based on them and not least in its opening scene on which Brecht concentrates.

D. H. Lawrence once wrote about the fruitful tension in art between 'the aspiration and the resistant', and he clearly detected in his own critical writings an equivalent tension between the urge to appropriate (he 'rewrote' the Wessex Novels in his 'Study of Hardy', it is sometimes said) and a respect for the stubborn otherness of the work being interpreted. In what Brecht actually did in his performances and adaptations of *Coriolanus* you'll find him intent, if not on grabbing Shakespeare for Marxist purposes, on relentlessly relating him to the mid-twentieth-century class struggle.[9] But the fun of the Dialogue derives from another struggle, between that political aspiration and the resistant play itself.

Under consideration by fictionalised versions of Brecht and his theatre colleagues is the opening scene, in which first the conciliatory if complacent patrician Menenius Agrippa and then the contemptuous and inflammatory Caius Martius (later titled Coriolanus) confront citizens rebelling at a food shortage. Who gets 'privileged' in this scene? In the Dialogue it is speaker 'B' who almost immediately gives a longish disquisition about 'how hard it is for the oppressed to become united'. But 'R' objects that 'I don't think you can find that in the text, just like that'. Not, B concedes, in just the first scene: 'quite right. You have got to read the whole play. You can't begin without having looked at the end.' But it's soon B's own turn to object. 'For the moment we are making an analysis. Go on,' he says to R, but he soon interrupts R's attempt at impartial description – one ought to be objective, but it's clearly impossible to give an objective description washed clean of interpretation. R ends by asking of their findings, 'Do you think that all this and the rest of it can be read in the play?' and B answers, 'Read in it and read into it.' Some introduced touches are indispensable stage projections of the text (the Tribunes entering with the Senators, easily overlooked 'because they got no welcome or greeting'). Others depend on the paucity of stage directions in the original text: could we have Marcius, with armed entourage, enter menacingly *earlier* than Agrippa's 'Hail, noble Marcius!'? This in turn suggests ways in which 'we can strengthen Shakespeare's text still further'. About one such intervention – making the newly-elected Tribune Sicinius act the role of First Citizen and thereby leader of the revolt – B soon has scruples: 'That's a major intervention.' W replies that 'there wouldn't have to be any change in the text'. B: 'All the same. A character has a kind of specific weight in the story.'

But what specific weight has each character; and what weight is given to individuated characterisation as against larger social contexts and issues? That last phrase of mine is woolly; this is Brecht's way of putting it:

P
We're talking about the people all the time. What about the hero? He wasn't even at the centre of R's summary of the content.

R
The first thing shown is a civil war. That's something too interesting to be mere background preparation for the entrance of the hero. Am I supposed to start off: 'One fine morning Caius

Marcius went for a stroll in the garden, went to the market place, met the people and quarrelled', and so on? . . .

W

I'm still bothered by P's question whether we oughtn't to examine the events with the hero in mind. I certainly think that before the hero's appearance one is entitled to show the field of forces within which he operates . . .

P

And *Coriolanus* is written for us to enjoy the hero.

R

The play is written realistically, and includes sufficient material of a contradictory sort. Martius fighting the people: that isn't just a plinth for his monument.

As P says, the play is realistic – and (therefore) contradictory. These collaborators alternately agree on or argue over the relative degrees of weight of individual and society, the relative respect given to 'hero' and to people. But mainly they collect contradictions. Menenius Agrippa's fable is ineffectual but has an effect. Marcius's public service is both mentioned and disputed. He is both admirable and beyond contempt. His pride includes modesty. 'His switch from being the most Roman of the Romans to becoming their deadliest enemy is due precisely to the fact that he stays the same.' The rebellion is desperate but not serious, treated with understanding but with humour. The people show determination but not solidarity. They are helpless, but not pathetic or negligible – 'They can go in rags, but does that mean they have to go raggedly?' More broadly, B invokes Mao Tse-Tung's essay 'On Contradiction' to illuminate the way that 'we've got a contradictory union of plebeians and patricians, which has got involved in a contradiction with the Volscians next door'.

But contradictions spell not problems but plenitude. Witness this volley of exclamations:

B

Lovely stuff.

R

The wealth of events in a single short scene. Compare today's plays, with their poverty of content!

P

The way in which the exposition at the same time gives a rousing send-off to the plot!

R

The language in which the parable is told! The humour!

P

And the fact that it has no effect on the plebeians!

W

The plebeians' native wit! . . .

R

The crystal clarity of Marcius's harangue! What an outsize character! And one who emerges as admirable while behaving in a way that I find beneath contempt!

B

And great and small conflicts all thrown into the scene at once . . . Well, how much of that do we see in the bourgeois theatre?

B later notes 'your astonishment and inquisitiveness as you move around within this play and within these complex events on a particular morning in Rome, where there is much that a sharp eye can pick out'. This excitement at richness and liveliness is picked up at the end:

P

Is it for the sake of these perceptions that we are going to do the play?

B

Not only. We want to have and to communicate the fun of dealing with a slice of illuminated history. And to have first-hand experience of dialectics.

Elsewhere Brecht says that the bourgeois theatre always aims at 'smoothing over contradictions' with 'conditions . . . reported as if they could not be otherwise' and 'characters as individuals . . . cast in one block'. Whereas

The theatre of the scientific age is in a position to make dialectic into a source of enjoyment. The unexpectedness of logically progressive or zigzag development, the instability of every circumstance, the joke of contradiction and so forth: all these are ways of enjoying the liveliness of men, things and processes, and they heighten both our capacity for life and our pleasure in it. (Appendix to 'A Short Organum for the Theatre', Willett, p. 277)

The dialogue ends with P wondering whether all the dialectics business isn't a 'refinement reserved for a handful of connoisseurs'. B replies:

No. Even with popular ballads or the peepshows at fairs the simple people (who are so far from simple) love stories of the rise and fall of great men, of eternal change, of the ingenuity of the oppressed, of the potentialities of mankind. And they hunt for the truth that is 'behind it all'.

That last remark touches on a tension that lies behind all this book of mine: the tension between responding to detail and to design. But Brecht's ending makes 'responding' a pale and pious word: rather, 'we want to have and to communicate the fun'. Communicate *with* fun, too, in that dialogue. Modern criticism, clogged with solemn talk of the Carnivalesque, goes on about 'Brecht's concept of *spass*' (Howard and O'Connor, 1987: 272) but has little time for his actual *spass* or fun. Not all criticism can be amusing; not all can be itself in dramatised, dialectical form. But there ought to be some kindling spark jumped between emotional response and intellectual analysis, as well as between responding to a play's substance and to the liveliness with which it is conveyed, such as there usually was until the 1980s. You recall that McLuskie's account of *Lear* seems to see them not in tension but in irreconcilable conflict. Most 1980s critics regard attempts to incorporate emotional response in accounts of a play as woolly humanist empathising. If, in Johnson's words, they achieve motion without progress, what they aspire to is progress without emotion. So a remark of B's, early in the Dialogue, can appropriately be appropriated as this book's last word: 'We don't have to do the play if we don't enjoy it.'

*   *   *

Appendices to Chapter Five

5A

Feminist criticism: these recommendations will serve to temper my negativity.

(a) of the three surveys cited in my Introduction, Ann Thompson's is obviously most relevant here. Her account is brought up to date in Holderness's *Shakespeare Recycled*, pp. 40–2. Very recent works are *The Matter of Difference: Materialist feminist criticism of Shakespeare* by Valerie Wayne, and *Woman and Gender in Renaissance Tragedy* by Dympna Callaghan (both 1991).

(b) other 'historical' feminists have tracked the after-life of Shakespeare's women. Thus Elaine Showalter (in Parker and Hartman) documents 'Ophelia's history on and off the stage and its alignment to wider cultural history', especially to the changing perception and treatment of female insanity; while Irene Dash (in Lenz *et al.*, 1983) diagnoses 'A Penchant for Perdita on the Eighteenth-Century Stage'.

(c) Madelon Gohlke (Lenz *et al.*, 1983: 156) sees the point of Lear's resistance to tears:

> the perception of the masculine consciousness is that to be feminine is to be powerless, specifically in relation to a controlling or powerful woman. For Lear, rage as an expression of power acts as a defence against this awareness, while tears threaten not only the dreaded perception of himself as feminine and hence weak but also the breakdown of his psychic order.

(d) The play with which I began this book is the subject of Graham Holderness's 'Patriarchy and Gender: *Richard II*' (reprinted as Chapter Three of his *Shakespeare Recycled*). This develops the suggestion that 'women may not be much in evidence in the play, but femininity is' (Holderness, 1992: 77).

(e) *Problems for Feminist Criticism* ed. Sally Minogue (London, 1990) provides an excellent overview, particularly in the editor's Introduction and long final chapter: see also Barbara Hardy's chapter on 'The Talkative Women in Shakespeare, Dickens and George Eliot'.

5B

Robert Greene's *Pandosto. The triumph of time* (1588) begins thus:

> Among all the passions wherewith human minds are perplexed, there is none that so galleth with restless despite as the infectious sore of

jealousy; for all other griefs are either to be appeased with sensible persuasions, to be cured with wholesome counsel, to be relieved in want, or by tract of time to be worn out, jealousy only excepted, which is so sauced with suspicious doubts and pinching mistrust, that whoso seeks by friendly counsel to raze out this hellish passion, it forthwith suspecteth that he giveth this advice to cover his own guiltiness. Yea, whoso is pained with this restless torment doubteth all, distrusteth himself, is always frozen with fear and fired with suspicion, having that wherein consisteth all his joy to be the breeder of his misery. Yea, it is such a heavy enemy to that holy estate of matrimony, sowing between the married couples such deadly seeds of secret hatred, as, love being once razed out by spiteful distrust, there oft ensueth bloody revenge, as this ensuing history manifestly proveth: wherein Pandosto, furiously incensed by causeless jealousy, procured the death of his most loving and loyal wife and his own endless sorrow and misery.

5C

Poetic drama and realist fiction: jealousy in *The Winter's Tale* and *Anna Karenin*. From Part Seven of Tolstoy's novel:

Chapter Twenty-three

BEFORE anything can be embarked upon in married life, there must necessarily be either absolute antagonism between husband and wife or loving agreement. When relations are uncertain, neither one thing nor the other, no move can be made.

Many families continue for years in the same old rut, which both parties heartily detest, simply because husband and wife are not sufficiently united to agree upon anything or sufficiently disunited for one of them to take things into his or her own hands.

Both for Vronsky and Anna life in Moscow in the heat and dust, when the spring sunshine was followed by the glare of summer and all the trees on the boulevards had long been in leaf and were already covered with dust, was intolerable. But instead of going back to Vozdvizhenskoe, as they had long ago decided to do, they still stayed on in Moscow, which they had both grown to loathe, because of late there had been no harmony between them.

The irritability which kept them apart had no tangible cause, and all efforts to come to an understanding only made it worse, instead of removing it. It was an inner irritation, grounded in her mind on the conviction of a decline in his love for her; in his, on regret that for her sake he had placed himself in a difficult position which she, instead of trying to ease, made harder still. Neither would give expression to their grievance, but each thought the other in the wrong and seized every opportunity to prove it.

In her eyes Vronsky, with all his habits, ideas, desires – his whole spiritual and physical temperament – could be summed up in one thing – love for women, and this love, which she felt ought to be wholly concentrated on her, was diminishing. Therefore, she reasoned, he must have transferred part of it to other women, or to another woman, and she was jealous. She was jealous not of any particular woman but of his love. Not having as yet an object for her jealousy, she was on the look-out for one. At the slightest provocation she transferred her jealousy from one object to another. Now she was jealous of the low *amours* he might so easily enter into through his bachelor connexions; now it was the society women he might meet; now she was jealous of some imaginary girl whom he might want to marry and for whose sake he would break with her. And this last tortured her most of all, especially since in an expansive moment he had unwarily remarked that his mother understood him so little that she had even tried to persuade him to marry the young Princess Sorokin.

And being jealous made her quarrelsome, and she was constantly seeking grounds for her discontent. She blamed him for everything she had to bear. The agonizing state of suspense in which she lived in Moscow, Karenin's procrastination and indecision, her own loneliness – they were all put down to him. If he had loved her he would have realized the misery of her position and rescued her from it. It was his fault, too, that they were living in Moscow instead of in the country. He could not live buried in the country as she would have liked. He must have society, and so he had put her in this awful position, the bitterness of which he wilfully shut his eyes to. And it was likewise his fault that she was parted from her son for ever.

Even the rare moments of tenderness that came from time to time did not soothe her: in his tenderness now she saw a shade of complacency, of self-confidence, which had not been there before and which provoked her.

It was already dusk. Anna all alone, awaiting his return from a bachelor dinner-party, paced up and down his study (the room where the noise from the street was least audible), going over in her mind every detail of their quarrel the day before. She recalled the words that had hurt her most cruelly and traced them to the thing that had occasioned them, finally arriving back at the beginning of their conversation. For a long while she could not believe that the dispute could have arisen from such an inoffensive exchange about a matter that was not close to the heart of either. But so in fact it had been. It had all begun by his laughing at high schools for girls, which he considered unnecessary and she defended. He had spoken slightingly of women's education in general, and said that Hannah, Anna's little English *protégée*, did not at all need to know physics.

This irritated Anna. She saw in it a contemptuous allusion to her own occupations, and bethought herself of an answer that should make him pay for the pain he had caused her. 'I don't expect you to understand me or my feelings, as anyone who loved me would, but ordinary delicacy I did expect,' she said.

And he had actually flushed with anger and made some disagreeable retort. She could not recall her reply but remembered that in response he had said, with obvious intent to hurt her too:

'You are right: I can take no interest in your passion for the child because I can see in it nothing but affectation.'

The cruelty with which he shattered the world she had so laboriously created for herself to enable her to endure her difficult life, the injustice of his accusation that she was false and affected, stung her.

'I am very sorry that only the coarse and material things are comprehensible and natural to you,' she flung at him, and walked out of the room.

When he came to her in the evening, they did not refer to the quarrel, but both felt that it was only smoothed over, not settled.

Now he had been away from home the whole day, and she felt so lonely and wretched at being on bad terms with him that she was ready to forget and forgive everything in order to be reconciled with him. She would even take the blame on herself and justify him.

'It is my fault, I am irritable and unreasonably jealous. I will make it up with him, and we'll go back to the country. I shall be more at peace there,' she said to herself.

'Affectation!' She suddenly recalled what had hurt her most of all – not so much the word itself as the intent to wound her with which it had been said. 'I know what he meant: he meant that it is unnatural to love someone else's child and not my own daughter. What does he know of love for children – of my love for Seriozha, whom I gave up for him? And this desire to hurt me! No, he must be in love with another woman: it can't be anything else.'

Suddenly she realized that in her attempt to regain her peace of mind she had only gone the round of the circle completed so often before, and arrived back at her old state of irritation, and she was frightened at herself. 'Is it possible that I can't . . . Is it possible that I can't take it on myself?' she wondered, and began again from the beginning. 'He is upright, he is the soul of honour, he loves me. I love him. In a day or two the divorce will come. What more do I want? I must be calm and have more faith in him; and I will take the blame on myself. Yes, now, as soon as he comes home, I will tell him I was wrong, though in fact I was not, and we will go away.'

And to avoid further thought and irritation she rang and asked for her trunks, ready to pack their things for the country.

At ten o'clock Vronsky came in.

Chapter Twenty-four

'WELL, did you have a good time?' she asked, going out to meet him with a penitent, meek expression on her face.

'The same as usual,' he replied, perceiving at a glance that she was in one of her good moods. He had become accustomed to these transitions, and to-day especially was glad to see her happier, as he was in the best of spirits himself.

'What do I see? Ah, that's right!' he said, pointing to the trunks in the passage.

'Yes, we must go away. I went out for a drive, and it was so lovely I longed to be in the country. There's nothing to keep you here, is there?'

'My one wish is to get away. I won't be a moment, and we'll talk it over. I must just go and change first. Order tea, will you?'

And he went to his room.

There was something offensive in the way he had said, 'Ah, that's right!' – the sort of thing one says to a child when it stops being naughty – and still more offensive was the contrast between her penitent tone and his self-assurance. For a moment she felt a desire to fight rising up in her, but with an effort she mastered it and met Vronsky with the same good humour as before.

When he came in she told him, partly repeating words she had rehearsed, how she had spent the day, and her plans for their departure.

'You know, it came over me like an absolute inspiration,' she began. 'Why should we go on waiting here for the divorce? Won't it do just as well in the country? I can't wait any longer. I don't want to go on hoping – I don't want to hear any more about the divorce. I have made up my mind that it shan't influence my life any more. Do you agree?'

'Oh yes!' he replied, looking uneasily at her excited face.

'What did you do at your dinner-party? Who was there?' she asked, after a pause.

Vronsky mentioned the names of the guests. 'The dinner was first-rate, and the boat-race and all that quite enjoyable, but in Moscow they can't manage without doing something ridiculous. Some lady or other appeared on the scene – the Queen of Sweden's swimming-instructress – and gave a display of her art.'

'What? Do you mean to say she swam?' asked Anna, with a frown.

'Yes, in some sort of red *costume de natation* – a hideous old creature she was too. Well, when are we off?'

'What an absurd idea! Was there anything particular about her swimming?' said Anna, not answering his question.

'Absolutely nothing at all. I told you, it was awfully silly. . . . Well, when do you think of going?'

Anna shook her head as though to drive away an unpleasant thought.

'When are we going? Why, the sooner the better! We can't get off to-morrow, I'm afraid, but we could be ready the day after.'

'Yes . . . oh no, wait a moment – the day after to-morrow is Sunday and I have to go and see *maman*,' said Vronsky, embarrassed, for no sooner had he mentioned his mother than he felt Anna's eyes fixed on him suspiciously. His embarrassment confirmed her suspicions. She flushed and turned away from him. Now it was no longer the Queen of Sweden's swimming instructress who was uppermost in her mind but the young Princess Sorokin, who lived with the Countess Vronsky in the country outside Moscow . . .

5D

Auden's poem 'Musée des Beaux Arts' describes how everyday life continues as tragedies are acted out. This is its last stanza:

In Brueghel's *Icarus*, for instance: how everything turns away
Quite leisurely from the disaster; the ploughman may
Have heard the splash, the forsaken cry,
But for him it was not an important failure; the sun shone
As it had to on the white legs disappearing into the green
Water; and the expensive delicate ship must have seen
Something amazing, a boy falling out of the sky,
Had somewhere to get to and sailed calmly on.

John Bayley's *Shakespeare and Tragedy* (London, 1981) develops similar thoughts, beginning with the lack of connection between Gloucester's attempted suicide and the Dover fishermen and sampire-gatherers.

Notes

Introduction

1. Wilbur Sanders, 1987:1. Writers may add that they want critics like cabbages crave slugs.
2. Ben Jonson, 'To the Memory of . . . Mr William Shakespeare: and What He Hath Left Us': poem printed at the front of the First Folio of Shakespeare's Works, 1623. Reprinted in Riverside: 65–6.
3. Contrast his reasons for running away from Shakespeare: 'he that peruses Shakespeare [a description of night in *Macbeth*] looks round alarmed, and starts to find himself alone' (Johnson, 1968, I: 132). When he was nine years old, and was reading *Hamlet* alone in the family basement kitchen, the ghost scene made him rush upstairs to the street door so that he might see people around him.
4. I have been encouraged by these critics: E. A. J. Honigmann, 1989; M. M. Mahood, 1972; Kristian Smidt, 1982 (especially Chapter 10, 'Shakespeare at Work'). I am also influenced by, and later quote from, Alfred Harbage, 1966, although I am aware of Drakakis's (to me unpersuasive) attack in his Introduction to *Alternative Shakespeares*.
5. I borrow Henry James's description of sprawling realist novels.
6. Preface to *The Nigger of the 'Narcissus'*.
7. George Orwell, 'Why I Write'.
8. 'This is indeed the everlasting difficulty of Shakespeare criticism, that the critics are so much more moral than Shakespeare, and much less experienced. The ready judgments which are often passed on Shakespeare's most difficult characters are like the talk of children. Childhood is amazingly moral, with a confident, dictatorial, unflinching morality. The work of experience is to undermine this early pedantry . . .' (Walter Raleigh, quoted by A. P. Rossiter, 1989: 54).
9. Cf. the 1980s' awareness that 'modern Shakespeare criticism is full

of . . . apparent movements forward which surrender to a ubiquitous tradition the very ground which they seek to occupy' (Drakakis, 1985: 22). Ryan makes the same complaint about the 1980s critics themselves.

10. Reports of the death of 'humanist' Shakespeare criticism are grossly exaggerated, and Evans's dancing on the grave is premature. Very much alive and going swimmingly are Jonathan Bate's *Shakespeare and the English Romantic Imagination* (Oxford, 1986); Graham Bradshaw's *Shakespeare's Scepticism* (Brighton, 1987); and Barbara Everett's *Young Hamlet: Essays on Shakespeare's tragedies* (Oxford, 1989).

11. No book can tackle everything. Any insight this one provides can of course be supplemented by theatre visits and watching videos. But my comments aim to cut across any distinction between stage and page, reader and spectator. In her first book, *Shakespeare's Art of Orchestration* (Urbana and Chicago, 1984), p. 3, Jean Howard takes her cue from Michael Goldman's remark that 'it is a mistake to speak as if we have a choice between a literary Shakespeare and a theatrical Shakespeare. The choice is rather between some of Shakespeare and more of him.' I agree.

Chapter One

1. Don't blame me for dwelling on an uneventful excerpt; I haven't made an untypical selection in order to encourage the reader at the expense of the spectator. The play's 'stage-centred' editor Andrew Gurr points out that the entire play 'is remarkable in the Shakespeare canon for its lack of movement on the stage' (Gurr, 1984: 37).

2. F. R. Leavis, *Revaluation* (London, 1936), p. 11.

3. The foregoing analysis is indebted to M. M. Mahood (1957: 85–6).

4. The analogy is suggested by Wilbur Sanders in *The Dramatist and the Received Idea* (Cambridge, 1968), p. 99.

5. C. W. R. D. Moseley, *Shakespeare's History Plays: Richard II to Henry V* (Harmondsworth, 1988), p. 120.

6. Coleridge (1989: 26) is speaking of the dramatic characteristics of Shakespeare's poems. Incidentally he reminds us of what must fill out the words in a play when he says that in the poems imagery provides 'a substitute for that visual language, that constant intervention and running comment by tone, look and gesture, which in his dramatic works he was entitled to expect from the players'. (Note, however, the resemblance to Conrad's view of the novelist's art, quoted above, Introduction, Note 6.)

7. D. J. Enright's phrase: see Introduction, p. 14 above.
8. The main source for this play is Arthur Brooke's *Tragical History of Romeus and Juliet*, 1562; most editions of the play reprint excerpts. But the poem is in rhymed couplets of twelve- and fourteen-syllable lines. And instead of Shakespeare's *sotto voce* squabble between Capulet and Tybalt, Brooke merely says that 'The Capulets disdain the presence of their foe:/Yet they suppress their stirred ire, the cause I do not know' (lines 183–4).

Chapter Two

1. Of the phrases in this sentence, the first draws on Hamlet's metaphor of 'spread[ing] the compost on the weeds/To make them ranker' (III, iv, 151–2). The other phrases come from III, iv, 153; III, iii, 81; III, iv, 92; and I, v, 32–3. Riverside's 'roots' comes from both Quartos: I prefer the Folio's 'rots', perhaps influenced by *Antony and Cleopatra* (I, iv, 47) on the vacillations of popular enthusiasm that will 'rot itself with motion'.
2. Other links missing from the Quarto: Hamlet's 'I will speak daggers to her' (III, ii, 396) and Gertrude's 'These words like daggers enter in my ears' (III, iv, 95: in turn a reminder of her late husband poisoned through the ears?); and the offer to 'silence me even here' (III, iv, 4) by the 'foolish prating knave' Polonius (III, iii, 215) whom Hamlet's dagger makes 'most still, most secret and most grave' (III, iii, 214).
3. That's a bit strong. But I think Bradley was right to speak of her 'soft animal nature', loving 'to be happy, like a sheep in the sun' (Bradley, 1905: 135). If I again recall Denis Healey's observation that attacking Geoffrey Howe was like savaging a dead sheep, the parallel reminds me of the gratuitousness of Hamlet's attack. In any case, as Bradley also says, the good in her comes alive 'through the heavy mass of sloth' (*ibid.*, 135). These remarks won't please feminists. But even Rebecca Smith's attempts to rescue her from prejudicial stereotyping end up calling her 'compliant', 'malleable', 'unimaginative' (in Lenz *et al.*, 1983: 207).
4. Eliot's essay of 1920 is in both *Selected Essays* and *Selected Prose*. Freud's principal British disciple Ernest Jones's essay on Hamlet and Oedipus, first written in the 1910s, was expanded into its final, book-length form in 1949.
5. Drakakis (1985: 18) calls Knight's work a 'celebration' of 'mystification'. The section of Ryan's book which is called 'Questioning the Consensus' echoes the consensus in speaking of

Knight's 'rapturous rhetoric', 'surrendering rational analysis to the sway of the awesome and ineffable' (Ryan, 1989: 44–5).
6. See Granville-Barker (1972, I: 224); Michael Hattaway, *Hamlet: The critics' debate* (London, 1987), p. 99; Sanders and Jacobson (1978: 23–4).
7. In one paragraph Hamlet, 'and the audience, must at least fleetingly experience a conflict' about whether the ghost exists outside Hamlet's mind. The next paragraph is bolder: 'By stressing the epistemologically doubtful status of the ghost we can usefully supplement the classic psychoanalytic explanation . . . outlined by Freud . . . and elaborated by Ernest Jones . . . Jacques Lacan, in his brilliant, albeit elliptical essay, speculates . . . Building on both Freud and Lacan, we might read Hamlet's frantic efforts to draw a clear epistemological distinction between his father and Claudius as his perception of an excessive degree of *likeness* between himself and Claudius, or more precisely, between his desires and Claudius's' (Ferguson, 1985: 296).

Chapter Three

1. Some original texts have the more boring *female buds*. The New Cambridge edition, which is among those adopting *fennel*, calls it 'a fragrant yellow-flowered plant, believed to cleanse the stomach and preserve and clear the sight [and] supposed to awaken passion, was thrown in the path of brides, and was especially associated with newly married couples'. Its delicate ferny-lacy foliage also seems to me appropriate. Again, how much lies in one little word!
2. R. W. David, *Shakespeare in the Theatre* (Cambridge, 1978), p. 190.
3. D. H. Lawrence, letter of 26 April 1911: *Letters*, I (Cambridge, 1979), p. 261.
4. From Coleridge, *Literary Remains* (1836–9): reprinted in *Coleridge, Shakespearean Criticism*, ed T. M. Raysor (London, 1960) I, p. 49, and *Coleridge on Shakespeare*, ed. T. Hawkes (Harmondsworth, 1969) p. 179.
5. Frank Kermode, Introduction to *Coriolanus*: Riverside, pp. 1394–5.
6. F. R. Leavis (1975). A very recent discussion of *All for Love*, Tate's *Lear* and other works, seen much more in terms of 'political rather than aesthetic motives' for rewriting, occurs in *The Appropriation of Shakespeare: Post-Renaissance reconstructions of the work and the myth*, Jean I. Marsden (ed.) (Hemel Hempstead, 1991) (on which see, p. 218).

7. The phrase comes from Johnson's *Life of Cowley* (1968, I: 13), describing what in the Augustan view needed doing to the 'grossness of expression' in Metaphysical poetry. Early eighteenth-century revisions of Donne's satires, by Parnell and Pope, acted on this perceived need: Dryden and Tate got to work similarly on Shakespeare.

8. The Signet edition reprints Knight on the flower symbolism of the pastoral scene, but not his preceding commentary on the party atmosphere, and on Autolycus in particular. He speaks of the latter's 'spectacular entry', of 'the richest humour' in this 'figure of absolute comedy' whose tricks are 'supremely satisfying', 'crying out for stage realization' and thus providing a 'delicate balance of unmoral humour' of which 'no finer examples exist than the early Falstaff and Autolycus' (Knight, 1967: 99–105).

Chapter Two

1. This miscellany of passages comes from Byron, in a letter and in *Don Juan*; Jane Austen, *Mansfield Park*; D. H. Lawrence, *Women in Love* and *The Rainbow*.

2. Richard Flecknoe, 'A Short Discourse of the English Stage' (1664) reprinted in *Critical Essays of the Seventeenth Century*, ed. J. Spingarn (Oxford, 1908–9), II, p. 95.

3. Margaret Cavendish, letter of 1662, reprinted in *Shakespeare: The critical heritage*, ed. Brian Vickers, vol. I (Routledge: London, 1974).

4. Keats, letter to Richard Woodhouse, 27 October 1818.

5. Hazlitt, *Complete Works*, ed. P. P. Howe (London, 1930–4), VIII, p. 42.

6. Cited in Jonathan Bate (1986: 43).

7. No use of the term in Shakespeare himself helps define it. When Autolycus tells us he 'was born under Mercury' he has in mind his nimbleness at pickpocketing – by this meaning-in-extension Mercury was the patron of thieves. His kindred spirit Falstaff comes close to the root meaning when he extols the mercurial properties of 'a good sherris-sack': it 'warms the blood and enlivens the brain, making it "apprehensive" [perceptive], "quick", "forgetive" [inventive], "full of nimble, fiery and delectable shapes"' (*Henry IV, Part Two*, IV, iii, 99–100).

   But again, don't lock yourself up in Shakespeare. The best evocation of mecuriality I know is D. H. Lawrence's description of the sudden violence of a thunderstorm on a mountain that is aptly topped by a statue of Mercury (Lawrence, *Phoenix*, ed. E. McDonald (London, 1936), pp. 35–9). Primo Levi has a relevant fable about mercury in *The Periodic Table* (London, 1988), pp. 96–108.

The Romantics perhaps preferred 'protean' to 'mercurial' because several of them were suffering the side-effects of mercury taken as a medicine for syphilis. But Hazlitt (1957: 117) calls Mercutio 'one of the most mercurial and spirited' of Shakespeare's creations.

8. 'Spannell'd', an eighteenth-century emendation of 'pannelled', is glossed by Riverside as 'spanieled' – a spelling adopted by Signet and several other modern editions.
9. Thompson and Thompson (1987: 208).
10. John Danby (1952) repr. in Signet (1988: 248).
11. Anne Barton, in *English Drama to 1710*, ed. C. Ricks (London, 1971), pp. 241–2.

Chapter Five

1. Ann Thompson (1988b: 75) warns feminists against being 'tempted to spend all their time and energy on re-building their own ghetto and rendering it as cosy and unchallenging as possible'.
2. J. D. Wilson, *Hamlet* in the Cambridge *New Shakespeare* edition, 1934 (but still being reprinted in the 1970s), pp. 74 and 90.
3. Tolstoy's 'Shakespeare and the Drama' was reprinted in Volume 21 of the Centenary Edition of his *Works*. The most interesting responses are by Bayley and Orwell (whom I discuss), and by Wilson Knight in *The Wheel of Fire*, Chapter XIV, 'Tolstoy's Attack on Shakespeare' (Chapter XI, 'Shakespeare and Tolstoy', is less relevant).
4. I have appropriated T. S. Eliot's metaphor about 'the chief use of the "meaning" of a poem': it is to keep the reader's 'mind diverted and quiet, while the poem does its work . . . much as the imaginary burglar is always provided with a bit of nice meat for the house-dog' (*The Use of Poetry and the Use of Criticism*, 1933, reprinted London 1964, p. 151). Knight dismisses as 'futile' any attempt to analyse Macbeth and Lady Macbeth in terms of individuated character or specific motives (Knight, 1989: 153); more helpfully, he reminds us that 'motive is always vague, a complex woven of conscious desire, semi-conscious promptings, opportunity', and much else (*ibid.*, 279).
5. Lawrence, 'The Novel', repr. in *Phoenix II*, ed. W. Roberts and H. T. Moore (London, 1968), pp. 418–9.

6. Orwell, 'Lear, Tolstoy and the Fool'. As this essay is available in many different selections and editions of his work, it would not be helpful to cite page-numbers.
7. Kermode, *The Classic* (London, 1975), p. 40.
8. An English translation of the Dialogue is in John Willett's *Brecht and the Theatre* (London, 1973). (I have not interrupted with page-numbers the quick-fire of quotations from Brecht in the closing pages of this chapter.) It is symptomatic of pervasive joylessness and academic narrow-mindedness (critic = prof.) that the piece is not mentioned in S. Wells (ed.), *Shakespeare: a Bibliographical Guide*. Students find it exhilarating: one of mine recently wrote a successful sequel in which such characters as Granville-Barker and Plutarch argued about later episodes of the play.
9. See Margot Heinemann, 'How Brecht Read Shakespeare', in J. Dollimore and A. Sinfield (eds), *Political Shakespeare*, pp. 202–30; and Martin Scofield, 'Drama, Politics and the Hero: *Coriolanus*, Brecht, and Grass', in *Comparative Literature*, vol. 24, no. 4 (winter 1990–1), pp. 322–41.

Bibliography

This lists all works recurrently cited and/or recommended as useful. Others will be found in the Notes. All appear in the Index.

As the list is purely alphabetical, I preface it with several chronological and/or ideological groupings:

A. Shakespeare Editions

— Oxford: *The Complete Works*, ed. S. Wells and G. Taylor (1986), Compact Edition (Oxford University Press: Oxford, 1988).
— Riverside: *The Riverside Shakespeare*, general editors G. Blakemore Evans and H. Levin (Houghton Mifflin: Cambridge Mass., 1974).
— Signet: *The Complete Signet Classic Shakespeare*, general editor S. Barnet (Harcourt Brace Jovanovich: New York, 1963). (Contains a long general Introduction and individual editors' introductions to each play.)
— Signets: individual-play paperbacks, various editors (New American Library: New York, 1963): many reissued in late 1980s in New, Revised Edition, but few currently available in UK. (Contain editors' introductions and an anthology of criticism.)
— New Arden and New Cambridge editions: single-play volumes.
— *Hamlet*, the First Quarto (FQ), ed. Graham Holderness and Bryan Loughrey (Harvester Wheatsheaf: Hemel Hempstead, 1992).

B. Dr Johnson and After: 250 years of what the 1980s called 'humanist-essentialist' criticism

— see below under Johnson, Coleridge, Hazlitt, Bradley, Knight, Granville-Barker, Mahood, Orwell, Rossiter, Enright. (Many of these would resent being thus flung together into an extended family, Coleridge for instance denying any kinship with Johnson and Hazlitt being less than kind to Coleridge.)

C.   Its Survival (or Death-throes?) in the 1980s

— see under Bate, Bradshaw, Everett, Nuttall, Taylor.

D.   New Approaches in the 1980s

— Dollimore (1989), Eagleton, Greenblatt, Ryan, Tennenhouse; and the collections edited by Dollimore and Sinfield, Drakakis, Holderness, Howard and O'Connor, Lenz, Greene and Neely, Parker and Hartman. (The warning under 'B' also applies here.)

E.   Most Recently: The early 1990s

— Holderness, Kamps (ed.), Marsden (ed.).

F.   Critical Surveys of Earlier Criticism

— 'Introduction' by Drakakis and 'Post Structuralist Shakespeare' by Christopher Norris, in Drakakis (ed.), *Alternative Shakespeares*; Evans, Grady, Holderness (1992), Ryan.

G.   Introduction to 1980s Criticism

— The three essays recommended in the Introduction, p. 9 above.

H.   Working with Shakespeare: Practical guidance and examples of close stylistic analysis

— Heaney, Knight (esp. 'The Othello Music' in *Wheel of Fire*), Leavis, McDonald, Mahood, Roberts, Scragg, Wright.

I.   Shakespeare Working

— Harbage, Honigmann, Mahood (1972), Smidt.

Altick, Richard D. (1947), 'Symphonic Imagery in *Richard II*', *PMLA*, 62, repr. in *Richard II: A casebook*, ed. Nicholas Brooke (Macmillan: London and Basingstoke 1973), and in *Richard II*, individual-play Signet ed. K. Muir (New York, 1973).

Bate, Jonathan (1986), *Shakespeare and the English Romantic Imagination* (Oxford).

Bate, Jonathan (1989), *Shakespearean Constitutions: Politics, theatre, criticism, 1730–1830* (Oxford).

Bayley, John (1966), *Tolstoy and the Novel* (Chatto & Windus: London).

Bayley, John (1981), *Shakespeare and Tragedy* (Routledge: London).

Bloom, H., ed. (1988), *William Shakespeare's Richard II: Modern critical interpretation* (Chelsea House Books: New York).

Bradley, A. C. (1905), *Shakespearean Tragedy* (1904), 2nd edn (Macmillan: London).

Bradley, A. C. (1988a), 'Shakespeare's *Antony and Cleopatra*', in his *Oxford Lectures on Poetry* (Oxford University Press: Oxford, 1909), repr. in Signet Classic *Antony and Cleopatra*, new revised edn, ed., B. Everett.

Bradley, A. C. (1988b), '*Coriolanus*' (1912) in his *A Miscellany* (Macmillan: London, 1929), repr. in Signet Classic *Coriolanus*, new revised edn, ed. S. Barnet.

Bradshaw, Graham (1987), *Shakespeare's Scepticism* (Harvester Press: Brighton).

Brecht, Bertolt (1964), 'Study of the First Scene of Shakespeare's *Coriolanus*' and 'Short Organum for the Theatre', in *Brecht on Theatre*, ed. and trans. John Willett (Eyre Methuen: London).

Callaghan, Dympna (1991), *Woman and Gender in Renaissance Tragedy* (Harvester Wheatsheaf: Hemel Hempstead).

Cohen, Walter, 'Political Criticism of Shakespeare', in *Shakespeare Reproduced*, ed. Howard and O'Connor.

Coleridge, S. T. (1987), *Lectures 1808–1819 on Literature*, in *Collected Works*, *5* (2 vols), ed. R. A. Foakes (Yale University Press: London and Princeton).

Coleridge, S. T. (1989), *Coleridge's Criticism of Shakespeare, a Selection*, ed. R. A. Foakes (Athlone Press: London).

Danby, John (1988), '*Antony and Cleopatra*, a Shakespearian Adjustment', in *Poet on Fortune's Hill* (Faber: London) repr. in New Signet Classic, *Antony and Cleopatra*.

Dollimore, Jonathan (1989), *Radical Tragedy: Religion, ideology and power in the drama of Shakespeare and his contemporaries*, 2nd edn. (Harvester Wheatsheaf: Hemel Hempstead).

Dollimore, Jonathan (1990), 'Political Criticism of Shakespeare', in *Oxford Bibliographies: Shakespeare, new edition*, ed. S. Wells (Oxford University Press: Oxford).

Dollimore, Jonathan and Sinfield, Alan, eds (1985), *Political Shakespeare: New essays in cultural materialism* (Manchester University Press: Manchester).

Drakakis, John, ed. (1985), *Alternative Shakespeares* (Methuen: London).

Eagleton, Terry (1986), *William Shakespeare* (Basil Blackwell: Oxford and New York).

Eliot, T. S. (1932), *Selected Essays* (Faber: London).

Eliot, T. S. (1975), *Selected Prose*, ed. Frank Kermode (Faber: London).

Engell, James and Perkins, David, eds (1988),*Teaching Literature: What is needed now* (Harvard English Studies 15, Harvard University Press: Cambridge Mass. and London).

Enright, D. J. (1970), *Shakespeare and the Students* (Chatto & Windus: London).

Evans, Malcolm (1986), *Signifying Nothing: Truth's true contents in Shakespeare's text* (Harvester Press: Brighton).

Everett, Barbara (1989), *Young Hamlet: Essays on Shakespeare's tragedies* (Oxford University Press: Oxford).

Ferguson, Margaret W. (1985), '*Hamlet*: Letters and spirits', in *Shakespeare and the Question of Theory*, eds Parker and Hartman.

'Fitz, L. T.' (= Linda Woodbridge) (1977), 'Egyptian Queens and Male Reviewers: Sexist attitudes in *Antony and Cleopatra* criticism', *Shakespeare Quarterly*, 28.

Grady, Hugh (1991), *The Modernist Shakespeare: Critical texts in a material world* (Oxford University Press: Oxford).

Granville-Barker, H. (1972), *Prefaces to Shakespeare* (1930), 2 vols in one (Batsford: London).

Greenblatt, Stephen (1988), *Shakespearean Negotiations: The circulation of social energy in Renaissance England* (Oxford University Press: Oxford).

Gurr, Andrew, ed. (1984), *Richard II*, The New Cambridge Shakespeare (Cambridge University Press: Cambridge).

Harbage, Alfred (1966), *Conceptions of Shakespeare* (Harvard University Press: Cambridge, Mass.).

Hawkes, Terence (1985), 'Telmah', in *Shakespeare and the Question of Theory*, eds Parker and Hartman.

Hawkes, Terence (1986), 'Shakespeare and New Critical Approaches', in *The Cambridge Companion to Shakespeare Studies*, ed. S. Wells.

Hazlitt, William (1957), *Characters of Shakespear's Plays* (1817) (Everyman: London).

Heaney, Seamus (1980), *Preoccupations: Selected prose 1968–1978* (Faber: London). ('The Fire i' the Flint' begins with Shakespeare.)

Hill, R. F. (1961), 'Dramatic Techniques and Interpretation in *Richard II*', in *Early Shakespeare*, Shakespeare Institute Studies, general eds J. R. Brown and Bernard Harris (Arnold: London).

Holderness, Graham, ed. (1988), *The Shakespeare Myth* (Manchester University Press: Manchester).

Holderness, Graham (1992), *Shakespeare Recycled: The making of historical drama* (Harvester Wheatsheaf: Hemel Hempstead).

Honigmann, E. A. J. (1989), *Myriad-Minded Shakespeare* (Macmillan:

London). Chapter Eleven: 'Shakespeare at Work: Preparing, writing, rewriting'.

Howard, Jean and O'Connor, Marion, eds (1987), *Shakespeare Reproduced: The text in history and ideology* (Routledge: London).

Huizinga, J. (1955), *The Waning of the Middle Ages* (1924) (Penguin: Harmondsworth).

Humphreys, A. R. (1967), *Shakespeare: Richard II* (Arnold: London).

Hussey, S. S. (1982), *The Literary Language of Shakespeare* (Longman: London and New York).

Johnson, Samuel (1968), *Lives of the English Poets (1779–81)* (Everyman 2 vols: London).

Johnson, Samuel (1969), *Dr. Johnson on Shakespeare*, ed. W. K. Wimsatt (Penguin: Harmondsworth). (Recent alternatives are: *Selections from Johnson on Shakespeare*, ed. Bertrand H. Bronson with Jean M. O'Meara (Yale University Press: New Haven and London, 1986); and *Samuel Johnson on Shakespeare*, ed. H. R. Woodhuysen (Penguin: Harmondsworth, 1989).)

Jones, Emrys (1985), *Scenic Form in Shakespeare* (Oxford University Press: Oxford, 1971, paperback edition with corrections).

Kamps, Ivo, ed. (1991), *Shakespeare Left and Right* (Routledge: London and New York).

Kermode, Frank (1971), *Shakespeare, Spenser, Donne* (Routledge: London).

Knight, G. Wilson (1967), *The Crown of Life: Essays in interpretation of Shakespeare's final plays* (1947), paperback edn (Methuen: London).

Knight, G. Wilson (1989), *The Wheel of Fire: Interpretations of Shakespearean tragedy*, with an Introduction by T. S. Eliot (1930), paperback edn (Methuen: London).

Leavis, F. R. (1975), '*Antony and Cleopatra* and *All for Love*: A critical exercise', in *Scrutiny* vol. 5, no. 2 (September 1936), reprinted in *The Living Principle* (Chatto & Windus: London).

Lenz, C. R. S., Greene, G. and Neely, C. T., eds (1983), *The Woman's Part: Feminist criticism of Shakespeare*, Urbana and Chicago (1980), Illini Books edn (Illinois University Press: Champaign).

McDonald, Russ (1985), 'Poetry and Plot in *The Winter's Tale*', *Shakespeare Quarterly* 36.

McLuskie, Kathleen (1985), 'The Patriarchal Bard: Feminist criticism and Shakespeare: *King Lear* and *Measure for Measure*', in *Political Shakespeare*, eds Dollimore and Sinfield.

Mahood, M. M. (1957), *Shakespeare's Wordplay* (Methuen: London).

Mahood, M. M. (1972), 'Unblotted Lines: Shakespeare at work', British Academy Lecture, London.

Marsden, Jean, ed. (1991), *The Appropriation of Shakespeare: Post-Renaissance reconstructions of the works and the myth* (Harvester Wheatsheaf: Hemel Hempstead).

Mills, Howard (1989), 'Shakespeare Critics: Two-and-a-half nations', in *English*, vol. 38, no. 160 (Spring).

Minogue, Sally, ed. (1990), *Problems for Feminist Criticism* (Routledge: London).

Nuttall, A. D. (1983), *A New Mimesis: Shakespeare and the representation of reality* (Methuen: London).

Parker, Patricia and Hartman, Geoffrey, eds (1985), *Shakespeare and the Question of Theory* (Methuen: London and New York).

Peck, John and Coyle, Martin (1985), *How to Study a Shakespeare Play* (Macmillan Education: London, repr. 1992).

Roberts, Philip Davies (1986), *How Poetry Works: The elements of English poetry* (Penguin: Harmondsworth). (See index for Shakespeare.)

Rossiter, A. P. (1950), *English Drama from Early Times to the Elizabethans* (Hutchinson: London).

Rossiter, A. P. (1989), *Angel with Horns: Fifteen lectures on Shakespeare* (1961), ed. Graham Storey with an Introduction by Peter Holland (Longman: London).

Ryan, Kiernan (1988), '*Romeo and Juliet*: The language of tragedy', in *The Taming of the Text: Explorations in language, literature and culture*, ed. W. Van Peer (Routledge: London).

Ryan, Kiernan (1989), *Shakespeare* (Harvester Wheatsheaf: Hemel Hempstead).

Sanders, Wilbur (1987), *The Winter's Tale* (Harvester New Critical Introductions to Shakespeare, Harvester Press: Brighton).

Sanders, Wilbur and Howard Jacobson (1978), *Shakespeare's Magnanimity: Four tragic heroes, their friends and families* (Chatto & Windus: London).

Scragg, Leah (1988), *Discovering Shakespeare's Meaning* (Macmillan: Basingstoke).

Smidt, Kristian (1982), *Unconformities in Shakespeare's History Plays* (Macmillan: London).

Tate, Nahum (1975), *The History of King Lear* (1681), ed. James Black (Nebraska University Press: Lincoln, Nebraska).

Taylor, Gary (1985), *Moment by Moment by Shakespeare* (Macmillan: London). (Published in America as *To Analyze Delight: A hedonist criticism of Shakespeare.*)

Tennenhouse, Leonard (1986), *Power on Display: The politics of Shakespeare's genres* (Methuen: London).

Thompson, Ann (1988a), *King Lear*, in The Critics Debate series (Macmillan: Basingstoke).

Thompson, Ann (1988b), '"The Warrant of Womanhood": Shakespeare and feminist criticism', in *The Shakespeare Myth*, ed. G. Holderness.

Thompson, Ann and Thompson, John O. (1987), *Shakespeare: Meaning and metaphor* (Harvester Press: Brighton).

Tillyard, E. M. W. (1944), *Shakespeare's History Plays* (Chatto & Windus: London).

Tolstoy, Leo (1937), 'Shakespeare and the Drama' (1903), reprinted in the Centenary Edition of his Works, vol. 21 (Oxford University Press: Oxford).

Tolstoy, Leo (1978), *Anna Karenin* (1878), trans. with an Introduction by Rosemary Edmonds (1954), repr. with revisions (Penguin: Harmondsworth).

Wayne, Don E. (1987), 'Power, Politics and the Shakespearean Text: Recent criticism in England and the United States', in *Shakespeare Reproduced*, eds J. Howard and M. O'Connor.

Wayne, Valerie (1991), *The Matter of Difference: Materialist feminist criticism in Shakespeare* (Harvester Wheatsheaf: Hemel Hempstead).

Weimann, Robert (1987), *Shakespeare and the Popular Tradition in the Theatre* (Johns Hopkins University Press: Baltimore and London), written 1967, trans. 1978.

Wells, Stanley, ed. (1990), *Shakespeare: A bibliographical guide, new edition* (Oxford University Press: Oxford).

Wells, Stanley, ed. (1986), *The Cambridge Companion to Shakespeare Studies* (Cambridge University Press: Cambridge).

Wright, George T. (1983), 'The Play of Phrase and Line in Shakespeare's Iambic Pentameter', *Shakespeare Quarterly*, 34.

Wright, G. (1988), *Shakespeare's Metrical Art* (University of California Press: Berkeley and London).

Index